Stealth Camping with Hundreds of My Closest Friends

Stealth Camping with Hundreds of My Closest Friends

A Memoir

Zinnia Abbott

Book design by Ray Rhamey

ISBN 978-1-7360156-0-5

Library of Congress Control Number: 2020924200

Acknowledgments

For guidance and encouragement, thanks to my writing coach, Lee Heffner. Without her, you would not be holding this book.

For editing and proofreading, thanks to Genie Dailey and Laurel Robinson.

For their ideas and support, thanks to Lindsey Ryer, Caitlin Wahrer, Minal Patel, Chris Queally, Daniel Fontugne, Rose Marie Zurkan, Emily Morrison, and Michael Torlen.

For his time, support, and caring, thanks to Jeremy F.

For showing me that you don't need loads of money to have adventures, thanks to my parents, George and Ruth.

For having my back, thanks to my sons, Micah and Seth.

For camaraderie and tech support over the years, thanks to my foster daughter, Christina.

For consistently restoring me to sanity with her kindness and patience, thanks to my AA sponsor, Faith.

Contents

Author's Notes

Zinnia Abbott is a retired nurse, mom, and grandmother living in southern Maine. Since 1985, she has been in recovery from alcoholism. To this grown-up Girl Scout and flower child out of season, every day is a new adventure, and she was born ready.

This is a memoir, told from the writer's point of view. The author does not officially represent Alcoholics Anonymous, but offers only her own personal experience and thoughts.

Some identifying information has been altered in keeping with the AA tradition of anonymity. The author's name, Zinnia Abbott, is a pseudonym. Other names may have been altered to protect confidentiality.

If you're curious, more information about AA can be found in Appendix A. More information about Zinnia's travels can be found in Appendix B.

zinniaabbott.com

zinniaabbott@gmail.com

Part One

Spring 2018: Stealth Camping

"I think you should do it." That's what my AA sponsor says. We are having breakfast at Bernie's Diner, as usual. "You're energized just talking about it."

I'm telling her about my daydream to take a road trip across the country. She asks, "What *is* stealth camping?"

"That means nobody knows you're camping out in your vehicle, so you don't have to pay anything for lodging, or a campsite. Just park somewhere legal overnight."

My sponsor, Faith, knows me very well. She's been my sponsor for a couple of decades. She has seen me at my most miserable, and she has seen me at my most enthusiastic. Enthusiastic is what she's seeing now. I look across the table and see her in her typical pastel colors, short blond hair, and tasteful jewelry. I revere her. She's a great listener and usually doesn't give me advice unless I ask, or unless she thinks it's important. I feel safe enough to tell her anything and she doesn't even flinch. She's practical and level-headed. I value her opinion. She's my touchstone.

I say, "I've reached a point in my life where I can retire if I want to. I'm sixty-six years old. That's full retirement age for me. I've already arranged to collect Social Security starting in March. I'm still working, but when that first check comes, I won't have to work for money or health insurance. I can make other decisions. It's scary or exciting, I'm not sure which."

I like my job. Working has its benefits. I like being with people, accomplishing something. At one point in my career, I made a game of noticing, "What is the most common thing I say at work?" And the answer, my survey said, was, "You're welcome." Patients say thank you when I bring them a towel, or give them a medication, or spend some time listening. And my coworkers say thank you when I help them out with something, or give them a compliment. Where else, when I "retire," will I be able to find this satisfying situation? But the job is stressful, too. I have been wondering what it would be like if I didn't have that kind of stress in my life regularly. I've spent the last eleven years working as a psychiatric nurse.

I confess that part of what motivates me is that I don't want to just stay home alone with no job. That sounds too boring and depressing. I'm not good at doing nothing. I might get what we call in New England "cabin fever." I recently had a painful breakup. My kids are grown and independent. When I talk about stealth camping, people often say to me, "That takes courage." I don't feel courageous. I don't have the courage to stay home alone with nothing to do. I am running away from grief and loneliness. I can't even consider not going. Whenever I'm not busy thinking about something else, my head is full of thoughts of stealth camping.

The other part of what motivates me is that I have always loved travel. Ever since I was a little kid, when I heard the car start up in the driveway, I would run out and leap into the backseat in time to go with my father to the hardware store or with my mother to the grocery store. My father's blue-and-white '57 Chevy, the green '63 VW bus, and later that clunky blue Chevy van that I drove to pass my driver's test. I just wanted to go.

I had done stuff like this before. Camping and traveling cross-country with my family as a kid, bicycle tripping, hitchhiking in the seventies and roughing it (don't tell my parents), traveling, and traveling alone. This kind of a trip is easy to imagine. Having a van to sleep in seems to me like luxurious accommodations. And the timing. After I quit work, I'll have no job, no kids at home, no commitments. I'll have money from my Social Security check and income from my rental apartments. I have health and energy, and I just love the idea. I think, *Now is my chance.*

So, when I hear Faith's reaction, that's when I decide to go ahead and do it. That is the moment the daydream becomes a plan.

I have only two colossal decisions to make: I have to quit my job, and I have to buy a stealth camping vehicle. After that, the rest will seem effortless.

I go shopping for a minivan. I start looking at old beaters. Frugal me. When I talk with my dad on the phone, I say, "I'm looking at a 2006 minivan with about a hundred thousand miles on it."

He says, "I think you need something more reliable." I realize that I'd rather have something that won't leave me stranded on the side of the road in any random godforsaken wilderness with no cell phone service. Something I can show my father so he won't worry so much. I see that if I have a van he approves of, it will be a better van for me, too.

I shop around for about a month. I try out a few. I test-drive a five-year-old Dodge Grand Caravan. It doesn't seem Grand to me, which is good. I'm looking for something nondescript. Maybe this van should have been called the Dodge Nondescript Soccer Mom Caravan. It's something no one will notice. It has thirty-three thousand miles on it. The salesman, Tommie, says, "This one was previously owned by an elderly couple who left it in the garage for half the year every winter while they were in Florida." Sounds like a story, I know. But the mileage and the condition of the van make me think the story is true.

I need a ride back to the car dealer to buy the van. My tall, strong, handsome, brown-eyed son Micah steps up to the plate. He says, "I'll take you there, Mom. Plus, I want to check out the van, too." Bless his heart. So he and I drive up to Brunswick, Maine.

Micah and Tommie and I spend some time trying to figure out how to fold the backseats down into the floor. We can see that there is plenty of room for my necessities. Tommie opens the side door and says, "This is your porch. I can see you sitting here in Utah or some exotic place sipping a glass of wine." A nice idea. It isn't going to be wine, but I don't need to tell him that and spoil his fantasy.

Micah waits patiently while Tommie and I accomplish all the paperwork and get the thing insured. I pay for some of the van with my credit card, just so I can get points, and pay the rest with a check from my checkbook that's held together with duct tape. Frugal me. The first colossal decision is checked off the list.

I'm already in love with this van. The seats fold into the floor easily, once we know how, leaving a space in the back that's four feet by seven feet. It's a handsome shade of sparkly black. All the back windows are tinted. That's a feature that I appreciate for the privacy.

Well, that first Social Security check does in fact get deposited, and I give six weeks' notice at work. Second and final colossal decision is complete.

Coincidentally, a young popular tech gives his notice for the same day, so a party is organized for him and me at a local restaurant, Sebago Brewing. I get some gifts, including a number of blank journals. Maybe that means people want me to write about my travels? It would be nice to think so. As the introverted nondrinker of the group, I am one of the first to leave the goodbye party. When I stand up to go, my friend Mary Lou, the weekend charge nurse, stands with me and announces loudly, "Zinnia is leaving the house!" I look back and see all the smiling faces, some people raising their glasses, and all waving and shouting their well wishes. It's a picture that is burned into my memory and can bring me to tears.

I have an ambitious plan to visit all the people I know who will have me, to see all the national parks that I haven't already seen, and to go to an AA meeting in each of the forty-eight contiguous states.

AA is a place where you can be in a room with people who wish you well and want you to succeed. My recovering friend Lydia said, "You're not traveling alone, you have AA." A comforting thought. My faith in AA and AAA gives me courage to attempt this adventure.

Faith says she'll be available by phone in an emergency. She has an attentive energy that holds me with kindness and compassion. It's comforting to even think about her.

My tall, strong, handsome, gray-eyed son Seth is getting married at the end of June, and I can't miss that. My plan is to do my traveling in two chunks, a southeastern loop, a return to Maine for the wedding, and then a western loop. That's as far as I've gotten in my planning. Beyond that, I will take it one day at a time.

May 13: In the Van

I set out early for the four-hour trip from my home in Maine to my first stop. My parents, Ruth and George, live in a senior housing place in Newington, Connecticut, the town where I grew up. It's Mother's Day.

I'm confident about the travel but apprehensive about the loneliness factor. It wasn't that long ago that I had a sudden, unexpected breakup. That Guy and I had been together for over three years. The relationship was safe, comfortable, easy, and problem-free. Or so I thought. Neither of us had any complaints. That Guy broke up with me in an e-mail, allowing no discussion, and I still don't know why. It was a hard hit.

Traveling alone isn't my first choice. Usually when I travel, I'm excited and happy. This time, I'm sad, lonely, ashamed to be single and not knowing what, if anything, I did wrong. I grew up with brothers and sisters, lived with roommates, married, and had my own children who grew up and got their own lives. All that is over now, and I'm living alone. One can have close friends and dear family members and still feel lonely going home to find no one there. I'm trying to escape.

For years now, my Christmas gift to my parents has been a homemade certificate good for four lunches out in the coming year. That's what I would want most from my own kids. I take my parents out to lunch at the Wood-N-Tap restaurant on the Berlin Turnpike, my brother Mike's suggestion. We're joined by my siblings and in-laws: Mike and Alison, Martha and Tom, Sue and Gary. All couples, and me. Sigh. Eye roll.

We all get along pretty well in my family. No one is drinking, no one is fighting, everyone is on speaking terms. We are really quite civil. The only difficulty might be that we are all senior citizens and half of us are hard of hearing. "What?" is the most commonly heard response at our gatherings.

Back at my parents' place, I have a chance to show off my van to them and to my sister Martha and her husband, Tom. I slide open both side doors and pop open the rear door so they can see in. My dad says, "Looks like a good van." He checks out all my preparations, just like a dad.

I say, "I have this camping cot here. It came with a thin foam mattress, and I added another foam mattress topper to that. It's cushy and wonderful. Feel it." My dad pushes the mattress down to test it. "I have two sleeping bags in case it gets really cold." The bed has a lavender bottom sheet and pillowcase, a blue blanket, and a blue India-print cotton bedspread. "I would love to have a bright-colored old-school VW bus with the peace sign and flowers, but that would not be subtle enough for stealth camping. So I settled for this India print so I can still see myself as a hippie. A stealthy hippie. When I worked at the homeless shelter, one of the residents called me 'a flower child out of season.'"

"You're still that," he says. I have long, brown hair turning to gray. I rarely wear makeup, and I dress casually, usually jeans and a T-shirt and sweater.

I step into the van and sit on the cot. "I have plenty of room under the cot for boxes of food and clothes, and the spare tire. And I can sit up tall on the cot with a couple of extra inches between my head and the ceiling." I demonstrate.

"This milk crate holds four gallons of emergency water in case I'm stranded in a desert."

"Don't say that," my dad says.

"See how I used bungee cords to attach these plastic drawers to the milk crate? The weight of the water keeps the drawers from falling over. There are five drawers here, five departments: electronics, office supplies, health and beauty, accessories, and kitchen. The drawers are bungeed closed, too, so they don't fall open when I'm driving. This other milk crate is for holding laundry. I don't need curtains because of the tinted windows, but I'm hoping these sheer curtains will discourage the bugs. They're attached with Velcro."

"Are you going to be cooking?" my mom asks.

"I decided not to bother with pots and pans and a stove. I don't want to spend time making food and searching for enough water to wash dishes. But look at this." I show her an empty covered thirty-two-ounce yogurt container. "This is my emergency latrine. Remember the chamber pot you used back in our camping days?" We both laugh. "That's about it. Pretty basic."

My dad says, "What else are you bringing?"

"I have AAA maps of all the states." I show off a cardboard box packed full of maps. "I'm hoping to avoid fast highways and big cities, and the maps will help with that.

"I have this book called *Your Guide to the National Parks*, my National Park Senior Pass, a rechargeable clip fan, this sun shield that I can stick to the driver-side window, my old cigarette-lighter GPS, a box of CDs, including Spanish language-learning CDs, my journal and books, a knitting project, and a cooler to keep my dark chocolate from melting.

I have this little backpack to carry in the things I need for showering after my workouts at Planet Fitness. And of course, my smartphone." I point things out to them.

"I stocked up on supplements and things I might not be able to find on the road, like those weird Chinese batteries for my clip fan. I have to keep reminding myself that I'm only going to be in the United States and that I'll still be able to buy stuff. It's not like I'm going to Antarctica or anything. And I can use my phone. If you call and I don't answer, don't worry. It just means that I'm in a place with no signal."

"Who is taking care of business at home while you're away?" my dad asks.

"I put most of my bills on auto-pay if I could. My tenants are putting my mail in a box inside the porch. I gave them Micah's phone number in case they have a problem. I'm still not sure how I'll get my lawn mowed. Micah and Seth are wicked busy. My tenants declined my offer to pay them to do it. My friends are my age, and none of them are the lawn-mowing type. I didn't want to hire somebody off Craigslist, because then some random stranger would know that my place is unoccupied. I don't mind if my lawn looks neglected, but I don't want it to look completely abandoned and advertise the fact that I'm away. Micah said he'd check out the lawn now and then when he's in the neighborhood. I hated to ask him because he already has so much responsibility, but I didn't have any better idea, so I just said thank you."

"Good for him," my dad says.

Martha says, "I have a present for you." She hands me a pewter G clef, the symbol of music, on a ribbon.

"Oh, that's nice. Thanks," I say, and I hang it from my rearview mirror.

Tom points to my box of CDs. "You'll be speaking fluent Spanish by the time you get to California," he says. We laugh.

My dad asks, "Where are you going to stay tonight?"

I say, "I don't know—in the van I guess." We both smile.

After hugs all around, it's time to continue on with my grand stealthy adventure.

I go to a women's AA meeting in West Hartford, Connecticut. Only a half dozen women are in the meeting room of a church. This cozy and comfortable room has soft couches and rugs, and nice people. Here's what I hear:

"I make all these plans and God laughs."

"Every day I get a daily reprieve from the disease. It's really a stay of execution."

"I'm twenty-six years sober. I can go to a party and not notice the alcohol at all, but I've seen all the brownies!"

It's heartwarming and reassuring to be in a room where people get me. I feel more normal, more optimistic. Meetings have a way of putting things into perspective for me. And I can certainly relate about the brownies. I've been having more trouble staying away from sweets than staying away from alcohol lately. It's been over thirty-two years since I drank any alcohol. It isn't something I think about. Although the alcohol doesn't seem to be a current struggle for me, the "ism" of alcoholism still persists. The things that "drive me to drink" are the things that are addressed in AA. That's why I still find meetings to be helpful for my well-being. The meeting ends at five and I still have some daylight, so I move along.

It's a pretty ride to Yorktown Heights, New York. Leafy, green, lake-y, rural, cloudy, drizzly. The temperature is in the fifties. I stop at a scenic overlook to take a photo of the gray Hudson River with green trees on both sides and clouds overhanging.

I begin to think I won't find a sleep spot because it's so rural. I look behind churches, behind closed stores, on the roadside. It occurs to me that security cameras are common now, and they would record my license plate. Neighbors might report suspicious vehicles parked on roadsides overnight. I look for a place to park in town. I find a line of cars on the road and don't see any no-parking signs. I park. I hit the lock, and without getting out of the van, I go to the back and into my sleeping bag. Grateful for the tinted windows, I sleep.

May 14: Hiding in Plain Sight

While drifting off to sleep last night, I thought about old times. When I was a kid, my father was a teacher, and later, a guidance counselor. He worked other jobs in the summer, but in 1966, when I was fourteen years old, he took the whole summer off and took us all camping cross-country. There were seven of us—my mom, my dad, and us five kids: my two brothers, Mike and Andy, and my two sisters, Susie and Martha. We had that clunky Chevy van. My dad had made boxes out of plywood to store all our gear, and we used them as seats in the van. Seat belts were not required in those days. *Seats* were not even required. We had AAA maps and TripTiks and campground directories to guide us.

At night we had two options. If we were staying only one night, all the boxes would come out and two sets of bunk-bed cots would be set up in the empty van. Four of us kids would sleep there. The pup tent would be set up for my parents and littlest brother, Andy. If we were staying longer at the same place, we would set up our big old tent for all of us. My dad would get one kid holding up a pole on each of the four corners while he went inside and put up the ridgepole. Then my mom and the remaining kid would go around staking it all up. It was made of heavy canvas and was an ordeal to put up. Especially in hot weather, which was typical.

Cooking was mostly my mom's job. We had a gas camp stove and ate variations on Spam Delight. We kids took turns hauling water, doing dishes. Mornings when we were moving on, everything had to be packed up. I got skillful at rolling up sleeping bags.

Often while we were on the road, my mom would interrupt our squabbling by saying, "Hey, kids! Look at the view!"

That was the cue for all of us to make fun of her by hooting, "Lookit the view! Lookit the view!" It's a standing joke in our family now.

My dad's squabble prevention strategy was to say, "OK, kids. A dollar for the first person who sees an Alaska plate." We would all shut up and look out the windows. None of us ever saw an Alaska license plate. This was 1966. I don't know how many cars in Alaska were capable of making the trip to the Lower 48.

Last night, I slept fitfully in my first stealth camping spot. I'm not used to it yet. I wake up early. The seven o'clock meeting in Yorktown Heights is at a beautiful stone church where I hit the bathroom before the meeting starts. I enjoy the New York accents. They say:

"My sponsor told me my emotions are where my alcoholism lives."

"Somewhere along the line, the gnawing in my gut went away."

"I just hated everyone and everything. And I was stuck with the thing I hated most: me."

"My spiritual awakening is to see how Godlike I can act."

I like the idea of acting "Godlike." I don't know if there is a God or not. But I do have a goal to act "Godlike" or at least "goodlike." They talk a lot about God in AA. On paper, the AA program allows for people to find their own Higher Power that is true for them. But in practice, the culture of

AA seems to be that you should have a god that has your best interest in mind always, and you are the center of that god's universe. Like a Santa Claus God who gives you things or a 911 God for emergencies. As for me, I have never been able to find that. Not so it sticks, anyway. The AA group is a reliable power greater than myself. It has proven itself. No leap of faith is required. Step 2 says, "Came to believe that a power greater than ourselves could restore us to sanity." AA is that.

New Jersey has pretty towns and big houses with nice landscaping. Spring is a beautiful time. I am in love with those pink dogwoods. It is a treat to see flowery green lawns in springtime and smell the newly mowed grass.

I get a quick text from my son Seth, who is in Vegas for his bachelor party. And we have a brief text dialogue. Though I am happy to get his text, and impressed that he thinks of his mom at his bachelor party, I long for a real conversation with him. I miss my boys, who are men now.

Into Pennsylvania, I get a call from Micah. He's in Vegas at Seth's bachelor party, and he's impressed with how awesome the party is. He asks about my travels so far. I tell him, "I have decided to sleep only where I can park amongst other parked cars overnight."

He says, "Kind of like hiding in plain sight."

"That describes stealth camping exactly." There is a learning curve to this stealth camping thing. My heart smiles after this conversation with him.

I find a meeting in West Chester, Pennsylvania, at a beautiful new modern church with a large parking lot surrounded by greenery. Don't think I am going to do nothing but go to meetings on this trip. Have patience; you'll hear about plenty of other stuff, too. It's just that I don't quite know what else to do with myself at this point. Meetings are safe, interesting, and comforting. I can find the human connection I long for there. So why not? But here's what I hear at the West Chester meeting:

"I got sick and tired of the high cost of low living."

"All my struggles are between my ears."

At this meeting a woman says, "I saw a billboard advertising a trapeze school. I was longing to do that, but I thought that it didn't apply to me. Then I noticed there was a phone number on the sign, and that number is there for people to call. I realized that I am also people, and that even *I* could call that number. How many ways do I limit myself with my beliefs?" That's a good question for me to ponder, too, at this transitional time in my life.

I drive into town, where I find a residential neighborhood with cars parked on the street. Multiunit houses on the right and a park on the left. I just want to make sure I don't park in a neighborhood where mine is the most expensive-looking car in the bunch. Locked in with the tinted windows, I'm safe and snug as a turtle. So far, so good.

May 15: It's Not Just a Daydream

I sleep like a brick. Another van parks right in front of me, and I don't even hear it. I clean up with wet wipes, get dressed behind the tinted windows, and make a pit stop at a fast-food place.

Breakfast is grapes, cheese, and dark chocolate. And water. I have several one-liter soda bottles that I fill with water at Planet Fitness or at rest areas along the road. I have a brilliant plan to drink two liters in just the first half of every day so that I can stay hydrated and not have to get up to pee at night. Worth a try.

Delaware uses the mobile phone app called AA Meeting Guide. The app describes the meeting and tells you how far away it is from your current location and what time it starts. You can hit Directions, and that takes you to the GPS, which tells you how to get there. It couldn't be easier. Without the app, I'd have to Google meetings and attempt to fathom their various and differing websites, then find them on the map. That can be time consuming and frustrating. I rejoice when I find that I am in an area where this app is used.

The early meeting in Newark, Delaware, is a group called Dawn Patrol. Before the meeting they have a "group conscience" to discuss how to handle a difficult situation involving a man who is not present at the time. This man sometimes interrupts the meeting, walking around, moving chairs, making noise, speaking out of turn. It's agreed that if he is disruptive again, he will be asked to leave, and the police will be called if he does not leave. I hear them strug-gling with this decision. No one wants anyone to be asked to leave, and yet, people need to be able to focus on the meeting, too. Here are some other things I hear:

"People go chasing after that perfect material thing to make them feel better. That won't work. There is no perfect material thing."

"I used to act the fool. Now I can act the fool by choice. AA is a good deal for a dollar."

"On vacation I saw people drinking by the pool. Morning, noon, and night. Next day they were late to the pool."

"If I won the Powerball, it would kill me. I'm not spiritually fit enough to manage that."

"Faith can move mountains. Bring a shovel."

When people talk about faith, they are usually referring to a faith in God. I don't seem to be able to find that, so I look for other kinds of faith. Faith can move mountains, but you don't just stand there, scrunching up your face and clenching your fists, praying for God to move the mountain. You have to have faith that your action, and the actions of others, can move that mountain. Faith is how you keep going when the situation seems difficult or impossible. I've heard my mother say, "God helps those who help themselves."

I have faith that I can help myself to the support that the AA program offers and be restored to sanity. I have faith that AAA can help me if I have a car problem. I have faith in the people in my life who have been helpful and kind to me. I have faith in Faith.

In Bel Air, Maryland, I pull over and take a photo of what looks to me like a 1950s-era Chevy Bel Air sitting up on the roof of a restaurant. I text the picture to Micah. He and his wife, Melissa, own and run an ice cream shop in Maine. Micah had an old 1956 stretch Cadillac that he painted pink and put up on metal posts to draw attention to their business. It has become a landmark. This project involved months of work and planning, and plenty of worrying. I tend to notice stuff like that, now that I know a little about the difficulties of actually doing such a thing.

It's a long drive across Maryland. Scary traffic on I-695 around Baltimore. Mountains in the west. Pretty, but I have to contend with trucks blowing my van sideways by speeding past me on the downhills, then slowing me down on the uphills. Traffic has been the scariest part of the trip so far. I see Confederate flags and wonder, *What does that mean to me with my Maine license plates and New England accent?*

In Fairmont, West Virginia, I call the AA hotline and learn about a meeting at seven thirty. I have time to scout out a sleep spot. I find a residential street that would have cars parked overnight. I eat my picnic supper in the park by the river. And call the folks and let them know that I'm OK. More than OK.

When I was considering this adventure, I told my dad, "I have a daydream of traveling the country again and camping out in a van."

He pointed at me and said, "Make sure it's not just a daydream."

Our conversation continued, and I was chattering on about retiring. I said, "I wish I had a consuming passion so I could save the world and win a Nobel Prize."

And he said, "Well, that's not typical for people in retirement." After a pause he added, "Maybe something will come to you when you're traveling." That's my dad.

When seven thirty comes, I meet only two other women at the meeting. We have a deep discussion about spirituality. Some things I hear are:

"I don't know about God. But there are miracles in AA. That's a fact."

"Yeah, I could walk along hand in hand with God, and eventually He'd lean over and say, 'How about you and me have a drink.'"

"Prayer and meditation is completely opposite of drugs and alcohol. Drugs and alcohol give me permission to give in to my lower self."

"I don't usually know what God's will is for me. But I usually know what it's not."

"Drinking turns down the volume on God's voice."

One of the women at the meeting, Dawn, invites me to come to her farm to stay the night. I already have a sleep spot in mind, so at first, I almost reflexively want to say, "No thanks, I'm all set." Typical Zinnia. I stop myself and think, *Zinnia. You're on an adventure.* I say, "Sure, that would be great."

"I have a guest room."

"I've been sleeping in my van."

"OK, so stay in my driveway."

"All right, then."

I follow Dawn on the highway. She drives fast. Through rain and lightning. The roads keep getting smaller and more twisty. The potholes are outlined in white paint. A harrowing ride. Her farm is nestled in some green hills. I meet her husband, Dan, and her dog, who keeps smearing his wet face on my bare legs. *I wish I wasn't wearing shorts.*

Dawn is older than me, pretty, with long, straight white hair. Dan is eighty-three, with a trim white beard and white hair. They tell me tales of their trip from California. She says, "We slept in the back of our pickup truck."

And they talk about their pet bull. Dan says, "He kept breaking through fences to get to the neighbor's cows, in spite of the fact that there were cows in his own yard. We had to give him up." When he speaks of the cattle auction, she takes her glasses off and wipes her eyes. He says, "She won't eat beef."

Their house is cluttered with useful, interesting objects. She has painted the cabinets yellow with hardware shaped like fishes. An electric keyboard in the kitchen has a John Thompson grade three music lesson book on the stand.

Next to their house, they have a cabin. She says, "He sleeps next door because I am restless and he doesn't sleep well."

She draws me a map to get back to Route 50 in the morning, because she plans to sleep later than me. She says,

"Since I retired, I sleep later and later all the time." I sleep in the van. It's raining. Cool, dark, and quiet.

May 16: You Can't Be Hateful when You're Grateful

I sleep well with the sound of the rain on the van roof. I love rain, and water in all its many forms: mist, snow, icicles, clouds, the river behind my home in Maine reflecting the evening lights of town. I take some pretty pictures of Dawn's farm in the early morning mist, when all the world is asleep except for the birds. I can see the broken split-rail fence, the green field, the red barn with the shiny metal roof, the leafy hills and misty mountains beyond. My mother might say, "My Lord, what a morning!"

Back in the van, I start my morning routine: install contact lenses, brush my hair, wash up with wet wipes, get dressed, put on sunscreen, take my supplements, eat something, check the weather on my phone, look at the map, make the bed. I decide to keep the bed made so that I won't be embarrassed when people ask to see my home, as they often do. I'm proud to show it off, and I imagine myself a young hippie again, free and adventuresome with my blue India-print bedspread.

I take a back road to Route 50. Homes in disrepair, slanted porch steps, peeling paint. Mobile homes. Gardens waiting to be planted. Rain. The gas-and-fast-food place is crowded in Ellentown, the local morning rush. After using the restroom, I eat the last of the dark chocolate I brought. *Before it can melt*, I tell myself.

I've been to six meetings in six different states in the past two days: New York, New Jersey, Pennsylvania, Delaware, Maryland, West Virginia. (More information in Appendix B.) I wonder if that's a record of some kind. I want to call my sponsor, Faith, and brag. I know I will not be keeping this up, though. The states will be getting bigger and the meetings farther apart, and I will be getting the hang of finding other stuff to do. Still trying to figure out what to do with myself.

For several hours in the morning, I listen to CDs on the way to Dunbar, West Virginia. Beatles, Tchaikovsky, Spanish language-learning. I shout out all the vocabulary words in my best Spanish accent, and no one judges me. At this age, I find that I learn it, forget it, learn it, and forget it again. I remember my high school French better than the Spanish I tried to learn last week. In high school, I never imagined I would actually be traveling to places where Spanish is spoken: Oaxaca, Guatemala, Puerto Rico, Cozumel, Honduras. I wish I had taken Spanish in school instead. So much more useful.

Back in 2007 in a conversation with my friend Lee, we discovered that we each had a sponsored child in a program called Camino Seguro in Guatemala. Right at that moment, we both agreed, "We are going there." We spent a week doing volunteer work at the program, and a week touring Guatemala and Honduras.

She spent her week in the library working on art projects with the kids, and I worked with Ruth in the kitchen. I had a chance to practice my limited Spanish. Ruth said, *"Frijoles, frijoles, y mas frijoles."* Meaning that what they had to eat at the program was "beans, beans, and more beans." Camino Seguro means "Safe Passage," and it was a program to help kids who were living in the Guatemala City dump by getting them to school and giving them meals.

Ruth and I had prepared the lunch that day. I was hungry, and we ate frijoles with the kids. I was thirsty, too, and chugged down a big tall glass of Kool-Aid before I remembered that I, myself, had made it out of tap water. I thought, *Oh crap, I'm in for it now.* I idled in bed most of the next day with aches and fever. Luckily, it wasn't as bad as I had feared. They tell you not to drink the water, but they never specifically tell you not to drink the Kool-Aid. Note to self.

It had been Lee's idea to stay in the town of Antigua, Guatemala, during Semana Santa, or Holy Week. It was the week before Easter, and the locals were in mournful religious mode. People spent hours covering the streets with *alfombras*, which were intricate carpets painstakingly made of stuff like colored wood shavings, flowers, leaves, and vegetables. Parades moved all through the town, day and night. When the parades passed, they just scuffed up the alfombras, and after the parade, the scuffed-up alfombras were scooped up with push brooms and tossed into a dump truck that had been following along. The parade floats represented the Stations of the Cross. These "floats" had no wheels, and it took a couple of dozen people to laboriously haul them down the street on their shoulders. I could see the heavy floats swaying from side to side as they moved slowly, in step with a brass band that played gloomy music. I saw people walking alongside the floats in hoods and robes, and I smelled the incense they carried. The scene was visceral, a devotion, an offering to Christ.

On the Guatemala trip, we also had a chance to visit Mayan ruins, Lake Atitlan, and Tikal National Park. Lake Atitlan is the most beautiful place I have ever seen. Tall mountains surround the lake. Small villages are accessible only by boat. We stayed at a lakeside bed-and-breakfast with a front yard full of trumpet flowers.

The thing I remember most about Tikal National Park is leaping out of bed, startled awake at four in the morning by a screaming roar that made my hair stand up. I found out later that I'd had my first howler monkey experience.

But now I arrive at the neighborhood in Dunbar, West Virginia, where the meeting will be. I'm early, as usual, wanting to make sure I can locate the place before the meeting starts at noon. I walk around the neighborhood, seeing broken windows, offices where people can apply for various types of assistance, a child-care center in a storefront with a collection of different bedsheets used as curtains, counseling offices, a "Groups Recover Together" office, and the Serenity Club, where the next meeting will be. I go into the thrift store that benefits the Anchor Program, and donate a bit of extra money. I get some music CDs and a book called *A Thousand Places to See Before You Die*. A thousand is a lot. I guess I better get going, then.

The Serenity Club may have been a storefront in the past. It's a large room with a dirty tile floor and mismatched chairs. Whispering, giggling, disruptions, people walking around, getting coffee. A generous share of tattooed and pierced people, some men with their ball caps sitting high and tilted on their heads. Some people are required by probation to go to AA meetings, and they have to get a paper signed by the chairperson of the meeting. Kind of a weird situation, since last names are not used in AA, according to the AA tradition of anonymity. They could have even gotten their bartender to sign those papers. I'm sure that has been done sometimes. Don't tell anybody. Some meetings have more of these mandated participants than other meetings do. Even with all the disruptions, I hear:

"You can't be hateful when you're grateful."

"I had to get honest with myself. Not just cash-register honesty."

"I thought the problem was the wife, the wife, the wife, the job, the job, the job, the boss, the boss, the boss. But it was me."

"There are only two times I need a meeting: when I don't want to go and when I do."

"Some people have to get a nudge from the judge."

"I really minimized my drinking. I told myself, everybody pisses the bed, right?"

In many meetings, they go around the room having people introduce themselves and I have a chance to say, "Zinnia, recovering alcoholic." If not for this custom, people in AA would hardly know me at all. Doggone my shyness. What a predicament: a shy person who is lonely.

Often, the chairperson asks who is new, or who is visiting, so I take that opportunity to say that I'm from Maine. I speak about how comforting it is to have a place to go when I'm traveling, where people are friendly and they understand me, and how AA is my home away from home. That's my standard spiel.

People might think I'm texting in a meeting because I use my phone to take notes about things people say so I can write them up later for you. By writing for you, I can imagine I have a companion with me. I considered bringing in a notebook. But I think it might be intimidating to people in the meeting to see someone spying and taking notes, because really, who does that in a meeting?

After the meeting, I hit the road with Stevie Wonder and Linda Ronstadt to keep me company now. I drive through a full-on thunderstorm east of Lexington, Kentucky. I find full-on thunderstorms exciting and beautiful, especially when I can sit under cover and watch them.

In Kentucky, I stop for gas at a rural crossroad with rolling green fields all around and a few houses in the distance. As I begin the task of feeding my van, a polite young man wearing clean jeans and a T-shirt approaches me. He says,

"Ma'am, I dropped my gas cap under your van, just so you're not surprised to find me under there."

I laugh and say, "Thanks for the warning." He ducks around the front of my van and I continue with my task, still smiling.

I'm on my way to visit Megan, my friend from junior high. The roads to her house are narrow, curving, with drop-offs on both sides. Her home is a white Cape-style house with an inviting open porch, sitting up on a rise with fields all around, a barn in back. Her steep driveway is paved with meatball-sized stones. The van is skidding on the stones and I think, *It would be ironic if I came all these miles only to get stuck in her driveway.* After a few attempts, I make it to the top and park in front of her house. And breathe a sigh of relief.

I haven't seen Megan since I visited her six years ago, when I was on another road trip with my parents to visit my brother Andy in Knoxville. Megan greets me with a hug and we get right down to it, talking about Medicare, cholesterol, carbohydrates, organic gardening, politics, grandkids. The usual subjects that are interesting for women who are sixty-six years old.

I see that Megan has given up on trying to straighten out her curly hair, and it's beautiful and still dark brown. Back in the sixties, when straight hair was the thing, she used to set her hair at night using huge rollers made of empty cans, then try to sleep that way.

We reminisce about old times. We were in the same class in junior high school in Connecticut. She and I used to take the city bus every Saturday into downtown Hartford to poke around in stores and window-shop. The bus cost twenty-five cents then, and the cigarettes that we sneaked cost thirty-two cents a pack. We were underage at that time, but we could write notes, supposedly from our fathers, asking the store clerk to allow us to pick up a pack of cigarettes for him. And we got away with that every time.

We especially liked shopping for patterns and fabrics. We sewed our own clothes in those days, after we had learned how to do it in home ec class. We did that until we discovered thrift stores. Sundays, we sang together in the church choir, both altos. Just for entertainment purposes, we learned the sign language alphabet so we could amuse each other during boring sermons, talking about parties, boys, school, or shopping. I hadn't realized at the time how cool it was being her friend and having all that fun together. But I realize it now, in hindsight.

I sleep in the van in Megan's driveway. I tell her I'm used to it and it's comfortable. And it's the easiest thing to do.

May 17: Edible Garden

For breakfast, Megan makes us a smoothie from strawberries, bananas, spinach, and almond milk.

Megan's dogs rub their soggy faces all over my bare legs. So gross. If you are around dogs, you have to expect to get mucus and saliva on you. Why are people so attracted to this? I am not a dog person. I have taken criticism about that. People have said to me, "You can't trust a person who doesn't like dogs," and "Not liking dogs is a form of mental illness," and "What are you, some kind of germaphobe?" and "You are so cold-hearted." OK, so yes, I am a social outcast, a freak of nature, a person who is not a dog person. Sorry. I know you hate me now.

Sometimes I believe I have been born on the wrong planet. I'm not a dog person, not even a pet person. I don't drink, drug, smoke, vape, use caffeine, or take any prescription medications. I avoid sugar and processed food. I exercise regularly. I don't care to watch sports unless I know someone on the team. I don't buy things just for fun. I don't wear makeup or go to the hairdresser. I don't have cable TV. I see TV news as traumatizing propaganda. I don't like violent movies. I don't think violence is entertainment. I have an aversion to guns, and I don't celebrate war. I see gender inequality and I object to it. I like Tchaikovsky and contra dancing. I read books. I play the bassoon. I walk in nature and wonder why others are not doing that. I believe there may or may not be a God. This is why I treasure people who "get me."

Megan takes me on a long drive to the Bernheim Arboretum and we wander around in the sunshine looking at plants and trees. Her son, Cole, works here. We meet up with him at noon, and I treat them to lunch. The restaurant at the

Arboretum is sunny, and we sit outside on the patio. The menu offers things that are organic and features vegetables, various teas, and politically correct coffees. Cole talks with enthusiasm about his work.

After lunch, he shows off the "edible garden" he created with raised beds full of compost. He says, "All the plants in here are things you can eat." He has dark hair and startlingly blue eyes for the son of a brown-eyed mom.

Megan takes a picture of me on the boardwalk at the Arboretum for me to post on my Facebook page, which is called Wander Woman, for all my friends to like.

When I set up this private Facebook group page, I wrote this description: "It has been suggested that I create a group to stay in touch with people while I am WANDERing around the US this summer. I would like to keep in touch, but I don't want just any random people to know that my house is left empty. You can choose to follow this group, or unfollow if you are bored. Looking forward to staying connected!" Then I invited only people I know to join the group. None of them have unfollowed, I'm happy to see.

On the way home, we stop to pick up spice jars for a sale Megan is doing on Saturday. She has a business growing organic garlic. We spend some time filling jars with garlic salt and other flavored salts, then labeling and sealing them. Lots of talking during that process. I'm getting a headache from breathing in all that salty garlic dust.

She has been with her husband, Jimmy, for a long time. Cole is from a previous relationship, and Jimmy is ten years younger than Megan. Megan says, "Our daughter, Elizabeth, is married to a Brazilian guy and they have two kids. Our son-in-law plans to speak Portuguese to the kids so they will be bilingual."

"They're lucky kids," I say. "Too bad Jimmy is away working. I enjoyed meeting him last time I was here. He has that southern courtesy. And it seems like he is good to you, right, Megan?"

"Yes, and I'm lucky, too."

Sometimes I feel shame that I am single, like I've failed. Even though people tell me it's not a failure, it still feels like it is. I've learned that you can't predict or control what other people will do. The men I've been in relationships with have either turned mean, or left me, or both. I say, "I have tried everything in relationships, except getting lucky."

Megan makes chicken, pineapple, and asparagus for supper. I am well fed today. She's having drinks. We watch *Jeopardy.*

I tell her, "My son Seth's wedding is coming up on June thirtieth. Let me show you a picture of my dress." On my phone, I show her the photo of me in my red formal gown. "I'm looking for a pair of chunky high-heeled sandals to wear so I can be dressed up and still be able to walk on the grass."

She goes to her closet and pulls out a pair just like that, and gives them to me. She tells me, "This is perfect! I've been trying to get rid of stuff."

When I talk about the narrow roads, she says, "I've gone to the town so many times and requested that a line be painted down the middle of the roads. But they won't. They said that the roads are technically not wide enough for two lanes."

In the evening, in the van with both back doors open, I enjoy a nice cross-breeze as I write this in my journal.

May 18: Not Much Can Top That

In the morning, Megan and I say our reluctant goodbyes. She says, "Come see me on your way back."

My GPS leads me along a seven-mile narrow, curvy, hilly one-lane road that is actually a two-way road. Like the ones Megan complained to her town about. I see abandoned trailers, farms, run-down houses, hills, trees, meadows. It's frustrating. I can't enjoy the beautiful countryside. I have to watch the road closely because I'm worried that I won't see a car coming toward me around all those curves and hills.

I go to a meeting in Danville, Kentucky, in the Presbyterian Church Annex. Because it's during a weekday, all dozen people tend to be retirement age, even older than me, if you can believe that. It's a topic meeting, and we go around the room one by one, talking about the question, "How has AA changed you?" Here are some quotes I hear at that meeting:

"Alcohol solved all my problems. Until it started causing them."

"An alcoholic is the only person who can be lying in the gutter and look down their nose at another alcoholic."

"It's a simple program. All you have to do is change every damn thing in your life."

When my turn comes, I mention not knowing what to do with myself in retirement. After the meeting, a gray-haired man touches me on the shoulder and says, "Hey, you know I retired at age fifty-five and I didn't have much of a plan, either. My Higher Power gave me new opportunities. Some part-time or volunteer jobs. Things like being a coach, a board member, a Scout leader. I learned a lot and met a lot of new people." I find this to be encouraging, because I don't know what to expect from life after leaving my job. Eventually, I will go home. I won't be traveling forever. I will find new opportunities, too, I just don't know what they'll be yet.

The road from Danville into Tennessee, is pretty straightforward. Highway. And nothing remarkable happens. Just me with my Spanish language-learning CDs and the voices in my head. I know you're thinking, *I'm glad* I *don't have voices in my head.* Well, that's the voice I'm talking about.

My brother Andy's house is in one of the historic districts of Knoxville. It's a gray two-story house with a slate roof, surrounded by tall trees. It has a big open front porch with a porch swing that I love. I'm greeted at the door by Andy and the dog, Lucy. He says, "You will not be sleeping in the van when you're at my house. You should get out of Dodge...Caravan." I'm shown to the upstairs front bedroom where I am to stay. It seems to be the former bedroom of my grown-up nephew Richard. On the desk is a birthday card that I sent him.

I have an hour to myself while Andy showers and gets dressed up in his tux, his concert uniform. He's a cellist in the Knoxville Symphony Orchestra. Andy's wife, Helen, is off in Johnson City for the weekend preparing for her concert with the Johnson City Symphony. It's nice to have some time to write. I didn't write on the second day of my trip, and by the third day, I had trouble remembering much of what happened on the second day. I decide to write in my journal every day.

Andy's cat keeps rubbing up against my legs, getting hair all over the black pants I'll be wearing to the concert. These pants are actually scrub pants, but they look real nice and have side-seam pockets only, no patch pockets to give them away. I like wearing scrub pants when I travel. They have pockets, they're lightweight, cool, and comfortable, they wash and dry easily, and they pack up small and don't show wrinkles. What's not to like about scrub pants?

We drop Andy's cello off at the Tennessee Theater. At the door, I take a picture of him standing with his cello in its case. He is six foot three and slim, and looks like a handsome Ichabod Crane in his black tux with tails. Hard to believe I once carried this kid around on my hip.

We walk together, him with his tails and me with my dress-up scrub pants, to a restaurant called Not Watson's. He says, "There used to be a business here called Watson's that everyone was familiar with, so they call the restaurant Not Watson's."

We sit outside under an awning on the pedestrian mall. Suddenly, a crashing thunderstorm sends everyone, except us and our fellow diners, running for shelter. I say to Andy, "Eating good food under an awning in a crashing thunderstorm with my brother while waiting for a symphony concert. Not much can top that!"

Bernstein, Gershwin, and Copeland are on the program. The comp ticket (complimentary) that Andy gave me has me sitting in the orchestra section of the theater. At intermission, I move to an unoccupied seat in the balcony for a better view.

I'm remembering once, years ago, when I was visiting Andy, I went to a Knoxville AA meeting that ended when his symphony concert was about half over. I walked into the theater without a ticket and stood up in the back of the balcony during intermission and waited to see which seats were empty, then went and sat down, and again watched the second half of the concert I had seen the night before. At the time, I was feeling thrifty and smug and lucky.

On that occasion, the Mahler First Symphony was on the program. Andy had invited me to a party with his symphony colleagues after the concert. In addition to my shyness, I was in early recovery then. I was nervous about the party, so I made a plan. I listened to the Mahler a number of times at home before the concert so I could talk intelligently about it. I made it a point to remember the parts I liked. When I was introduced to people at the party, I could say things like, "I loved that bass solo you did where it's like 'Frère Jacques' in minor." People seemed to love hearing that kind of talk. I had been making a personal study of how to socialize without drinking. *My plan worked out well*, I congratulated myself.

Every year, I used to feel awkward at Faith's New Year's Day party at her house. I didn't know many people there. The first few years, I tended to arrive late or leave early. Then, when I was reading a book about shyness, I learned that shy people can actually be likeable. That was news to me. I came up with a strategy. I tried it out at Faith's next party and shared the results with her. "I found a way to deal with my awkwardness at your parties. I looked around the room to find someone who seemed more miserable than me. Then I went over and talked to that person."

Faith said, "Thank you."

"You're welcome," I said.

May 19: A Jaw-Dropping Solo

Helen arranged a comp ticket for me, so I'm debating whether I want to go all the way to Johnson City to hear her play with the Johnson City Symphony. It's a two-hour drive. I try to find out if I can take a bus or a train, but no. I decide to go ahead and take the van. I know it will be memorable. And I want to think of myself as someone who goes out of my way, someone who shows up.

In Johnson City, I gas up my beloved van and locate Milligan College, the place where the concert will be. I have some time to spend before the concert.

I stop in at Sycamore Shoals State Park. It's sunny and pleasantly warm. I wander down the easy paved walkway in the woods along the river. I sit for a while on a fallen tree, watching the current. I'm reminded of my riverfront home, my shoulders relax, and I take a breath.

The visitor center features a movie, totally from the settlers' point of view. *Biased*, I think. In a grassy field nearby, I see a replica of a fort where settlers defended themselves against the Cherokees. I see white tents and people in period costumes. Some kind of reenactment. I think, *Why reenact this? Wasn't it bad enough the first time? And what would the Cherokees have to say about this?*

Back at Milligan College, in the van, I change into my Best Jeans outfit to wear to the concert. Best jeans, blue India-print top, black sweater, amethyst polished-stone necklace that I got at a church rummage sale. And the chunky-heeled sandals Megan gave me. At the door, the woman can't find my comp ticket, so she just hands me one and says, "We know Helen."

I sit in the balcony on the side with the best view of Helen and the rest of the violinists. The program is all John Williams movie music. Some kids are in movie costumes for a costume contest at intermission. Helen plays some spectacular solos. One is from *Schindler's List* and makes me cry, remembering the emotions in the movie. Then, in another piece, she does a downward run that is so fast, it's a jaw-dropping solo. I want to stand up and yell, "That's my sister-in-law!"

The orchestra gets a lengthy standing ovation.

After the concert, Helen is sitting on the conductor's podium chatting with two other women. I can tell they're from the orchestra because they're wearing all black. She looks beautiful, all dressed in concert black, with stage makeup and her dark curly hair. We hug and I say, "Your solos were amazing! Stunning. I loved the whole concert."

She says, "Thanks! I'm glad you could come. It's so good to get to see you."

We chat for a while about the performance. I say, "I better get going. It's a long ride back, and it's already after ten."

She says, "I'm staying here tonight, but I'll see you tomorrow. Have a safe trip."

I hit the highway for the journey back to Andy's. I drive through three separate blasting thunderstorms along the way and it's well past my bedtime. People often say, "You're brave," when they hear about my travels alone. It does take some perseverance to "brave" this weather. But I make it back, and in Richard's comfortable bed, I fall asleep almost immediately.

May 20: A Real Home-Cooked Meal

I have tea with Andy in the morning and we talk about sibling-ish things: kids, music, work, our parents. I say, "I'm so glad they're in senior housing. They're much safer where they can ask for help if they need it."

"I agree. Well, I have stuff to do…"

"OK. I'll just hang out on the porch swing." I look at maps, write, read my Maeve Binchy novel.

Helen gets home from Johnson City, and we chat on the porch while she waits for her violin student to come. We talk about traveling, traveling alone, and her trip to see her son Thomas in Denver. "I took the car," she says. "I don't fly. I always go by car. You can see so many interesting things along the way, like the National Grasslands. Who knew there was even such a thing?"

"I'll be looking for stuff like that, too. I'm planning on stopping in to see Thomas when I'm out west later this summer."

When Helen's violin student leaves, the three of us and Lucy the dog go to Ijams Nature Center. We stroll the path through the woods and the boardwalk along a cliff-like area above the river. Helen has another student at five o'clock, and Andy has rehearsal with his jazz group from five to eight. The life of musicians. I'm thinking of going to a meeting at six thirty. So supper is planned for eight. Helen will be cooking beef in the pressure cooker. A real home-cooked meal to look forward to.

At the AA meeting, seven people sit in a downstairs room of a church. A woman with tattoos and piercings keeps getting up, walking around, touching and picking up things, making random statements. When her turn comes to share, she gives a lengthy, rambling, tangential speech. She is treated courteously and familiarly by the others in the group. One of the guys in the meeting says:

"Oh, I always had a job, so I could support my best friend, alcohol."

"I'm not responsible for what goes through my mind, but I am responsible for what comes out of my mouth."

This last quote makes sense to me. I have made a practice of trying to keep my words kind and clear. It's my belief that, if I try, I can find a way to say what I need to say without being abusive or mean. I think it's easier for people to hear a request than a criticism.

After the meeting, I'm sitting in the van in the parking lot. A man from the meeting notices that I'm lingering and says, "Is everything all right?"

"I'm just writing in my journal. I'm fine, but thanks for noticing and for checking in."

On the way back to Andy's, the dashboard engine malfunction indicator light comes on in my van. *Oh, well, I was fine*, I think. *Now what?*

Andy's house smells like supper. I tell Andy about the problem in my van. "It seems to be running OK. What would you suggest?"

"If it's running OK, don't bother with it."

I think about that. *That might be good advice if I were staying in Knoxville, but I'm planning to travel to who knows where. I don't want the van to die in a desert or on some remote mountaintop where I get no phone signal.*

Besides, with the light on, I won't know if something else goes wrong, because the light won't come on, because it will already be on.

"Well, I'd feel safer if I get it seen to. Do you have a mechanic to recommend?"

Andy tells me a place where I can get it fixed in the morning.

I get a text message from my sister-in-law Alison. She and my brother Mike live in the same town where my parents live, so she is up on the latest news about them. I sure do appreciate that. The message says, "Your mom is in the hospital with fluid around her heart. She's expecting to be discharged tomorrow."

I text her back, "Thanks so much for letting me know. I will call them."

I call my mom in the hospital. She says, "Oh, I'm OK. They gave me a diuretic and I'm going home tomorrow. I'll just be peeing all night."

Then I call my dad at home. He says, "Ruthie's coming home tomorrow. I'm doing OK, too, for an old guy." Neither of them seems upset at all, so I'm reassured. My mom is ninety and my dad is ninety-one. They have their ongoing health issues, but nothing terminal or life-threatening. I am grateful for cell phones and to be able to stay in touch with people I love. It's a great relief to me that Alison and Mike are nearby and paying attention.

May 21: People Don't Notice Much of Anything

I'm up at seven and ready to go. But I want to say goodbye and thanks to Andy and Helen. Musicians have concerts and rehearsals in the evening, so they are on a sleeping-late schedule, like I was when I worked the evening shift at the hospital. I wait around, looking at the map, checking the weather, metaphorically tapping my foot and looking at my watch. When they get up, we chat a short while in the kitchen.

Andy says, "Where are you off to next?"

"I'm going up to Mammoth Cave National Park after I get the van taken care of."

"Well, good luck with that. And be safe. Let us know if you need anything."

After hugs, I am good to go.

Now, on to the subject of car trouble. At one time, Micah offered to fix the check-engine light on my old Subaru. He said, "I'll just put a piece of electrical tape over the light. Problem solved." Once when I heard a knocking sound on my old VW bug, I fixed it by turning up the radio. Not this time. I am depending on this van, and I have to take good care of it if I want it to take good care of me.

I find the Firestone Complete Care that Andy suggested, and they take me right in. It's $99.00 for diagnostics, and the vapor canister valve will be removed and replaced, for a grand total of $263.43. The man tells me, "It will be done in an hour."

While I'm waiting, I cross the street to a shopping center and poke around in a Goodwill, my favorite store, and buy nothing. Sometimes I go into stores as if they are museums. In the Kroger store, I buy carrots, grape tomatoes, apples, cucumbers, and bananas.

While walking back to the Firestone place, I cross a bridge that overlooks a large stream. On the banks of the stream, some trees and weed bushes make a contrasting vision of wild nature surrounded by concrete and tar and metal and cars. I notice the sound of the water, and the leafy greenness, and it draws me in to pause at the scene. A man is camped out down by the water, out of sight from all the traffic and city bustle. He has found his oasis. He doesn't notice me, and I am sure that no one but me is noticing him. One thing that helps me feel safe while traveling alone is that I can be confident that I will probably not be noticed. There is a safety in that, for a stealth camper. In general, I can trust that people don't notice much of anything.

I bail out my van and begin the trip northwest back into Kentucky to visit Mammoth Cave National Park. I gain an hour because of the time change. I arrive just in time to take one of the ranger-led tours, one of my favorite things in the world to do. The cave tour that I want is sold out. The courteous southern lady at the ticket counter upsells me, saying, "Try the Domes and Dripstones Tour. It includes everything you want to see, plus more. You also get a fifty-percent Golden Age Discount because you have the Senior Pass for

National Parks." I end up paying less and seeing more. My lucky day. I'm learning that being a senior has its advantages.

It's a two-hour tour, including the bus that brings us to and from the cave entrance and the walk through the cave. I keep thinking of the melody of the *Gilligan's Island* theme song, changing the lyrics to "a two-hour tour."

The ranger says, "The place is called Mammoth Cave because there are more than four hundred miles of caves, and more that have yet to be explored. It's the longest-known cave system in the world." The tour of the cave is cool, literally. The ranger shows us where to go. I'd be lost without her. Steep stairs go down, walls dripping. There are large dry rooms, too, and a formation called Frozen Niagara. I can easily see why it's called that.

At one point, the ranger turns off the lights so we can experience true darkness. Impressive. Sounds are much more noticeable in the darkness—breathing, rustling of clothing.

A middle-aged man wearing a ball cap with a letter *G* on it is also here alone, and we tend to hang out together and exchange comments during the tour. I find that when I am traveling alone, people talk to me more, and that is one advantage. I think a person is more approachable than a couple. For some reason.

The ranger says, "There is a fungus that causes white-nose syndrome in bats. It's contagious, and it's harmful to them, so on the way out of the cave, we want you all to 'cleanse your soles.'" We're asked to step on a tray of spongy stuff that gets the bottoms of our shoes wet with disinfectant.

In the parking lot, the man and I finish our conversation. I say, "Where are you from?"

"Georgia."

"What do you do there in Georgia?"

"I'm a psychology professor at a college."

"Oh. I was a psych nurse. I think I might be retired now."

"Lucky you."

"Where are you staying?" I ask.

"I'm camping out here. I'm on vacation. How about you?"

"Toward Missouri. I'm off to see the country."

"Lucky you."

I'm getting good at saying goodbye and letting go.

When Micah was just a baby, I took him into a movie theater. It wasn't long before he started fussing, and then crying. So I let go of the movie and took him out of the theater to take care of him. I didn't see the whole movie, but I did get to see a sampling of it. That's when I made a decision to allow myself to be satisfied with samples of things and to let go of the longing for more.

I'm aware that if I'm visiting a town or a park for a week or even a month, I will get to know very little about the history, the geography, the culture of the place. Spending a day gives me just a sample, and I am satisfied. I am content to be on a road trip of samples.

I follow my GPS to the Green River Ferry. The narrow shady road leading to the ferry goes down a hill, under the river, then up the hill on the other side. This ferry can hold only three cars. It's unattended. There are no other cars, no human being on the ferry except me. It's all automated. Signs tell me what to do. I drive onto the platform. The platform is pulled across the river by a metal cable, a journey of about twenty feet. I drive off the platform and back onto the road on the other side. No word is spoken, no smile, no nod. No time to get seasick. The Green River Ferry.

Not all ferry trips have been as pleasant for me. When we were young and foolish, my kids' father, Joel, and I went on a bicycle tour from Hartford, Connecticut, to Martha's Vineyard. We camped out by the roadsides, sometimes in a pup tent and sometimes just under the stars. On Martha's Vineyard we—well, just I—drank wine in the evening. In the morning, we needed to get on the ferry to head home. We didn't have time for a real breakfast, so I just got coffee in the store and a half-sour pickle. I had just learned about half-sour pickles and was enamored of them. Then we got right onto the ferry. Nausea is what I remember best about that boat ride. Undaunted, I still love boats, but I have left the wine behind.

My GPS takes me on narrow, twisty, woodsy roads. I'm looking for Central City, Kentucky, because it's red on the AAA map. I'm under the impression that towns printed in red are larger towns. I'm hoping I can find a place to park on the street. When I arrive, I see that this is a town of single-family houses with driveways. My van would be the only vehicle on the street. That would not be stealthy. I stumble upon a twenty-four-hour Walmart. Cars will be parked here all night. I hadn't planned to park at Walmart, but here I am. I've found another option.

May 22: A Heavy Dose

This Walmart parking lot is my liveliest sleep spot yet. I park off to the far side, thinking, *I'll be out of the way here.* But it turns out to be next to the route the eighteen-wheelers take to get to the back of the store. Loud trucks wake me up multiple times. But it's a safe place, and it does work. I decide that if I have to stay at Walmart again, I will find the truck lane and not park there. They do have a bathroom at Walmart. So, there's that. And soon I am headed west to Missouri.

While I'm on the highway, my friend Lydia calls. She's just gotten back from a women's spiritual retreat. We have a conversation about thriving. We agree that the quality of your life is consistent with the quality of care that you give yourself. I tell her about another traveling experience I had. "I have hearing loss in my right ear, and sometimes I hear the funniest things, I misunderstand. I don't always hear consonants. Once when I was on an airplane, the flight attendant was doing her speech, describing how to use the oxygen mask. I knew she was saying, 'Please be sure to secure your own mask before assisting others.' But what I *heard* was, 'Please be sure to secure your own *ass* before assisting others.' At the time, it made me laugh right out loud. That's become my mantra for recovery and self-care. If I take care of myself first, I will have much more to offer others."

Dead armadillos are here and there along the roadsides. We're not in Maine anymore, Toto. Just like in Kentucky, the Missouri roads are narrow with no place to pull over. I see an eighteen-wheeler off the road, smashed up and covered with grass and dirt. A pickup truck driver suddenly jerks back into his own lane just before he would have hit me head-on. A little adrenaline to wake up with.

Cape Girardeau, Missouri, has a nice downtown area with a park, a college, restaurants, a walk along the Mississippi River, and, best of all, a port-a-potty. And there is great rejoicing. I meander along the river in the hot sun and eat some lunch in the shady grass. Some fruit and cheese and a small zucchini, which I chomp down raw and enjoy because it is cool and wet.

The meeting is in a room in the basement of what used to be a church. The interior walls are of stone, with plastic wisteria climbing on them. In this meeting, they go around the room so that everyone can have a chance to speak. The chairperson says, "I think what you're doing is really cool, Zinnia." Other people speak, too:

"I was drinking without my permission."

"I woke up alcoholic again this morning."

"The opposite of addiction is connection."

Connection is what I crave, and it seems to be the medicine for the symptoms, the "ism," of my alcoholism. A daily dose of positive human contact is what I look for, at home and away. On some days, I want a heavy dose.

Leaving Cape Girardeau, while I am on the road, Seth calls. After a short conversation, he asks me, "Hey Mom. Where are you staying tonight?"

"I don't know, but tomorrow I'll be in Hot Springs, Arkansas."

Later he calls back and says, "Check your e-mail." I pull over, and in my e-mail, I'm delighted to find that he has booked me a room at the Embassy Hotel in Hot Springs. Here is my heavy dose for the day! So much cause for rejoicing.

I find a rest stop on Route 40 just before Forest City, Arkansas. I have never stayed at a rest area before, but I don't see any sign that says I can't park overnight, so I decide to try it. Worst case is that I get asked to move along. In which case, I will put on my glasses, pick up my keys, and move along. I make sure to keep them in an easily accessible place in the van. With a restroom and drinking water available, what more could one want?

May 23: Marinating in the Luxury

Well, it turns out I have no need to worry about getting caught sleeping at the rest area all night. The place is jammed with all kinds of vehicles. It's noisy. Big trucks running continuously. People coming and going. Lights going off and on. Car locks beeping, doors slamming. I wake up at three, and this time I don't get right back to sleep. I go up to the bathroom, an unsavory place, dirty and smelly, and then take a walk around, surveying the mess of rigs parked here. I go back to my cot and put in my earplugs. I've been hesitant to use them because I want to be able to hear if there's something I need to pay attention to during the night, like maybe a cop knocking on the window. But nothing like that is going to happen in the midst of this circus. I might be the most normal person here, which would be saying something. With the doors locked, I sleep a bit longer and hit the road early.

In Hot Springs, Arkansas, I drive around town not finding anything that looks like it might be a national park. *When all else fails, ask directions.* I'm in the middle of town, on Central Street. The man on the sidewalk says, "It's right here," and he gestures to a couple of three-story bathhouses, one of which is the visitor center. The man says, "You are in Hot Springs National Park now. Right here on Central Street."

Inside, I am given a couple of brochures that describe places where I can spend buckets of money getting mineral baths and massages and so on. A small museum shows photographs of local history. Pictures of rich White people who used to come to the inn here for the healing properties of the natural hot mineral water. I watch a video about the history of this place. The Native American tribes shared the hot springs. Even warring tribes were peaceful here. Then the Europeans came and built bigger and better structures and "owned" stuff so they could charge money for people to enjoy the hot springs. Later, it became a national park. And now this place can again be enjoyed by all, even warring tribes.

Behind "Bathhouse Row" is a broad sidewalk and a small brook of hot water streaming down the hill through trees and weeds, and pooling at the bottom in a space created by a stone wall. And yes, it is steaming, and hot, but not so hot that it would burn.

Up the hill from this pool, behind the bathhouses and parallel to Central Street, is the "Promenade," with a self-guided tour that you can get for free by calling a number on your cell phone. The recording describes the history of the places down on Central Street that can be seen from the Promenade. Of course, I do call that number and put my earbuds in to stroll along and listen. I never want to miss out on anything. Especially if it's free.

Across Central Street from Bathhouse Row is the Duck Tour. Naturally, I check that out. I love boats and I love informational tours. So what could be more perfect? A couple of tourists my age are taking a selfie. I'm still on the sidewalk, so I offer to use their camera to get a photo of them on the duck. They seem pleased at this offer, and he hands me down his camera. Nice photo. This is something I enjoy doing. I have confidence that I know how to use other people's cameras and phones, and I've found that everyone I have done this for has been appreciative. That makes me feel good and costs nothing. And I get to say, "You're welcome." Plus, the added bonus is that they usually offer to take one of me. That is a real advantage for a solo traveler who has no one to take her photo. When I board the duck, this man gets off and takes my phone and gets a photo of me grinning on the duck. That is a treasure.

Our duck driver is an entertaining fellow who says he is a college student and has aspirations beyond being a duck captain. We drive through town, then down a ramp and into a human-made lake, where our driver describes the rich people and the mansions they built here. He tells stories. "Hot Springs has a colorful history. The whole center of town has burned down three times that I know of. There have been two major shootouts on Central Street: gangsters versus police, and county police versus local police. Gambling has been legal, not legal, legal, and not legal, depending on politics, economy, religion. Casinos are currently illegal. Here's a pawn shop right across the street from the place that is 'not a casino.' Bill Clinton graduated from high school in Hot Springs, though he doesn't seem to advertise that fact."

My duck tour ticket is a package deal that includes the wax museum. I've never been to a wax museum before, so since I'm on an adventure, I do it. I pull that "generous offer" photo maneuver and get some unsuspecting tourist to take a photo of me with all three of my best friends at once, Donald Trump, Jimmy Carter, and Clark Gable. What a conversation we could have if they were not just made of wax. Probably Clark Gable would end it by saying, "Frankly, my dear, I don't give a damn."

There's another section of the national park that you can drive to. A paved road goes up a mountain—we'd call it a hill in New England—to where a tower overlooks the town. In the gift shop, you can buy a ticket to go up in the elevator, which naturally I do. From the tower, I can see the town, the highway, and the Embassy Hotel, where I will be spending the night.

Central Street is lined with expensive, touristy shops. I walk along for a while and buy nothing. I'm waiting till check-in time at the hotel.

In the van, all my things are distributed in boxes and drawers where they belong, just like yours are at home. So in order to stay at the hotel, I have to pack my bags. I have my Planet Fitness showering backpack and a large tote bag for this. I have my big Subway sandwich with me for supper.

My room is luxurious. It has a living room and a bedroom. A beautiful clean bathroom. A large comfortable bed. I take photos of it and make that my post of the day on my Facebook group page, Wander Woman, with a thank-you to Seth and his fiancée, Nicole. I text them, too, to say thanks. I do the exercise bike, then the swimming pool, then the shower in my room. Oh, sweet heaven.

When I walk out the door of my room, I'm in a hallway that's open to the glass-ceilinged courtyard below. I can look down and see people gathering for the "complimentary snacks and adult beverages" that I was invited to when I checked in. I'm showered and wearing clean shorts and tank top, my usual uniform now. I take the glass elevator down for free snacks and some non-adult beverages. A man plays piano and sings. Besides him, I'm the only person alone. People are drinking and chatting in pairs or small groups, and no one notices me.

This is the loneliest I have felt so far. What is it about hotels? Or is it just that I have all my needs met effortlessly and have nothing else to think about for the moment besides the loneliness that lurks, waiting?

Back in the room, I look at TV. I don't have TV at home, so when I'm visiting or in a hotel, I check it out. Then I remember why I don't have TV at home. I write postcards and eat my Subway supper, read my Ann Patchett novel, enjoy the air-conditioning, and stretch out on the big bed. I'm marinating in the luxury of the generous gift from Seth and Nicole.

May 24: The Happiest Place in the World

Because of the bed and the air-conditioning and my wakefulness the night before, I sleep soundly until six thirty, just in time for the breakfast buffet. At breakfast, I see a gathering of middle-aged women, casually and comfortably dressed, mostly overweight. I think, *Hmm. They look like nurses.* I look in the lobby at the Embassy convention center schedule, and sure enough, a conference for nurses. Do I miss doing stuff like that? Umm. No.

I decide to take advantage of my hotel stay while I still can. I go to the workout room, finish writing postcards, read my book in air-conditioned comfort. Make a second trip to the breakfast buffet. Because I can. And now it's checkout time.

At a small white building that used to be a church, in the steeple where a bell used to be, hangs a large AA logo, the triangle inside the circle. That calls to me like a candle in the darkness. The three sides of the triangle in the AA logo symbolize recovery, unity, and service. It's nearly noon, and people are gathering inside, seated on folding chairs, mostly men. A sign on the wall says, "You Are Not Alone." I feel that hit my heart. People say this:

"In this program, if you ain't having fun, it's your own damn fault."

"I can reset my attitude any time I choose."

"I tried to run away from myself, but I'd always show up."

"This is a room full of miracles. It's the happiest place in the world."

Paradoxically, the happiest place in the world is also the place where one man has a son in jail for murder and another man has a son who killed himself. These men have their sorrows, but they have a place to go where their situations can be accepted and they can get support and friendship without judgment. So, yeah, probably the happiest place for them, too.

I'm chatting with a guy named Gary, a man roughly my age, after the meeting, and he invites me to lunch at the Hungry Greek. I'm on an adventure, so I accept. I get an unimpressive salad, mostly iceberg lettuce.

We talk about this and that. He says, "My wife and I travel a lot, and we have homes in three states—Arkansas, Texas, and California."

"You get around. What else is there to see in the Hot Springs area?"

I've long since finished my lame salad, and I'm waiting politely for him to labor through his lunch. He says, "Garvan Gardens is nice."

When we say goodbye in the parking lot, I know I'm having a conversation with someone I will never see again. I do want to be able to be open to experiences, even though they may be bittersweet.

It's hot and humid, in the upper eighties at Garvan Gardens. A long walking trail goes past woods and gardens, flowering plants, a stone bridge, bugs. I enjoy places like this partly because I like taking pictures of flowers and other interesting things.

At home, I've been making my pictures into note cards and bookmarks. That's becoming a dying art because people don't send note cards much anymore, and they are tending to read e-books that don't require paper bookmarks. I'm old-fashioned that way. I love taking pretty pictures. But what to do with them?

I used to carry a camera with me, looking for beauty, but now I just carry my smartphone. One time, I went with a group of people to clean up the trash in a local park. I was supposed to be looking for trash. Instead, my mind was telling me, *Look, what an interesting mushroom.* And I took a picture of it. That was when I realized that taking pictures had become a spiritual practice for me. I had unintentionally trained myself to see beauty. I had to force myself to see trash.

Toward evening, I stop at a rest area on Route 40 near Russellville. It's still hot. I open the van doors for some air, and immediately bugs come in. So I hit the road again, watching the sun set, and watching the temperature on my dashboard go from eighty-five to seventy-five. I stop at another rest area near Ozark, Arkansas. When the temperature is seventy-five, and I park in shade, I can be moderately comfortable sleeping in the van. I decide that from now on, I will wait until full dark before parking for the night.

May 25: Nothing Bad Happens

The good thing about rest areas is that you can use the bathroom anytime and get drinking water. The cars are parked up behind the bathrooms, and the trucks are parked out by the road. I park near the bathrooms, thinking that the building will muffle the sounds of the truck engines running and the highway noise, and it does, to some extent. I wake up briefly a few times, and drift right back to sleep. When I get up, only two other vehicles are here, one on either side of me. Much less chaos, the opposite of that other rest area.

I have a hard time finding a meeting in Kansas. I call the AA hotline, and I'm on the phone with two women for twenty minutes while they work with their unfathomable new computer system. They tell me about a noon meeting in Parsons.

Parsons is a town of run-down single-family houses and businesses, some open, some closed. Flat, straight roads. The meeting is in a white stucco building that used to be a church. It's not marked in any way, not even with a street number, and the only way I know a meeting is here is by looking at the cars that begin arriving. Some have AA-related bumper stickers. I have a gold-colored sticker of the AA logo, the triangle in the circle, on the back of my van. If you see a knot of people smoking or vaping outside a church, you are at an AA meeting. Or if you see a biker guy in leather laughing with an old lady in the parking lot, you have found AA.

Inside, I see the John Deere wallpaper border on the walls up along the ceiling. In the bathroom, a sign on the mirror says, "You are looking at the problem." The chairperson opens the meeting and goes right into the readings from the literature, without qualifying.

In New England, the chairperson starts the meeting by "qualifying." That means that the chairperson talks about what qualifies them to be a member of AA. In other words, they share "what it was like, what happened, and what it is like now."

Coffee is made in glass pots, and a woman circulates, offering refills. I'm remembering the first AA meeting I ever attended, on a field trip from rehab. I asked how much the coffee cost, and that gave them all a good laugh. Here is some of what I heard at the Parsons, Kansas, meeting:

"My perspective is broken."

"My brain is hardwired to overlook the many blessings in my life and focus entirely on the made-up stories in my head."

"I'm working on trying to be comfortable with being uncomfortable."

"Now the cops see me and wave."

"We don't shoot our wounded."

So great to know there is a place where I won't be shot for being wounded. Outside, after the meeting I ask the smokers, "What is there to see locally?"

After some general head-scratching and shrugging among the group, one man says, "Turner Falls. It's the tallest waterfall in Oklahoma." I haven't ever thought of Oklahoma as a land of waterfalls. No one comes up with anything of interest to suggest here in Kansas. So I look for Turner Falls on the map.

I'm following maps whenever I can. I like maps because I can look ahead and see what my choices will be. I can see lakes, cities, complicated highways, parks, small towns, state lines, time zones, back roads. AAA maps mark the scenic roads with a dotted line. My GPS just tells me the next turn. If I rely only on the GPS, I might miss something. At times, though, I have to rely on the GPS to get me to where I can identify my place on the map.

I consult the Trip Advisor app and learn that the Little House on the Prairie Museum is on my way to Oklahoma, so I make a stop here. I pay the three-dollar admission. This is supposedly one of the sites where Laura Ingalls Wilder lived during pioneer times. Her book, *Little House on the Prairie*, describes her life during those times. But nothing here is original. There are life-sized reconstructed buildings: a post office, an example of her home, a one-room schoolhouse with an American flag with fifty stars on it.

When I was a kid, I read all of the books in the Little House series and just loved them. I'm nostalgic, missing the child I was who could be so delighted with such simple things as these books. A trip to the library made me overjoyed in those days. And the adult me? My joys are more complicated now, seasoned with loneliness, losses, grief, responsibilities.

Feeling sad, I check the AA meeting app and find one listed in Coffeyville, Kansas, this evening, where they will probably serve "coffey." In Coffeyville, no one is at the Alano Club. I wait around, but no cars show up. This time, I'm not just exploring. I'm looking to bring my nostalgia and my sadness to an AA meeting. Ironic. I decide to continue on into Oklahoma. I know the sadness will pass, as it always does.

I stop at a park and polish off my picnic. Fruits and vegetables are not lasting in my cooler. They're turning to mush because I've given up looking for ice. Every day is so hot. That's when I decide to get food for only one day at a time. I start using my cooler to store my books and notebooks.

I see some rural roads called "YY" or "N," and I have no idea what that means. I see roads labeled just "166" with no *W* or *E* to help me decide which way to turn. I have to do some guessing, especially around midday when the sun is high and I can't use it to get my bearings. Route 16 West takes me to 75 South.

Looking at the map, I know I will have to pay attention to stay on 75 South through Tulsa, Oklahoma, with all the exits and entrances. It's getting dark, and fast traffic weaves in and out, changing lanes, and my GPS is busy giving me instructions. This is why I try to avoid cities.

But I make it through Tulsa and nothing bad happens, and I get on a smaller, slower road south of the city. I'm exhausted, sad, and stressed-out by now. It's dark, and a bright neon sign shouts, "Casino 24/7!" It might be safe to stop, because cars will be parked here all night, including mine.

May 26: A New Custom

It seems OK at the casino parking lot, not too noisy. I wake up around two thirty and some people are just leaving. Many more are still inside. I think, *This place is full of broken hearts.* A couple of guys patrol the parking lot in a golf cart. *Security, probably. Have they noticed how long I've been parked here?*

I remember this story I heard at a conference on the topic of gambling addiction: A guy was sitting in his car in the casino parking garage with a gun to his own head when he heard a shot. Another person had just killed himself in a nearby car. The security team came and cleaned up the mess so quickly that this man believed he was the only customer who even knew what had happened. He did not kill himself. Instead he made an appointment with our conference speaker for help with his gambling addiction. I start wondering, *What would it be like if I were in my van when some dude offed himself right next to me in a parking lot in Oklahoma? No way I want to be involved with anything like that.* I am spooked. You know how things can get big at two thirty in the morning? So I put on my glasses, grab up my keys, and drive away.

Soon I come to a place called Creek Nation Travel Plaza. It's a gas and convenience store. A few people are smoking and chatting out front, even at this hour. I park around the side, near some trucks. I use the restroom, which is an outhouse—a really nice one, though. And sleep again.

In the early morning, on the road in Oklahoma, I savor the bright golden haze on the meadow. I see a white horse that my sister Sue would love. I stop to take pretty pictures of the horse in the sunrise, standing by a fence decorated with spiderwebs that are glowing in the low sun.

My GPS directs me to a park called Honor Heights. I'm the only visitor here, so I have the place to myself at first. Then some guys show up to do yard work. I have a brilliant creative idea that I could make a collection of photos of license plates from all the different states, and use them to invent an inspired work of art. I take one license-plate photo. I feel self-conscious doing it because I wonder if people will get paranoid thinking I'm spying on them with the intention of reporting them for something. I immediately quit the license-plate photo collection idea.

I've seen ads for the Renaissance Faire, so I decide to check that out next.

The Renaissance Faire reminds me of the one I went to with Seth when he lived in Florida. At the Florida one, Seth was enjoying the rotten tomatoes booth where a man with his face in a hole in the plywood was shouting insults at Seth, and Seth was trying to hit him in the face with drippy red tomatoes. The insults were interestingly creative. Seth was wearing a checked shirt, and the man said, "What's up with that shirt? Did your mom make it for you out of her old tablecloth?"

These Renaissance Faires must all be similar. Maybe they are the same one traveling from place to place. I see people eating funnel cakes and huge turkey legs. Pony rides, period costumes, a parade, and music and dancing. And many ways to spend money. Some people are acting overly polite, saying things like "Good day, m'lady." And some people are overly rude. As part of their act, three men are covered in mud and yelling random nasty comments. It seems that I am the only visitor here alone.

I set off for Turner Falls to see the tallest waterfall in Oklahoma, the one that my Kansas AA colleague recommended. On the way, I stop at a farm stand and buy two peaches and one big tomato. This is living. The woman tries to upsell me a basketful, but I tell her, "I'm traveling, and I haven't brought my refrigerator with me."

I find the entrance to Turner Falls Park, and the man says, "We're sold out." *What? How could a falls be sold out?* He won't let me in past the gate. I turn around and drive back to the main road.

Up the hill, I come to a place where a store and restaurant overlook the park and the falls. The falls don't seem that huge, but below the falls is a large pool crowded with swimmers. It's ninety-five degrees on a Saturday. No wonder the place is so popular.

My dashboard has been flashing a notice that warns, "Change oil." But according to my precise calculations, the oil change is not due for another thousand miles. Now the message stops flashing. Sometimes I wish I had someone with me to talk over things like this.

I'm happy to see windmills in Oklahoma. Some people complain that they are ugly, but when I look at them, I see a free, renewable, clean energy source, and I love them.

One thing that made me hesitant to do this road trip was climate change and the effect that driving a van might have on the environment. After the 2016 presidential election, I got advice from a friend. He said, "Just choose your most important issue and put your energy into working for that." My most important issue is climate change. I looked for organizations working on this issue and found a group called 350 Maine.

I attended a few of their meetings but soon felt overwhelmed and out of my league. I have no skills, no knowledge. I can't speak intelligently on the subject. My shyness is an obstacle. I went to some rallies and protests. I heard so much denial from people in power. In despair, I stopped attending.

I talked with some friends about my guilty feeling. No one had an answer. People said things like, "At least you're not driving one of those big honking houses on wheels." And "The problem is bigger than you. Think of all those corporations and politicians. That's where the real problem is."

Everything I buy is encased in plastic and has a carbon footprint. Heating my house has a carbon footprint. Everywhere I go has a carbon footprint. Everything I eat has a carbon footprint. Everything I do has a carbon footprint. Breathing has a carbon footprint.

I am defeated. I surrender. So I put my environmental guilt up on a high shelf where it won't be in my face. Feel free to judge me. I deserve it. Still, I'm happy to see windmills.

The AA app tells me about an evening meeting in Ardmore, Oklahoma. Good timing. On my phone, I see that there's a Goodwill store, a 24-hour Walmart, and a 24/7 Planet Fitness in Ardmore. What else could one want? I've discovered 24-hour Planet Fitnesses, a new option in lodging. Using the maps and the phone, I can look ahead and find places like this and know that I will have a safe place to park for the night, and that's reassuring. It's still ninety degrees, though.

In Walker Park, my picnic is cheese, peaches, and a tomato, which I eat like a peach and love it.

The Tradition Two club is in an abandoned shopping center. The AA logo is plainly visible, and two benches are set outside for smoking. During the introductions, I mention that I am from Maine, as I always do. I'm asked to be the chip club person and present people with their chips. Many AA meetings give out chips that look like poker chips with numbers on them that represent the number of months, or medallions that represent the years, of sobriety the person has achieved. In Maine, when a person gets up to receive a chip, the chip club person hugs them. So, when I am presenting their chip, I hug them. People seem taken aback at first, but then they hug back. Oops. Have I started a new custom? Here is some of what I hear:

"There's not one day I don't find something I like better about myself now."

"I thought I was Don Knotts, but when I drank, I was Cary Grant."

"Good things happen to alcoholics who don't drink."
"I am perfectly flawed."
"I realized that every time I drank, I missed the party. This is the party. Life is the party."
"If I make good choices, bad stuff quits happening."

An AA white chip is the one you get when you are "new or coming back." It means you are starting your recovery in AA. Rumor has it that in Portland, Maine, a certain bar gives out a free drink in exchange for a white chip. That's demonic! When I was new, I was too shy to pick up a white chip. But I did get my one-year medallion, and I've gotten many medallions since.

May 27: Be Safe and Enjoy Every Second

I have trouble sleeping, for some stupid reason. This seems to happen at random frustrating times. The temperature is still eighty-five, so that's probably part of the problem.

I take a drive, looking for the center of Ardmore. I find it. Dead center. Most of the buildings are empty and run-down. Very few signs of life at this early hour. There is no such thing as a working downtown in most places, it seems.

A big Methodist church boasts a nine o'clock service. I put on my dress-up black scrub pants and Megan's sandals, and go to church. I am not religious, but churches are interesting to me, for the local color if nothing else. People are friendly here. Because I went to Protestant churches when I was a kid, the service is familiar. There is comfort in the familiar. It makes me teary. Church has that effect on me for some reason. Maybe because it's about the only time I ever sit quietly. Maybe because I wish I could believe the things they preach, and I wish I could belong. I'm nostalgic for the little girl I used to be who loved the Little House books and believed church stuff. I can't take it literally, like they do. I try to listen to the words as if they're metaphoric, so I can get some value from them.

I see the minister's jeans and cowboy boots underneath his robe.

After the service, I mosey back for a cup of decaf in the fellowship hall. I'm invited to stay for Bible school, and I stay. I'm introduced to the group of about a dozen people. The topic is the story of Jesus raising Lazarus after he was dead for four days. One guy says, "If Jesus can help someone that long gone, I guess He can help us." It reminds me of how in AA we believe no one is too hopeless to recover. Men do almost all of the talking. I do not speak, nor am I invited to.

An "Epic Service" is scheduled after Bible school. It turns out it will be the same sermon, the minister now sans robe. The music is different, loud, amplified, like religious country rock. I insert my earplugs. I stay for a while, but leave before I hear the sermon instant replay.

It's ninety-five degrees at Lake Murray State Park. The place is packed. I notice Texas plates and hear Hispanic music. The human-made lake is huge, shallow, and muddy. I swim around for a while and lunch alfresco. I try to read my book, but it's annoyingly windy, and I have no comfortable place to sit in the shade.

I move along and drive up to Tucker Tower, part of the Lake Murray Nature Center. Up in the tower, I discover a glorious view of the lake. And downstairs, I take a look at their displays of local wildlife.

I don't know what to do with myself. I want a rest from driving. But it's so hot, and where can I go? It's Sunday of Memorial Day weekend, and places are closed. I find a shady picnic table near the tower to write this.

On my GPS, I scout out an open laundromat. At home, I have my own washer and dryer, so laundromats are an adventure to me. At least half of the machines have handwritten signs saying "Out of order." A slim, pretty older woman is working here, older than me, even. She helps me figure out how to use the machines.

We get talking. She says, "Where are you from? I can tell you're not from Oklahoma."

"I'm from Maine. Traveling this summer."

"What do you do back home in Maine?"

"Well, I was a nurse, but I'm not working now. I don't know what I'll be doing when I go home."

"Oh, yeah? Me, too. I used to be a medical assistant, but now I'm retired. I'm helping my nephew with his laundromat business, and I'm really enjoying it. Where have you been staying?"

"Just sleeping out in the van, anywhere I can park over-night."

"All alone?"

"Yes. I'm alone by choice, but not by *my* choice."

She laughs. "You can do just exactly what you want every moment. My advice to you: Be safe and enjoy every second."

To keep cool after the laundromat, I make an entrance at a movie theater for the movie *Book Club*. The movie is about a group of mature women who read the same book and discuss it. The book they read in the movie book club is *50 Shades of Grey*. So they're all out to have sex. I thought I would like this movie, but I don't care for their choice of book, or how they react to it.

I haven't read the Shades of Grey books, but I've heard enough to know that they are not about love, or even sex. They are about dominance and submission. That thought keeps nagging at me throughout the movie. I dunno. But at least it's air-conditioned in the theater. And when the movie ends, it's much cooler outside, which had been part of my movie plan.

So now I'm off to find a man to whip me. Ha-ha. Not.

May 28: Achy Breaky Corazon

On the Planet Fitness TV, the Weather Channel talks about Hurricane Alberto coming through the Florida panhandle, and record heat predicted for Texas and Louisiana in the foreseeable future. Well, that's where I'm going, so I have that to look forward to.

Route 39 South takes me into Texas. I stop at the visitor center and get some literature. I find out about some state parks where I can go swimming while it's so hot. The hospitable visitor center has a couple of big comfy rocking chairs where I sit and watch all the traffic.

The Trip Advisor app informs me of a huge junk/antiques place called Southern Junkers, so how can I resist stopping in? But when I find it, it's closed. It's Memorial Day. I visit a Goodwill. I'm looking again for chunky-heeled sandals for Seth's wedding, because I've gotten a blister from the ones Megan gave me.

I buy shorts and tank tops. When I left home, the temperatures were in the fifties. I'm finding out that I'd like to have more shorts and tank tops. Now I'll be able to go longer before having to visit the laundromat. Not that there's anything wrong with visiting the laundromat, though. You can meet nice people there.

Lunch is at a roadside stop that has only a picnic table and a trash barrel. I left a can of chili on the dashboard earlier, and by lunchtime it's all warmed up. All I have to do is open it with a can opener and eat it with a spoon.

Thanks to the literature from the visitor center, I make it to Eisenhower State Park. I pay the five dollars to get in, and the old gent in the admission booth says, "It's standing room only in the park." The swimming area is down a steep hill, with stairs made of stone. It's crowded and uncomfortable at the "beach," which is mostly a collection of sharp rocks and some silty water.

I get into the water deep enough to stop hurting my feet on the rocks. Hispanic music is playing, something about my "achy breaky corazon." So often when I hear songs in Spanish, I notice the word *corazon*. I do have an achy breaky corazon at times, but hearing it sung that way makes me smile.

I can't get comfortable at the so-called beach, so I trudge back up the hill to the parking area. In the van, I'm half out of my wet bathing suit when a man and two girls get into the car next to me. The man takes three empty soda bottles and throws them into the bushes in front of his car. If I wasn't soaking wet and half naked, I would pick up the bottles and hand them back to him. I have been known to do that kind of thing. He probably wouldn't have done that if he thought someone would see. But this experience does tell me how much privacy I have in my tinted-window van. I'm glad of that.

Sometimes when I'm sitting in the back of the van, I can see people walking right by me picking their noses or scratching their butts. Another indicator that they don't see me in the van.

Once clothed, I sit at a shady picnic table and look at the map and brochures. And write.

May 29: Bugs

In the morning, cherries are on sale at Albertsons. I get some, and bananas, cheese sticks (individually wrapped and don't especially need refrigeration), and milk. Sometimes I don't eat supper, or sometimes it's just some trail mix or something. I've been eating less and craving food less.

After a shower at Planet Fitness, and filling my water bottles, I take off. I fill my water bottles whenever I can, at rest stops, AA meeting rooms, visitor centers, Planet Fitness. I know that the water will soon be warm, and I'm getting used to drinking warm water.

I like to explore a "business route" when I come across one. I remember downtowns when I was a kid. They usually were busy with a grocery store, a drugstore, a post office, a church, a school, and other shops. Sometimes a movie theater. Most of the "business districts" that I pass through are like ghost towns. Most of the shops are vacant or closed, or they're antiques shops, most of which are closed, too. Lots of antiques shops. And the Angela Davis School of Dance.

It's still hot, so I search out Atlanta State Park in Texas. In the swimming area, only two other families are here besides me—a blessed contrast to the last two holiday weekend days when the state parks were jam-packed. The swimming area sand is mucky where it's wet. Bugs like deerflies are stinging, and ants are stinging, too. And there are other buggy things. After a swim, I have a picnic table all to myself.

Around this time, Micah calls. "Hey, Mom! Just calling to check in." He's not on Facebook and doesn't see my posts on my group page, so he calls. And I'm all smiles.

I tell him where I am, and he tells me about the latest flip house they've got under contract to buy. I say, "You know, the change-oil indicator light kicked in, but the oil is not due to be changed, and I've been wondering whether to take it seriously."

"Don't worry about that. As long as there is oil in it, you can run it till you get home."

I get a chance to FaceTime with my four-year-old granddaughter Kennedy, too. She makes sure I can see Charlotte, the dog, in her living room in the background. In my background she sees trees and the lake of Atlanta State Park. I say, "I'm so glad you called. It's a real gift for me!"

I check the oil. And it's OK. I feel reassured.

Now the bugs drive me on.

May 30: Uncertain

After a breakfast of cherries and bananas, I follow Route 59 down to Jefferson, Texas. I see a sign that says "Uncertain 5," meaning that the town of Uncertain is five miles out of the way. I'm uncertain whether it will be worth the drive. But my plans for the day are uncertain, so I make an attempt to visit Uncertain. I'm certainly interested. At certain intersections, I'm uncertain which way to turn. I make my best guess and proceed without being certain. After a while, I become certain that I've gone more than five miles, and I'm uncertain whether to turn back toward Jefferson or continue to search for Uncertain. I think, *I may or may not have already passed through the town of Uncertain. I'm not sure.*

These towns can certainly be so small as to be unnoticeable. Signs directing me to Jefferson are certainly clear. I head back that way because there are certainly things to do in Jefferson. I am uncertain whether I have been to Uncertain, but I am keeping an open mind.

I drop in at the Chamber of Commerce in Jefferson, where I'm greeted by a friendly, dressed-up blond woman with a southern accent who encourages me to take armloads of brochures. I'm drawn to a brochure about a ten-dollar riverboat tour, cash only. I call and make a reservation for the two o'clock tour because by that time, my stomach will have settled from all the cherries I binged on. I spot a public restroom near the park in Jefferson. Good to know.

Meanwhile, I follow the walking tour of the town of Jefferson. I've been given a map that shows the historical houses, churches, schools, and such with a brief history of each. I even wear my big straw hat, it's that hot. While walking down the street in town, I go through a section of sidewalk that's shaded by a building. Two girls pass me, and I hear one girl say to the other, "I love shade!" I do, too, certainly.

I visit a couple of shops and stop for lunch at the Riverport Bar-B-Cue. A large man is standing next to me in line. I say, "What's good here?"

He laughs, "Everything's good here. I'm getting the chopped brisket sandwich." I get the chopped brisket sandwich. You can tell a place is good when it is crowded with locals and people in work clothes. I have the Texas barbecue experience, with extra barbecue sauce. So tasty. Memorable.

Continuing on the walking tour, I come across the Jefferson Historical Museum, so I enter to get cool and wait for it to be two o'clock. The museum is in a brick building that used to be the post office and some other offices. Four stories are packed with stuff. Collections of things that used to belong in the mansions of rich people. My favorites are the doll collections, the quilts, and the collections of dishes. And three fat ivory Buddhas positioned like see-no-evil, hear-no-evil, and speak-no-evil. And who knew there are over a hundred different types of barbed wire to be seen?

Captain John runs the boat tour. He has a little shack by the water where he takes your money, cash only. He has some books for sale, too. The boat is small and looks like it might hold no more than twenty people, and it's covered with a blue tarp to protect us from rain and sun. The customers are two older couples and me. Sigh. Eye roll.

Captain John is also a historian. He says, "Jefferson used to be the last riverboat stop upriver from New Orleans until the Army Corps of Engineers changed the flow of the water and the bayou became too shallow for riverboats. So Jefferson's heyday is over."

A white-haired gent, a curious fellow named John, is keeping the conversation going by asking Captain John questions. He asks, "What's the difference between a bayou and a river?"

"I guess you could say that a bayou is a slow river."

"When was Jefferson founded?"

"They think around 1841. They got the land from the Caddo Indians."

"What's the population of Jefferson?"

"It's about twenty-five hundred now, but just after the Civil War, during the heyday, they think the population was about thirty thousand. It was the sixth-largest town in Texas at that time."

"What is Jefferson known for?"

"Now? History mostly, and tourism."

John and his wife, Sue, chat with me after the tour. They're both college administrative types, in their seventies or so, retired. They are interested in my travels, and I show off my luxurious accommodations. I'm glad I made the bed and kept the van neat.

John says, "We're going down to Caddo Lake for the afternoon. I'd like to treat you to supper later." Naturally I accept. I give him my phone number, thinking, *As if this is really going to happen.* We go our separate ways for the afternoon.

When I am rambling around in the downtown area of Marshall, Texas, I am surprised by a call from John. "We're in Marshall, too. Let's meet at a pub called OS2 on the square near the courthouse." I'm only a few blocks away. I'm on my way to where my van is parked when I see them drive up.

I say, "I was about to brush my hair and put on a clean blouse." My hair is all frizzed and blown and tangled. I've been sweating in this blouse all day.

He says, "Never mind, you look great."

I order a salad, and so does John. Sue orders chicken. They're drinking wine, I am not. So the topic of AA recovery comes up. They're open to hearing about my recovery and my travel experiences.

John, being John, has questions about AA. "If meetings are anonymous, how do you find them?"

I say, "In the olden days, there used to be an eight hundred number in the white pages. Remember the white pages?"

They laugh. He says, "Yes, I do."

"You could call that number and they would give you information about the times and locations of the meetings. You could get printed meeting lists at the meetings. Now, you can just Google it and find meetings on the local AA website. There is an app, too, now." And I describe my beloved AA app to him.

The waiter brings our salads and Sue's chicken. He says, "Can I get you anything else?" We all shake our heads. "No, thanks."

John says, "What does *anonymous* mean?"

"It means you don't say your last name, or give any identifying information. And you don't talk about the meeting outside of the meeting. It's an agreement. I won't tell anyone I saw you here and you won't tell anyone you saw me here. Some people have reputations to protect, like for their careers. People can go to AA and be confident that it's private."

"What do they talk about in meetings?"

"This salad is great. The balsamic vinaigrette is really good." I take a breath. "Ideally, people talk about problems they've had and how they used the AA program to rise above their problems. When you hear people talk about problems that are similar to your own problems, you can talk with them after the meeting. People exchange phone numbers and stay in touch. They support each other. Usually people save their juicier problems to talk about privately later, not in the meeting."

Sue speaks up now. "I've heard about sponsors. What's a sponsor?"

"If you find someone you think can help you, you can ask them to be your sponsor. If they agree, they are making a commitment to be there for you and help you work the AA program. The sponsor and 'sponsee' decide together what kind of relationship they'll have. Sponsors don't get paid, but they say that they benefit from helping someone, and that helping other people helps their own sobriety."

John says, "You say 'use the AA program' or 'work the program.' What does that mean?"

"It means reading AA literature, going to meetings, and working the twelve steps. The steps are a process of 'clearing the wreckage of the past,' as they say. You admit a problem, find help, take an inventory to identify character defects, make amends. There's a lot to it, and it is so healing. Medicinal."

"Does it cost anything?"

"No, but they do take up a collection to pay for the coffee, and the literature and the rent for the meeting room. Usually people put in a dollar."

"Does the meeting have a president?" John sips his wine.

"No. Someone volunteers to keep the key and open the meeting room. They have a secretary or a treasurer for the group, but these are voluntary jobs, and temporary. A different person chairs the meeting each time. No one is the boss. Newcomers are welcome. They remind us of how bad our drinking career was and refresh our commitment to stay in recovery. The groups do have business meetings, usually after the AA meeting, where they discuss issues that concern the group. And they send representatives to the larger business meetings in the districts and areas."

"Who goes to AA?"

"Anyone can go. The AA Traditions say, 'the only requirement for membership is a desire to stop drinking.'"

John says, "What are the rules in AA? Are you required to go to meetings? Forever?"

Sue is listening, too. She must get quite an education hanging around with this inquisitive guy.

"There are no rules. The AA Big Book says that the steps are suggested. People are free to go or not go to meetings, but if you've been a regular and you don't show up for a while, someone might check in with you to see if you're OK."

"The 'Big Book'?"

"That's the AA book. It's technically called *Alcoholics Anonymous*. It has the steps, and people's stories, and information you might need for your recovery."

"What if an AA member drinks again?"

"When that happens, they're welcome to come back to meetings and start over. AA is abstinence-based, though. The hope is that people will be abstinent, because if a person is an alcoholic, by definition they won't be able to control any amount of drinking. Or using. That applies to drugs, too, if you're an addict."

The waiter refills our water glasses and asks, "Everything tasting OK?" We all nod with our mouths full, and smile.

"How does a person join AA?"

"Just keep showing up, I guess. If you want to be a group member, you can get your name on the list. Some meetings celebrate sobriety anniversaries. When it's your anniversary, you might be invited to chair the meeting, or share your story, and they'll probably have a cake for you. It's a good excuse for cake." We laugh.

"Does AA have social events?"

I can't remember a time when anyone has been so interested in what I have to say. But then again, this is John. "Yeah, sometimes they have a potluck for Thanksgiving, or a picnic in the summer. Sometimes AA dances. There are retreats or weekend gatherings that are organized, too."

"Could I sit in at a meeting? Even though I'm not an alcoholic?"

"You could if you look at the meeting list and find meetings that are called 'open' meetings. That means anyone can come, like family members or friends, or someone like you who is AA-friendly and curious. You'd want to make sure it's not listed as a women's meeting, though."

John smiles. "Do you feel like you're being interrogated?"

I laugh. "I'm enjoying the attention. I like a chance to talk about AA because it's so important."

We talk for an hour and a half. Sometimes you meet people and feel like you are coming home. They are sweet, open, curious, interested, welcoming. They invite me to visit them at their home when it comes time for me to go through Iowa.

When I mention that I am sixty-six years old, John says, "You don't look a day over fifty-two."

I like them.

May 31: Spooky Trash Bag

During the night, I wake up hearing a weird, rustling sound at random intervals. In the quiet darkness, I suspect that a person or a creature is creeping around my van. I wait for it to go away, but it doesn't. I'm spooked. After a while, I sit up and investigate. I realize it's just the wind rattling the plastic bag lining the trash can in the parking lot.

It's still dark when I go into Walmart to use the bathroom. On the PA system I hear Rossini's "William Tell Overture," loud, with full orchestra. I think, *That'll keep the employees awake.* Bugs Bunny cartoons have introduced a generation to opera music.

I haven't dared to bring water bottles into Walmart to fill. I don't want them thinking I'm trying to shoplift water bottles.

On the way to Galveston through Baytown, fast traffic is zipping through lane changes. This kind of thing has been the scariest part of the trip so far, except for that spooky trash bag.

Adrift in Galveston, I stumble upon a visitor center. The nice lady hands me a street map of Galveston so I can take a stroll around. I say, "My van is in your parking lot. Is it OK for me to park here for a while?"

"You can park here all day."

The historical district is now touristy shops and restaurants. At Pier 21 Theater, I take in a documentary video about the Galveston hurricane of 1900. My book club back home read a book about this called *Isaac's Storm*. I have been haunted by that story because the book describes so well what the people went through during that storm, and I could picture it. That's why I wanted to visit Galveston. The documentary gives more information about the situation. Six thousand people died. The bodies were buried at sea, but they got washed back ashore. So they had to be burned along with the rubble left by the storm. Men were forced to do this job under threats of getting shot if they didn't. Now they have built a seventeen-foot seawall and raised up the whole town behind it.

At the seawall, wind blows hot air and sand around on the beach. Such a harsh environment. I don't know how or why people can stand it. There's a section of shops, restaurants, amusements. On the beach by the roller coaster, I hear the song lyric, "Back to life, back to reality." And I think, *No, I could live just like this. Wait, I* am *living just like this. This* is *my reality now.*

I look for the ferry to Bolivar Peninsula because, well, I like boats. I wait in line in the hot, hot heat for twenty minutes. Then I get "screened." The attendant directs me to open the hood of the van so she can see into the motor, and then she looks into the back of the van. I don't know what she's looking for, but she passes me anyway. I drive onto the boat and I'm first in line in the front, and first getting off.

Ferries remind me of my uncle Russell. He was a bachelor living on Staten Island in New York. He worked in an office in Manhattan. I grew up in Connecticut, not far from the city, so sometimes we all went down to stay at Uncle Russell's house. We would all take the Staten Island Ferry from his house into Manhattan to see all the standard tourist sights. Uncle Russell and I would go to the bottom level where the cars were so we could be close to the ocean, in the wind and spray and salt-smelling air. He said, "I like it down here. It's wild." I liked it, too. He died from an illness just a bit before the World Trade Towers went down. I am glad he didn't have to see that, but I miss him, and I miss visiting him in New York. Since he's gone, there is nobody there now.

Bolivar Peninsula is a long, skinny spit of sand with houses raised on stilts. Like Galveston, hot and windy. No businesses for miles. Why would anyone come here, much less live here?

I see flocks of pelicans, though. Pelicans make me smile because they're so awkward, they are graceful.

At a farm stand farther up on Bolivar Peninsula, I want to buy a tomato, or a peach, or something. The man refuses to sell me just one because he wants me to buy the whole pot. His produce is sold in flowerpots.

I search for a shady place to pull over and look at a map, and plan, and eat. No shade. No trees.

I have some kind of bug bites all over me. They're a torment, especially when it's hot, which is always. Must have been from those buggy things at Atlanta State Park. Seems like I'm in a complaining mood.

June 1: Fighting Is Not the Way

During a phone conversation with my friend Janet, she says, "Thich Nhat Hanh has a meditation center in Mississippi. It's called Magnolia Grove." I am impressed with Janet because she meditates, and proud of her because she won a humanitarian award for volunteer work. She is a nurse, too, and I met her when we were on a trip to Cambodia to do a medical clinic. I'll tell you more about that later.

I say, "What a great idea. I'm so glad you mentioned that."

The Magnolia Grove website welcomes people to come and stay for their day of mindfulness every Sunday. I call, hoping to make a reservation to visit and stay overnight. The woman who answers seems to be willing to have me come, but with her accent, I can't be sure. Then she hangs up on me. Not on purpose, I assume. I send an e-mail as well. Later, when I get no reply, I send another e-mail.

In 1999, I went to a weeklong meditation retreat led by Thich Nhat Hanh in Ascutney, Vermont. We were in silence most of the time. Meals were a vegetarian buffet. People were asked to not start eating until all the places at the table were taken, then to start eating together in silence. This method would have solved my worries when I was in school. *Who should I sit with? Maybe they don't like me. What should I talk about?* Everyone was happy to see me sit down because that meant they could start eating.

Every morning at the Vermont retreat, Thich Nhat Hanh gave us a Dharma talk. I remember during the question and answer period, one man asked, "How do I decide what is worth fighting for?"

Thich Nhat Hanh said, "Nothing is worth fighting for."

And I thought, *What?*

"Because fighting is not the way."

Oh!

I felt calm and clear and content when I left that retreat. I know Thich Nhat Hanh won't be at Magnolia Grove himself, but I crave some of that Zen energy.

Today I am in Louisiana. The walls inside the Allen Parish Welcome Center are covered with framed pencil drawings of the faces of all the veterans from Allen Parish. The artist himself is here, a Vietnam vet with a potbelly and long gray hair underneath his ball cap. He's accompanied by an Asian woman about his age. I'm impressed and tell him so, while she beams. He made the drawings by looking at photos. Well over a hundred of them.

Trip Advisor advises me about things to see in Alexandria. First, the Louisiana History Museum. The guy at the museum tells me, "Don't miss seeing the lobby of the Hotel Bentley. It's spectacular. Joseph Bentley built the hotel after he was denied service in another place because he wasn't dressed correctly. It's on the National Register of Historic Places because generals had their headquarters there, including Patton and Eisenhower."

Entering the hotel lobby, I see extravagant Ionic columns, a mosaic floor, a painting inside the domed ceiling. So naturally, I sneak a photo, even though a sign tells me "No Photos."

A weird thing happens when I start up my van. No air comes out of the AC, and when I put it into gear, it won't move. I turn it off and start it up again, and now it's OK. I call my mechanic at home and explain the whole situation. He says, "I have no idea what happened, but don't go too long without an oil change." Contrary to the advice Micah gave me, which was not to worry.

Steve's Lube is listed on my GPS. I'm second in line. They change the oil, top off all the fluids, put air in the tires, and wash the windshield. And they're very polite, as men here seem to be. Like when I was driving down the street signaling to turn left, a man was coming toward me on a bicycle on the other side of the road. I waited for him to pass, and when he went by, he doffed his hat to me.

I have more confidence with the van after getting it some attention. Like a good van mom.

Darkness comes and I don't know where to stay, so I just keep going. Crossing over a big bridge into Natchez, Mississippi, I spot a visitor center. It's closed, but some other vehicles are parked here. It's late and I'm tired, so I take a chance. What could happen? If I get asked to move, I will move.

June 2: You Are Never Alone

It works out fine at the visitor center. Nothing bad happens. In the town of Natchez, I visit Bluff Park for a view of the river and Vidalia, Louisiana, on the other side, and the bridge I crossed last night. It's cloudy and cooler than it has been. I pick up some plums, peaches, and a cuke at the farmers' market, and have pleasant conversations with vendors.

The Natchez Trace Parkway goes toward Jackson, Mississippi. No trucks are allowed on this road, so there's little traffic. If you want to get to a town or a business, you have to take an exit. Nature-y, quiet, and pleasant. Trees and a field of yellow wildflowers.

Oh, but the roads in Jackson are horrible. It seems there's been no attempt to fix the mess. Potholes are outlined with white paint, and some potholes loom large and deep and have makeshift fences around them.

The YANA Club in Jackson is a converted multistory home in a neighborhood where Black people are out and about. Around thirty people gather at the noon meeting. More than half of them are Black, I'm glad to see, because it seems the random meetings I've stumbled upon have been attended mostly by White people. I ask the man next to me, "What does YANA mean?"

He looks me in the eye and says to me, "You are never alone." And in fact, a sign on the wall says that, too. As a solo traveler, and a single person, I breathe that in. Some people speak at the meeting and say:

"If they're ready for recovery, you can say anything and they'll be OK. If they're not ready for recovery, no matter how politically correct you try to be, they'll find fault."

"If I really had really taken account of my life, I would have collapsed in despair."

"I don't have to lose my car now. I don't have to be afraid to go to the mailbox."

"I get my spiritual food here. When you leave here and go to LongHorn or Burger King, see if they serve spiritual food there."

Spiritual food is what I get when I hear "You are never alone" and know that it is true. It has the ring of truth.

For physical food I pull off into a rest area with a shady picnic table. My lunch is a warm can of chili that has been heating up on my dashboard in the sun, and half of a chocolate bar, which I also eat with a spoon. A security guard is keeping watch from a booth at this rest area. Makes you feel secure, right?

The Magnolia Grove Meditation Practice Center is in Batesville, Mississippi. I follow "Registration" signs to the kitchen, where I'm told, "Come back after dinner, six thirty." This Asian man has enough English to get me to understand that. Thich Nhat Hanh is from Vietnam, and I wonder if these folks are from there, too.

I linger outside. Eventually Brother Allen speaks to me in American-accented English.

I say, "I'm looking for Registration."

"I am Registration."

"I am hoping I can stay here for the day of mindfulness tomorrow."

"Well, we weren't expecting you."

"I called and spoke to a woman. And I sent two e-mails."

"Oh...well...I don't know about that. I'll see if we have any clean sheets."

"I don't need sheets. I have everything I need. I've been camping out in my van. I can just sleep there."

"No, no. I'll get you some sheets. You can stay in the Pink Lotus Room." He gestures to a nearby building.

In the room, three of the seven beds have other people's gear on them. I choose a bunk and plop down my belongings.

I take a walk around the grounds to the meditation hall. It's large, with a tall cathedral ceiling, all polished wood inside, and sunny windows. It brings tears to my eyes, the same way I tend to get in churches. I sense that spirituality is here, but that it is just beyond my reach.

It's so hot and sticky that I have trouble getting my clothes off to take a refreshing shower. Back in the Pink Lotus Room, I notice a message on my phone from my dad. I have to speak loudly to him on the phone because of his hearing loss, so for privacy, I sit in the van to return his call. That loud tone of voice would probably not go over well at a meditation practice center. But in the van, I get no phone signal.

I ask some brown-robed people, "Do you have a phone I can use?"

They silently point to a wall phone in the kitchen. I rotary-dial my parents' number. When my dad answers, I yell, "I CAN'T TALK LONG BECAUSE I'M AT A ZEN MEDITATION CENTER! I'M USING THEIR PHONE IN THE KITCHEN BECAUSE I DON'T GET A SIGNAL ON MY CELL PHONE! I'LL CALL YOU TOMORROW WHEN I CAN GET A SIGNAL!"

I imagine my voice echoing all over the grounds and throughout all the buildings. *How embarrassing.* But I do not want my dad to worry about why I'm not returning his call. I told him there would be times when I wouldn't be able get a signal. But I'm uncomfortable thinking about him lying awake, wondering.

On the Magnolia Grove website, I read the description of their "day of mindfulness" for visitors. It's to be from five thirty in the morning until after lunch tomorrow, Sunday.

A donation can be made for my room in a box in the dining hall. No one at the meditation center tells me what to do, or when, or how. *What am I doing here?* People are around, but they don't look at me and they don't talk to me. I don't dare talk to them in case they're in silence. No one has told me any rules about silence, but there seems to be a lot of silence going on around here.

I don't know what to do with myself. I start doing a walking meditation alone, looking down, mindfully aware of my feet as they touch the earth. I smash face-first into a massive metal bell that I hadn't seen, hanging from a tree. Right across my nose. It makes my eyes water. *Who would have expected that?* I hope nothing is broken, but I predict a couple of black eyes tomorrow. Welcome to the Magnolia Grove Meditation Practice Center.

June 3: She Fled a Zen Meditation Center

I'm a light sleeper in the Pink Lotus Room. I wake up off and on. My roommates have the AC going. I should have brought in my blanket. My three roommates are visitors from the same Sangha, or Buddhist practice community. Their names are Nicole, Tina, and Mina.

We've set our alarms so we all make it to the early meditation. The speaker uses a microphone, but I miss a fair amount of what she says. The sound is loud enough but unclear. Sometimes it takes me a while to decide whether she is even speaking English. We are given chant books in English, and we're told what page, yet all the chanting that's done is not in English.

Signs around the place say "You are home" and "You belong," and other welcoming messages. My roommates say that all are welcome, but the actions of all the residents are the opposite of welcoming. They're not speaking to me, or even looking at me. As if I don't exist. I walk off alone for a while, like the unwanted outsider.

I'm reminded of childhood times of being the shy, awkward, unpopular, left-out, overlooked child. *I don't belong.* I begin to cry. Definitely the low point of the trip so far.

Is it my fault for having had expectations of the place? Expecting to be welcomed with the open-hearted loving-kindness of Zen energy, and finding cold indifference instead? In AA they say that expectations are premeditated resentments. I try with minimal success to adjust my thinking and take responsibility for my experience.

We all hang around waiting for breakfast. I'm still teary. Mina notices and says, "What's wrong?"

"I don't know what to do with myself. I don't know what's going on here."

"The schedule is on the board."

"What board?"

She gestures toward the wall in the dining room. She says, "Meals are silent. When the bell rings, everyone stops. I've been here before, that's how I know. The senior nuns, the ones who speak English, they're away this weekend. They have no office staff and no answering machine here. Someone may or may not eventually answer your e-mails, or they may or may not return your call from your caller ID number. Come with me, I'll show you around." Mina walks with me past the vegetable garden and shows me the statue of Thich Nhat Hanh standing with Martin Luther King. "Did you know that Martin Luther King nominated Thich Nhat Hanh for a Nobel Peace Prize?"

"Yes, I have heard that. Mina, I am so grateful to you for helping me out here."

A morning Dharma talk is given by a soft-spoken German guy. He smiles all the time he's talking. His voice is amplified but sounds muffled. He talks on and on about enjoying every step, enjoying breath, enjoying trees. After a while, I give up trying to understand and focus on trying to stay awake. I see others dozing.

A Five Mindfulness Trainings recitation is next. I'm familiar with these since going to the retreat in Vermont, and I've also read about them in Thich Nhat Hahn's books. The Five Mindfulness Trainings are reverence for life, generosity, mindful sexual behavior, mindful communication, and mindful consuming.

There is much be said about each of these, and whole books have been written about them. They are a guideline for living, and I'm happy to make a commitment to these as my North Star. The ceremony involves Touching the Earth, which means that you lie flat on the ground—the floor in this case—to commit to each one of the Five Mindfulness Trainings. I feel more grounded.

They do a chant in English, and I can sing it because there's written music that I can read, feeling smug because I can read music. Finally, something that includes me.

Breakfast and lunch are vegan. Men's and women's tables are separate. They wait until everyone is seated before eating, in silence. After eating, we take our dishes out to the porch and wash them in a series of tubs.

The dishes are done and I'm all packed up. I'm bewildered to realize that I'm actually relieved to be leaving Thich Nhat Hanh's place. So not what I had imagined.

My next stop will be a contrast. Elvis was really famous, so it's natural for me to want to visit his birthplace in Tupelo, Mississippi. There was talk about Elvis in my family when Micah was working on his pink Cadillac project.

The home where Elvis was born is a two-room white cottage with an open porch. One room is a kitchen/living room, and the other is a bedroom. A gray-haired woman attendant is on hand to answer questions. I ask her, "How did Elvis ever get started?"

"Elvis had a twin brother who died when he was born. He had no siblings, so his mother was very protective of Elvis. He wanted a rifle for his eleventh birthday so he could go hunting. He and his mother went to the hardware store to buy Elvis a rifle. She thought the rifle idea was dangerous, so she asked the salesman to show him a guitar. Elvis played it. He liked it. She bought it."

I say, "Mothers can be influential, right? Just imagine if she had allowed him to get that rifle." We both laugh.

In the gift shop, I buy a postcard of Elvis with his pink Cadillac for Micah.

I track down an open laundromat that takes quarters. My thoughtful friend Sarah gave me a roll of quarters as a going-away gift. Wendy's for a baked potato supper. And a twenty-four-hour Walmart for lodging. A comforting end to a long, emotional day.

I can hear you thinking, *She fled a Zen meditation center for the comfort of Wendy's and Walmart.*

June 4: I Have an Army of People Behind Me

At Kroger's, I snag some carrots, apples, and bananas. Carrots and apples are lasting pretty well in my hot van. Grapes, forget about it. Breakfast is fruit and cheese at a picnic table in a park, where I pore over maps, guidebooks, and my phone to make a plan for the day. Before leaving, I wander around the pond, taking pictures of ducks.

I take Route 22 East, then 43 South.

The Tuscaloosa, Alabama, meeting is in a white cinder-block building, down a long driveway, with a dirt parking lot, obscured by some trees, right in town. A small orange neon sign glows "AA." Inside, I see old wooden school chairs with attached desks, and some people place their coffee cups in the holes that were designed to hold ink bottles.

I'm surprised and dismayed to find that it's a meeting where smoking is allowed. In Maine, there are no smoking meetings that I know of, mostly because smoking is not allowed in the buildings where the meetings are held. I remember some bitter disputes about smoking back in the nineties in AA business meetings in Maine.

Speaking of bitter disputes, I sure am glad that the culture of AA is to never talk about politics. That saves us a lot of bitter disputes, for sure.

At the Tuscaloosa meeting, some people say:

"If you ask God to remove your character defects and they are still there, that means you still have something to learn."

"I used to lie to my sponsor about my Higher Power so that I wouldn't get in trouble."

"I used to be jealous when people died from this disease. At least they don't have to fight it anymore. I was sick of fighting it. Now I say, 'Bring it on. I have an army of people behind me.'"

The idea of lying to your sponsor strikes me as funny. What would be the point of doing that? I tell Faith my truth as I know it. She has a Higher Power that she believes in, but she is accepting of my beliefs, or lack thereof.

And faith in that army of people is a huge part of what gives me the confidence to attempt a road trip like this.

A woman at this meeting says that while she was having a great time home alone dancing to praise music, she was thinking, *I'm so cool, someone should be watching me.* She calls that the character defect of pride. I feel that way at times, too. I don't call it pride, I call it loneliness, or just the human need to share. It's natural. We want a witness to our life. People get married because they want a witness to their life. That's why I write this for you. I want a witness to my road trip.

After the meeting, stinking of cigarettes, I ramble along the Riverwalk on the Black Warrior River of Tuscaloosa. It's calming, this quiet, tree-covered walkway between various buildings and the river. On my phone, I detect a Chipotle less than a mile away. So I get to eat a large wad of healthy food for supper.

Driving south on Route 43 toward Demopolis, I pass Bird's Farm, a field on the right, occupied by a number of silly sculptures made of hay bales, plywood, and old junk. I wish I could stop and take pictures, but, as usual, there's no place to pull over, and also, it's getting a little dark for photos. I see statues of a helicopter, the Tin Man, an octopus, a bull and a matador with a sign that says "Call 911," Snoopy crashing the Red Baron's plane into a tree, Big Bird. And more. Art is everywhere.

June 5: Wherever I Go, I Am Home

At first the temperature is around seventy, but then it drops into the sixties when it rains. I sing, "I bless the rains down in Alabama!"

The meeting at the Common Ground Club in Daphne, Alabama, is charming. The building is clean and attractive. The meeting room is large, with long tables arranged in a square, and three big identical patchwork quilts hanging on the wall.

"Those are beautiful quilts," I say to the woman next to me.

"We found these quilts at a thrift shop for ten dollars each and hung them on the wall because the room was too echo-y." In the meeting I hear:

"I was always kind of quiet. But it wasn't serenity quiet, it was more like serial killer quiet."

"I'm thankful to drug court for getting me here."

"If you do what you've always done, you'll get what you always get."

This is one of my favorite meetings, for the friendliness and optimistic energy. In addition to the chips that represent time in sobriety, this meeting gives me a "visitor chip." It's a poker-sized chip that reads, "There are no strangers here, only freinds we haven't met. Daphne, Alabama." Spelled "freinds." It's sweet, a lovely souvenir of a lovely meeting place.

A woman asks for my phone number after the meeting. We exchange phone numbers, but I doubt we'll ever be in touch. You know how life goes on, and way leads on to way.

On the road in Alabama, I'm reminded of old times. In 1977, I went with my friend Bob to the Mardi Gras celebration in

New Orleans. I had already quit smoking pot by that time because it made me wicked paranoid, but Bob was smoking in the car while driving through Alabama. Abruptly, we were stopped by a roadblock. When Bob rolled down his window, a vast, thick cloud of pot smoke wafted out and hit the state trooper in the face. The cop waved Bob to go on ahead. Apparently, and certainly luckily, we were not what they were looking for. You might remember that pot was illegal then, and you could go to jail for ages just for having a roach in your possession, or a few seeds mixed in with your pocket fuzz.

Not the sort of thing I have to worry about anymore.

I drive into Fairhope, Alabama. I park and cruise the town on foot. I pass tony, foo-foo shops, the kind where I will never buy anything. I enjoy walking along the Fairhope Municipal Pier, and I love the rose garden with its beautiful fountain. Along "Scenic Route 98," I explore a path by the water, shaded by Spanish moss–hung trees. Very few people are enjoying this beautiful place. But that's me. I go to the beautiful, less crowded, nature-y places while others flock to the foo-foo shops.

At the Piggly Wiggly, I get two boiled eggs and cool wet cottage cheese for supper. Sitting in the parking lot in Foley, Alabama, I read, write, study the map. Wherever I go, I am home.

June 6: Rich People Are Not Exempt

I'm early for the AA meeting in Santa Rosa Beach, Florida. So I keep on going down the road, which takes me straight to the Hogtown Bayou. In the shade, I watch a man and a little girl fishing in a rowboat. I put my feet in the water, eat my picnic, and miss my granddaughters.

The Camel Club is populated with rich White people. Just seeing the address on the AA meeting app gives you no clue about what you might find when you arrive. In the parking lot among other cars, I notice a Jaguar and two Range Rovers. This is a clean, new, well-furnished building with a patio and firepit. Membership in the club gives you a key and permission to use the facilities. There is a cost to become a member of the club, but as always, meetings are free to attendees, including the likes of me. I hear some interesting things:

"I had ten years sober, and I thought I had internalized the program to the point where I could now drink like a gentleman. And I did. For about an hour."

"I'm glad to be here with you sane people."

"I was having flashbacks of using so harsh it made my hair stand up. Finally, I prayed for them to go away. And they did. It was like God was saying, 'I was wondering when you'd ask.'"

"It's a simple program for complicated people."

This place is one of my favorites. I like it because it's clean and lovely and friendly. And, as you can see, alcoholism is an equal opportunity disease and does not discriminate. Even rich people are not exempt.

I continue along Route 98 East. At first, it's busy and commercial, then it becomes more and more rural and beachy. My friend Skip had recommended Port St. Joe's, so I'm checking it out. I wander around the town area, the shops, restaurants, and bars. The woman at the visitor center informs me, "Camping is allowed on beaches, but not at parks, so you can park overnight at beach parking lots."

I go to the beach. The signs in the parking lot are loud and clear: "No Overnight Parking." So that idea is out.

I swim in the tepid, shallow, seaweed-y water. Nice. I want to get some sun and salt on my bug bites so they can heal. It has been eight days, and they're still red and itchy and driving me mental.

Back to Port St. Joe's looking for a place to park. Marina? Visitor center? Park? No signs in these places, but I don't feel confident about any of them. Research on my phone reveals a twenty-four-hour Walmart in Marianna, Florida. That seems familiar to me, so I blow town.

On the way, I pass acres and acres of bonfires. It looks like trees have been harvested and the slash is being burned. Port St. Joe's is on Eastern Time, and then toward Marianna it goes back to Central Time again. I'm glad my phone can keep up with the changes.

June 7: Do Not Swim with Alligators

The Florida Caverns State Park cave tour is spectacular and beautiful, thick with stalactites and stalagmites. More to see here than at Mammoth Cave National Park, though Mammoth is more mammoth in size. The ranger gives an interesting talk. "The stalactites and stalagmites were formed from minerals in the dripping water." The air is cool in the cave, and the beauty of the formations is enhanced by strategic lighting.

It's a hot day, needless to say. After the cave tour, I drive around to the Blue Hole swimming area, a little grayish pond. Unfortunately, or maybe fortunately, the swimming area is closed because of the presence of alligators. I take a photo of a sign telling me, "For Your Safety. Alligators Are Dangerous. Do Not Swim with Alligators." OK, I can take the hint. I spot one alligator lurking in the gray water by the dock.

Along Route 84 East, I notice some prisoners all wearing gray and picking corn by hand. A school bus is parked nearby, with a sign that says prisoners are working.

In Cairo, Georgia, I take the road toward "Historic Downtown." Another ghost town. I think when they say "historic," they mean "like it was when I was a kid in the fifties and sixties, except without the human life." I have reached the age where my life is now "historic."

In Thomasville, Georgia, Trip Advisor sends me to the Jack Hadley Black History Museum. It's in an out-of-use one-story brick school, and it takes up the equivalent of maybe three classrooms. I see posters, newspaper and magazine articles, album covers. I see photos of sports teams, programs from plays and concerts, letters, documents, clothing, uniforms, team jerseys, statues, art. I look for and find Lena Horne, Stevie Wonder, Frederick Douglass, Little Richard. It's packed with memorabilia. Every Black person I can even think of is represented.

Jack Hadley himself is here, an elderly Black gentleman, and we chat a while. I ask, "How did this whole thing get started?"

"My son was doing a project, and it just kept expanding."

We talk about a situation that has been in the news lately. President Donald Trump has been critical of Colin Kaepernick, an NFL player who took a knee during the national anthem at games rather than standing, as is traditional, in order to protest police brutality against Black people. I say, "What do you think about that situation?"

"Aren't we supposed to have free speech in this country?"

"Yes, we are supposed to. And I think he has a right to do what he did."

"I agree. Let me show you this. It's called the *Green Book*." He shows me a small book with a green cover. "This book lists hotels that accepted Black guests around America. Because when this was printed, most hotels were turning Black guests away. You know, some of us are starting in on a project to restore some of those Black-friendly hotels that are in this book. If you want, you can write your address on here and get on our mailing list." He gestures to a clipboard on his desk by the door. I write down my contact information.

Jack says, "I'm going to have to excuse myself now. I'm going home to have lunch and watch the soaps with my wife."

The museum is impressive, and my talk with Jack is touching and inspiring. In one way, he is a lucky man to have a passion for something and be so successful at it. I envy that aspect. I'm looking for something like that for myself.

The Valdosta, Georgia, meeting is in a brick ranch house in a residential area, with chairs outside for smoking. Inside, some walls have been removed to make the meeting room bigger, and the ceiling is beginning to sag in those places.

They choose the topic of control issues. At one point during the meeting, a flurry of cross talk goes on, about people who hadn't been showing up to meetings. Cross talk is when people go back and forth with personal comments, and it is generally considered inappropriate at meetings. The norm is that others stay quiet when one is sharing until that person is done talking, and always avoid making judgments or criticisms of what that person said. A messy meeting, but here are a few of my favorite things I hear:

"Miracles come from action."

"I have difficulty adjusting my sails."

"I couldn't face life drinking. I couldn't face life without drinking."

"They said I couldn't do it. I was motivated to prove them wrong."

"The alcoholic is born two drinks short of normal."

This is one of the ways I can identify myself as an alcoholic. The first time I drank, I discovered what it would be like to feel like a normal person. I had been shy, sad, awkward, an outsider. When I drank, I felt happy, sociable, normal. And I found people who were happy to see me when I showed up with a six-pack. That's why I continued drinking, because it made things better.

Until it didn't.

After the meeting a gay guy says, "I like your shoes."

They're flats made of woven grosgrain ribbon. "Thanks. They're from Chez Goodwill."

"My favorite," he says.

June 8: It's a Mystery

At Okefenokee Swamp State Park, I buy tickets for the boat tour, the train tour, and the nature show. While I'm waiting for the boat tour, Micah calls. "You know, I stopped in at your house to mow the lawn, and it looked like it had already been done."

"I don't know who would have done that."

"Well, it hasn't rained much here, so maybe it hasn't grown much."

I text my tenant to say thank you, and she texts back, saying, "You're welcome, but we didn't do it."

Seth is in Maine now, and when I talk to him, he says, "I didn't do it, but would you like me to?" It's a mystery.

The boat tour with our guide, Allen, is a delight. The boat could hold about a dozen people, but only five of us are on board: Allen, me, and a small boy named Mason and his parents. I overhear Mason's mom lamenting, "I wish I had put sunscreen on Mason."

I fish out my sunscreen and hand it to her. "Here, use some of mine."

"Oh, thank you so much!"

"You're welcome."

The water is the color of iced tea and looks black, so it reflects like a mirror. Allen says, "The color comes from decaying plant material. The peat rises to form islands called 'trembling earth.'"

On the train tour, I can't understand most of what's being said because of the cheesy speakers and southern accent and loud train engine and my hearing loss. The smell of the exhaust gives me a headache. Other than that, it's a great train tour through the woods.

The nature show is a large young man who rocks back and forth while he speaks and shows us turtles, snakes, and a baby alligator. The turtles roam around the small auditorium. The little kids touch the snakes and then recoil. The grown-ups are having none of it.

I wander along the boardwalks, through the trees that are keeping their feet in the black water.

In the gift shop, I buy a small glass turtle, my mascot, my traveling companion. I feel like a turtle when I'm all tucked into my van at night.

St. Marys, Georgia, seems to be a likely next stop. At the visitor center, I pick up a map for the historical walking tour of the town. I browse the big old houses, big old trees draped with Spanish moss. Very picturesque, so I take some pictures. I stroll along Waterfront Park, taking even more pictures, eventually sitting on a bench to eat my dashboard-heated can of chili.

From this place, you can take a ferry to Cumberland Island. I've been there once already, so not this time.

It's a hot day. As usual. Why do I even bother saying that? My plan for the evening is to sit in an air-conditioned movie theater. I call my parents and check in while waiting for the movie. Now we all know that we all are OK. The movie is *Ocean's 8*, and I enjoy all the costumes and drama. When the movie ends, it's dark and substantially cooler outside, tolerably cooler.

June 9: You Belong

I get to the Publix grocery store early before it opens at seven. I see a man arrive in a truck that says "Fresh Produce." I think he's making a delivery, but instead he goes into the Publix and comes out with massive amounts of strawberries.

I'm continuing to appreciate the things I've done to prepare: the rechargeable fan, the sun shade, maps, Planet Fitness membership, the GPS, phone apps, and all my experience traveling and camping, even alone.

Another thing I've begun to appreciate is the ease with which I can move through the world. I am a White female senior citizen. I can go to stores and museums and parks, and no one blinks. No one notices me much. No one mistrusts me or suspects me of anything. No one is afraid of me. It's a form of freedom. White privilege? Old-lady privilege? Being an old White lady is an advantage to a stealth camper.

Traveling along the road today, I'm less lonely and more happy than I would have been if I had just stayed home alone with no job and no partner. I will need a new life when I get home. Then I will not have all this traveling to distract and entertain me.

Still in Georgia, I book the Jekyll Island State Park tour. A jeep pulls a train of open passenger carts with roofs, and information is given through speakers on each cart. Much better speakers than at Okefenokee, so I can hear all of what is being said. "Around this time, in the early twentieth century, you had to be a club member or an employee to live on the island. Club members owned one-sixth of the world's wealth. Super-rich people wintered here, mostly northerners. Because they were northerners, they had full basements.

"The locals had a laugh over that because there's no need for a basement in the South, and these northerners ended up having to pump out the water that seeped in. The season was about ninety days long. They went hunting and played golf. They ate four-hundred-dollar dinners every evening at the clubhouse, in formal attire. The women had a different formal gown for every dinner."

I have had only one formal gown in my entire life. I got it recently on Amazon for forty dollars, and I'm looking forward to wearing it to Seth's wedding. His fiancée, Nicole, told me that for the wedding, dress would be long, formal gowns.

We are escorted into one of the old Jekyll Island houses. Our tour guide says, "They would score the wood floors with a knife, then stain sections to look like inlaid wood. Paving was done with 'tabby,' a mixture of cement and oyster shells." One of the houses has a bright pink room, the color of Pepto Bismol. Our guide says, "Pink has not always been a color associated with femininity."

The tour continues inside Faith Chapel. "The club members hired a minister who preached to them that moral men are rewarded with riches. This signed Tiffany stained glass is insured for a million."

On my own again, I wander Driftwood Beach. It's long and decorated with small and large—even tree-sized—pieces of driftwood in most interesting shapes and arrangements. In one spot, white flowers and streamers and folding chairs are set up in the sand among the pieces of driftwood—wedding preparations. Smiling, I begin humming a song, thinking of Seth's upcoming wedding. The song is "Loves Me Like a Rock" by Paul Simon, the song I'm considering for our mother/son dance.

A sudden thunderstorm has me scurrying back to the van.

OK, so I don't know what to do next. Sighing and scratching my head and looking at the map. Sometimes that happens. That what-am-I-doing feeling. It's not enjoyable. But luckily, it only ever lasts until I make my next plan. One thing Faith noticed about me right away is that I don't do well with too much downtime. She often asks me, "What are you planning for your days off?" Or "What are your Thanksgiving plans?" Sitting in my van, I make a plan to go to Savannah, where I will find a twenty-four-hour Planet Fitness with a nearby botanical garden that opens at eight the next day. What could be better? Temporary emotional discomfort resolved.

One of the things I appreciate about Planet Fitness is that they all feature signs saying "You Belong." I take it literally. It is a comfort.

I've discovered that some Planet Fitness locations are open twenty-four hours, so this night will be my first experiment with being a Hotel Planet Fitness overnight guest. I like to park facing a security light so that I can read and write in the front seat. Then my cot, in the back of the van, will be in shadow for better stealth.

June 10: Two Asses Named Hit and Run

I take some more photos at the Savannah Botanical Gardens. Pictures of flowers, pictures of bees on flowers. Then I set my GPS for Edisto Beach, South Carolina, another place recommended by my friend Skip. When I get here, anything that might have interested me is closed because it's Sunday. I step out onto the hot, bright, sandy beach, a hostile environment. I spot an outhouse at a construction site, though. Small victories. Another what-now moment. I Trip Advisor a few nearby towns and don't find much, so I set out for Charleston.

Parking in Charleston is free on Sunday. Bonus. Sunday has its advantages. I park on Broad Street.

The carriage for the tour of Charleston is a surrey with a fringe on top. Our guide says, "We are being ushered through Charleston by these two asses named Hit and Run. This is the Slave Market." We see a long, low brick building with openings along the sides. The sign above the entrance calls it the Charleston City Market. "Vendors inside sell food and artsy stuff. This place is called the Slave Market because that is where slaves went to sell things, not where slaves were sold."

Someone mutters, "That's a lie."

He shares information about Charleston as he manages the "two asses." King Street has been closed off for Second Sunday street fair, which, unfortunately, I missed. They're just finishing packing up. There has been thunder and lightning all afternoon.

The "two asses" tour returns to the Charleston City Market. By then it's raining and I'm hungry, so I step inside and order a grilled pimento cheese sandwich. It takes a long time, but boy, is it worth the wait. This sandwich involves thick homemade bread with butter on both sides then grilled, with the grated cheese and pimento and mayonnaise salad inside. Perfection.

On the carriage tour, I saw a sandwich-board sign for "Jazz Vespers" outside the Circular Congregational Church, so I circle back. The service is not well attended, but the music is intriguing and enjoyable. The quartet consists of a piano, a clarinet, a stand-up bass, and some percussion. They play regular hymns, but with a jazzy style. It's a real church service, complete with a sermon and collection plate.

I locate another twenty-four-hour Planet Fitness in Charleston with some difficulty because of darkness, rain, one-way streets, and divided roads. A place to park, finally. Note to self: Try to find your sleep spot and take out your contact lenses before it gets too dark.

June 11: A Little Bit Pregnant

During the night, a motorcycle pulls up right next to my van with country music blaring. The guy lets the bike idle until the song ends. "Everything's Gonna Be Alright," but not the Bob Marley version.

When I wake up again, I see that I've parked in a handicap spot. Oops.

My GPS takes me on Route 26 to Route 95, then on a scenic tour of small highways through cornfields.

I arrive at my destination, Congaree National Park.

At the visitor center, I watch the eighteen-minute informational video. Alone. On the deck, I see the "Mosquito Meter" sign with six levels: All Clear, Mild, Moderate, Severe, Ruthless, and War Zone. The arrow is currently pointed at Severe.

I stride down the boardwalk trail through the woods. It's hot, humid, and buggy. Knowing that the mosquitoes will be Severe, I've covered myself with bug dope. Even so, I can't stop walking because when I do, the mosquitoes descend. This is making me cranky. *Why did this place get made into a national park?* I wonder. I guess because, as the literature says, it's "the largest intact expanse of old growth bottomland hardwood forest remaining in the southeastern United States." With arguably the largest mosquito population, I might add.

A summer camp group, all four- and five-year-olds, is lined up at the water fountain. When they're done and it's my turn, a little girl shows me where to push the button to fill my water bottle. I have always relied on the kindness of strangers, even in the form of five-year-olds.

I set the GPS for Myrtle Beach, South Carolina. I am taken on that roundabout rural ride again, and gradually the roads get bigger and more crowded.

Coming into town, I find the Alano Club on 67th Street N. I notice public parking every block or so in this neighborhood. I'm early, so I park and step out onto the beach. It's cloudy and breezy on the beach. I can hear the waves and smell the salt air, and I feel myself letting go of the tension I didn't even know I had.

The Alano Club is a big, well-maintained building with a large parking lot in the back, in a residential neighborhood. It has a lecture hall and a meeting room. It's a well-attended meeting with well-dressed, well-spoken, friendly, and happy people, hugging and laughing. If I lived in Myrtle Beach, I would definitely be frequenting the Alano Club. A lot of spirit.

Here is some of what I hear:

"I'm a newbie. I've been waiting for sanity to come. I guess I'm a tough nut to crack. Or maybe just a nut."

"Take my advice. I'm not using it."

"We're all here because we're not all there."

"Being a little bit alcoholic is like being a little bit pregnant."

That reminds me of what I was told when I went for an assessment with a substance abuse counselor. I told her, "I'm working to control it."

She said, "If it's work to control it, then it's a problem, and if it's a problem, it should be put into remission."

"You're telling me I'm an alcoholic and I should stop drinking."

She said, "No, *you* just said that."

That was it for me. I was done. My drinking was ruined. Before this conversation, I had been a woman enjoying a beverage. After this conversation, I had become an alcoholic, drinking.

Other people have had assessments that take multiple detailed sessions. Mine took four sentences.

Here's how I wound up in a position to get a substance abuse assessment. There was trouble in my marriage, so I insisted that we go to couples counseling. In those days, I had a deal with my ex, Joel. He could sleep late on Sunday mornings and I'd get up with the kids, and I could sleep late on Saturday mornings and he'd get up with the kids. So guess what I did on Friday evenings. Drink. Our couples counselor noticed a pattern of regular drinking, and she recommended an assessment. I was willing to do anything. I was so miserable that I was considering what minor crime I could commit so that I could get thirty days in jail. I was longing for a break from the job, the bills, the housework, the kids, the bad marriage.

I was delighted when the substance abuse counselor suggested I go to a twenty-eight-day rehab. My parents helped Joel with the kids. I got to spend a month talking about my favorite subject: me. And the rehab had a salad bar, a swimming pool, and a hot tub. Everyone else hated being there and couldn't wait to leave. But I loved it. And I learned a new way of life. That's where I was introduced to AA. That's when things started to turn around for the better for me.

I've always been annoyed by the saying, "When the student is ready, the teacher appears." I had been ready and searching fruitlessly for ages.

After the Myrtle Beach meeting, I call my parents and ask them to remind me of the name of the motel where they used to winter: South Seas. I hunt down the place and take a picture of it so I can show them it is still alive and well.

I sample a few of the many souvenir and gift shops and buy only postcards. It is so hard to find gifts for people. No one I know needs or wants more "stuff." I don't know what people would like. I want to get souvenirs for my granddaughters, but what? When my sons were young, I used to bring gifts home to them when I traveled, but I don't think they were ever impressed.

By now it's dark, with thunder and lightning.

June 12: A Lot of Gold Jewelry

Best kind of sleeping night. Rain, and temperatures in the seventies.

On the way to Wilmington, North Carolina, I stop at a visitor center. The woman recommends the Southport/Fort Fisher Ferry, saying, "Best entertainment you'll find for five dollars." She is right. The boat ride, the characters, the scenery, the atmosphere.

Southport is touristy. You can get your latte and expensive gifts. On the other side, Fort Fisher is beachy and also touristy. Route 421 North goes right to Wilmington.

Wilmington, like some other towns, has an area similar to Portland, Maine's Old Port, crowded with small shops and restaurants, and pleasant strolling along the waterfront. I walk along the river for a while and spot a boat tour deal. After a hunt-down for longer-term parking, I hop onto a water taxi that takes me to the narrated eleven-dollar boat tour called Wilmington Water Tours. It's a flat, covered boat, and it holds about forty passengers. We cruise the Cape Fear River and hear about the history of the area. I'm distracted by a boy sitting right next to me who keeps poking at his phone and spitting into the water. I want to ask him to stop in case the wind blows his spit in my direction.

After the boat tour, I stroll around that neighborhood of Wilmington. Expensive restaurants and shops. I'm losing interest in shopping. Most stores are chains, just like at home, and other stores are expensive and full of "stuff." I don't want any expensive restaurants, or any "stuff," and I'm ready to leave Wilmington.

The AA clubhouse in New Bern, North Carolina, is a big building in the part of town that I guess was downtown at one time. A Lincoln is parked outside. Inside, a lot of gold jewelry on some people and dirty clothes and greasy hair on other people. This is AA. People are friendly. One woman invites me to join them for an AA campout happening in the next month. It's tempting, but I don't plan to stay in

New Bern for a month. I hear some interesting things at the meeting:

"I've been to meetings at Grateful Dead shows."

"I'm an egomaniac with an inferiority complex."

"They're always looking for a pill to cure alcoholism. But it's not just the drinking. It's the character defects. AA will never be replaced."

"Even as a kid, I thought there was something fundamentally wrong with me. The drink was my solution."

"We are driven to come here, and that's an advantage. We can get the blessings of AA that others don't get."

"I feel at home in AA. It's good to know that when I travel, I can go home."

"I told myself I could have just one more drink. Then again just one more drink. And the next thing I heard was, 'You have the right to remain silent.'"

I have never been arrested, but I've been to jail many times. I volunteer with another recovering woman to bring an AA meeting in for the inmates. I tell them, "It's important to me to let you know about all the support you can get in AA, because it has meant so much to me." That's one way I practice Step 12, carrying the message. And after the jail meetings, so far, the authorities have always set me free.

June 13: Up Past My Bedtime

I'm craving milk. I drink a whole half gallon over the course of the morning. I told you about my plan to drink all my liquids early in the day, so that I won't have to pee during the night. I am happy to report the plan is working.

My ex-husband Joel lives in Wanchese, North Carolina, in the Outer Banks on Roanoke Island. My kids and granddaughters have visited there, but I've never seen the place. When Joel heard about my travels, he invited me to stop in.

After crossing the ridiculously long Virginia Dare Memorial Bridge, I arrive a little after noon. Kathryn, his wife, is home, too. Joel is an uprooted New Yorker from a Jewish family, and Kathryn is a blond New Englander.

They live in a white ranch house, on flat land close to the ocean. It's up on stilts. I say, "I can feel it wobbling ever so slightly. Do you ever get seasick?" The place is packed with books, musical instruments, art supplies. Quilts that Kathryn made hang on the wall.

We sit in the living room to catch up for a while, and then Joel says, "Let's go to O'Neal's for a seafood lunch. My treat."

But his card isn't working, so Kathryn pays. We eat on the deck in plastic chairs, next to fishnets draped on the wall. Then Joel drives us around for a short tour of the little town of Wanchese. I see the biggest pile of oyster shells I have ever seen in my life.

Back home, Joel and Kathryn have things to do, and they show me the room where they want me to stay. I pack a bag and move out of the van and into their guest room. I'm enjoying some introvert time to write postcards, write in my journal for you, and read my Nevada Barr book.

Kathryn appears at the bedroom door and says, "I have to go to work for a while. We're getting organized for next semester. So I'll see you later." She's been teaching jewelry making at a local college.

Joel says, "Let's take a ride to the botanical gardens at Roanoke."

I pay our admission. We wander around in the Elizabethan Gardens. Talking about the kids, what it's like to be in our sixties, health, careers, and what to do next in life. Joel and I have always been able to have good conversations.

Joel treats me to the evening play at Roanoke in a large outdoor theater. Our designated seats are right next to a big, fat, smelly guy, so at the last minute we sneak down to other vacant seats closer to the stage, giggling like teenagers.

It's a long play, told from the English point of view. A large cast of actors play the roles of Native Americans and English settlers, and act out the history of Roanoke—or at least their version of the history. I'm impressed with the effect of their ship moving in the background of the stage. After the play, Joel gives me a backstage tour and shows me how they make the ship move on rails. He used to work here, and he knows people.

Kathryn is home when we get back. We gossip about family and discuss holiday plans. I'm up past my bedtime.

June 14: I Can Hear My Hair

Joel makes oatmeal, eggs, and turkey bacon for breakfast. He says to me, "I have a doctor's appointment today. Do you want to come along for the ride?"

"Sure."

Then I find out that the doctor is in Virginia Beach, Virginia, and it's going to be a three-hour ride one way, and Kathryn is going, too. I'm starting to wonder if I'm staying too long.

While driving, Joel calls the doctor's office to find out what time his appointment is. Then Kathryn says, "After the appointment, I want to go to the Museum of Contemporary Art and the art show on the boardwalk in Virginia Beach." That's when I know it will be dark before we get back.

Joel invites us both to come in to meet with the doctor. He's getting new hearing aids. I decline. It's not my place. Kathryn declines, too.

Joel is grinning when he comes out with the doctor, with his new hearing aids installed. He asks the receptionist to take a picture of the four of us. Our son Seth paid for the hearing aids, and Joel wants to send him a photo of this triumphant moment. It seems a little weird for me to be involved in this, but I'm glad that Seth will be getting a picture that includes me. Like it's a way of saying hello to him.

Coming out into the parking lot, Joel says, "Everything's so loud! I can hear my hair!"

I catch sight of a Chipotle, one of my favorite places to eat. Kathryn has never been there, so I treat them to lunch.

Next, the Museum of Contemporary Art. I confess to you, I don't get contemporary art. So I have nothing more to say on that subject.

The boardwalk art show is right along the shore in a heavily populated area of Virginia Beach. The prices are high. Pottery, jewelry, paintings. I'm impressed with some intricate and detailed embroidery pieces. I see some wooden boxes you can sit on. They have sound holes, and make drumming sounds when you hit them with mallets. Cool.

We debate where to have supper and end up at Food Lion. I get cottage cheese with pineapple, Kathryn gets trail mix and diet Dr. Pepper, and Joel gets hummus, a cucumber, and coconut water.

Their place is so remote that I would have to drive a long way in the dark before I could find a place to park for the night. I don't want to do that, and I bet they wouldn't want me to do that, either. So I'm staying overnight, again.

I plan to leave first thing in the morning.

June 15: Dismal Swamp State Park

As usual, I'm up early, packed, and ready to leave. I want to be polite and say goodbye and thanks to Joel and Kathryn, so I wait for them to get up. And wait.

Joel gets up and cooks eggs and oatmeal. When Kathryn gets up, we all lounge around on the deck for a while.

Now I can gracefully make my exit. I hug them both and say, "Thanks so much for everything."

"Drive safe."

"Have fun."

Back across the ridiculously long bridge. Again.

I stop to use the restroom at a visitor center. When I come out, a man is also coming out, and apparently, we both hit our keys to unlock our cars at the same time. He starts getting into my van, then hesitates and looks at his key with a puzzled expression. I say, "I think that's my car," and I gesture with the key in my hand.

He steps back. "That explains it." And we both laugh.

Driving onward, I smile, seeing windmills and fields of solar panels in North Carolina.

If you come across a place called Dismal Swamp State Park, how could you not investigate? Their visitor center has a bunch of real animals that are dead and stuffed, and a little informational film. In the film, I hear, "Slaves were used to dig out the canal, which is now part of the Intracoastal Waterway. The slaves ran away through this area and camped out."

I had heard the same thing at Congaree National Park, too, a place equally dismal. I think, *Camping out along with snakes, bears, foxes, bobcats, and worst of all, mosquitoes. Life must have been pretty miserable for slaves if they thought this dismal place was preferable to staying put where they were.*

I post the photo of the Dismal Swamp State Park sign on my Facebook group page, Wander Woman. I look for something interesting to post most days.

I set out for Danville, Virginia, because it looks promising. Supper is a picnic at Dan Daniel Park, where I also take time to do some writing and immerse myself in nature on the trail through the trees along the river.

June 16: You Deserve a Medal

I wake up with that song in my head: "Unbreak My Heart." Sigh.

I wander across North Carolina and on into Virginia, taking mostly secondary roads. State Route 43 is a scenic, rural, twisty, green, gorgeous, and slow road that crosses Skyline Drive and comes to the valley on the west side of the Blue Ridge mountains. No phone signal. I've been on Skyline Drive several times before, so I don't go that way this time.

Natural Bridge State Park in Virginia is impressive. A long stairway goes down to the trail that leads to the natural bridge. It's 215 feet tall, a huge, natural hole through the rock, and my photos don't do it justice. I also take the mile-long walk through the woods to the thirty-foot waterfall, and that is underwhelming. I enjoy the woods walk, though, as always.

I also appreciate the scenic drive through Virginia, the green hills and mountains.

While waiting for the tour of Shenandoah Caverns, I poke around in the gift shop. I buy two heart-shaped polished rocks for my granddaughters, Hailey and Kennedy. Gifts can be difficult. I often feel like no gift can express my love. And yet, I want to try.

Our cave tour guide, Ashley, is yelling to be heard over the commotion of the visitors: a huge, noisy family consisting of eight adults and a pack of kids and babies, and three college-age couples who are goofing off and joking the whole time. And then there's me. This cave tour is the prettiest of the three I have seen so far, including Mammoth and Florida Caverns. We see a variety of formations in different cave rooms, lit up with colorful lights. In one stunning room, the colored lights on the stalactites are reflected in a mirror image on still water. On the way out, I give Ashley a tip and tell her, "You deserve a medal."

"Thank you."

"You're welcome."

The cost of the ticket includes two other attractions next door. The Yellow Barn is a museum that contains old vehicles and memorabilia of the history of Shenandoah Caverns. The American Celebration on Parade museum is huge and full of interesting and colorful parade floats. So cool. Cartoon and movie characters, a dragon, a train, polar bears, ducks, pelicans, a pirate ship, and whatnot. I'm wishing my granddaughters could be with me to see that.

At Food Lion along the way, I get some peanuts, bananas, cheese, canned pineapple. I have to pay higher prices than the marked prices because I don't have their discount card. Other grocery stores are like this, too. So annoying.

After some research, I decide to spend the night in Centreville, Virginia, because it will be a short drive from there into Washington, DC.

June 17: Happy Father's Day, Dad

Usually I want to avoid big cities, but it's Sunday and I know that parking is free in DC. And all the museums on the mall are free, too.

I park near the mall early and nothing is open. I move along to the Vietnam Veterans Memorial, which one can always see because it's outside.

One of the volunteers I speak with here says, "The designer of the memorial was an architect who was one of fourteen hundred applicants. She had done the design of the wall for a class project and had gotten a grade of B on it."

The Vietnam Wall is built into the side of a hill. The first time I ever saw the Vietnam Wall, I looked up and saw grass growing above it, and I got a chill when I realized that all these names are of people who are under the grass. Dead.

The Vietnam War years were chaotic and heart-wrenching times. The country was bitterly divided into pro-war hawks and peacenik doves. The hawks waved American flags and showed bumper stickers that said "America, Love It or Leave It," and referred to the peace sign as "the footprint of the American chicken." The doves wore black armbands and held antiwar protests. Four unarmed college students were shot and killed by the Ohio National Guard during a demonstration at Kent State. Seventeen-year-old boys, who were considered too young to vote or buy alcohol, were considered mature enough to be drafted and transported to the other side of the earth to kill and be killed in a war they couldn't understand. They could get a draft deferment if they were a student, or married, or gay. When my friend Glen dropped out of school, we reacted as if he had signed his own death certificate. My friend Sue married a guy she didn't know, just to protect him from the draft. There was a random draft lottery based on dates of birth. My boyfriend, Richard, and I made a pact that we would move to Canada if he was given a bad draft number. He got a lucky one, and we were able to stay in the United States.

Today is Father's Day, and roses are being sold to benefit the Vietnam Veterans Memorial Fund. People buy a rose and write the name of a loved one on a tag, then leave it by the person's name on the wall. I see some older gents, maybe my father's age, touch the rose to the wall, then set it down, step back, and salute the wall. They would have had sons or daughters my age. I'm crying, too.

After Vietnam, I get my free ticket for the Holocaust Museum, and I'm in line with a field trip of teenagers, waiting for the place to open. It's hot outside in the sun. I'm wearing shorts and a tank top, and I'm getting all sweaty. Inside finally, it's air-conditioned and cold. For once, I'm caught without my sweater. It's freezing and crowded and depressing in here.

I sit through a short film about the rise of Hitler's power, and it reminds me of what's going on with Trump now. German people were poor and looking for something different politically, there was no other leadership, and White nationalist propaganda and dehumanizing language were prevalent in their culture. I start to get nervous and look for a way out of the museum. Everywhere I turn, I see images of skeletal people, a pile of old shoes, anti-Jewish propaganda.

I see a sign that says "Exit," and when I get here, another sign says "Emergency Exit Only, Alarm Will Sound." I keep going from (emergency) exit to (emergency) exit, freezing, getting more and more anxious. Finally, I see daylight and head for that, the way out to the warm benign outdoors. Oh, sweet heaven.

I explore the National Air and Space Museum. I learn that the Wright brothers were raised by a mother who designed and built things. She invented appliances for herself and toys for the kids.

A planetarium show is narrated by Whoopi Goldberg. A little kid is chirping, as little kids do, and he and his mom are immediately asked to leave the show. That saddens me. Earlier, grandparents were yelling at some little kid, too, probably for doing something childish. There is infinite human pain in the world.

At the National Museum of African American History and Culture, I'm told, "You have to have a free ticket. You can get them online."

A man is trying to get tickets on his phone. I wait to see what happens. With a humorless laugh, he says, "The free tickets to this museum are sold out." We are turned away. This day is starting to become a bummer.

Time for a refreshing dose of art. *At least art will probably not be traumatizing*, I think. At the Smithsonian Sackler Gallery, I see some Swahili art. And Buddhist art at the Freer Gallery. And I mindfully breathe a sigh of relief.

Feeling restored, I also visit the United States Botanic Garden, the National Museum of the American Indian, the National Gallery of Art, the Hirshhorn Museum. And I enjoy a large, juicy burger with plenty of condiments from a food truck. I eat it with relish.

A late afternoon meeting is scheduled in a crowded section of DC in a neighborhood of restaurants and shops with apartments and offices above. I luck out and spot a parking space. But I have to parallel park. While I'm parking, people have no room to pass me. I am not a good parallel parker, and the van is longer than my Subaru, so I have to go back and forth about a million times while people are leaning on their horns and the temperature is around a hundred. Finally, I succeed in getting parked, so the rest of the world can pass me by and continue on their important missions. I rest my head on the steering wheel for a long moment.

The Dupont Circle Club is upstairs in one of these buildings. About a dozen people sit on folding chairs in the meeting room. They have a planned chairperson, but he's a no-show, so they improvise and someone else chairs. A few things I hear:

"I have given up all my bad habits: alcohol, Valium, cigarettes, caffeine, sweets, gluten. You can use the steps to stop bad habits or start good ones."

"I still have an anger management problem. They stole my anger management and stress management book at the shelter."

"My worst day sober is better than my best day high."

"Keep it in today. Open the present."

"Bring your ass to a meeting and your mind will follow. It's a form of mental hygiene."

Today has been an emotional roller coaster, and it's calming to listen to other people speak from the heart about how they live without using their addictions. Meetings have a way of putting things into perspective for me.

I call my parents, especially to say, "Happy Father's Day, Dad!"

June 18: Then Comes a Rainbow

It's early morning, and I'm exploring the small town of Denton, Maryland. Businesses are still closed. Trip Advisor lists a fiber arts place, but I find nothing at the address they give. On the brick steps of a shop, I take a photo of a life-size wire sculpture of a man holding a guitar that's inlaid with mosaic tiles.

Signs are posted around town describing historic places. Much of the history has to do with slavery, which I find depressing.

I walk around the back of the closed visitor center in Denton to the wharf. I linger and look across to the trees and green field. The historical marker says that Harriet Tubman had an Underground Railroad stop here. I am so impressed with the people who were involved with the Underground Railroad. I would like to think that I could have been one of them, but I don't know if I would have been brave enough.

I decide to go across to the Delaware shore on Routes 404 to 113 to 54. Solar panels on houses and in fields lift my spirits. In Bethany Beach are shops, but there's no place to park without paying. By now I know I want nothing at these kinds of shops. I discover a Dollar General with a parking lot in Bethany Beach. I tend to notice Dollar General stores because that's where I can most always get my favorite large dark chocolate bar for a dollar. I eat half of it and save the rest to eat with a spoon tomorrow.

I travel Route 1 because I believe it will be scenic, but dunes and houses obscure the view of the ocean. I continue to Lewes Ferry. For thirty-eight dollars, the ferry brings me the seventeen miles from Lewes, Delaware, to Cape May, New Jersey. The air is cool, and the long ride is hazy. It's foggy in Cape May.

South Jersey is rural. The Garden State. The traffic in Princeton is thick. The town is alive with pedestrians. It's getting toward evening, and everyone is out on the town, visiting shops and restaurants. I see plenty of expensive real estate.

I'm thinking about my own real estate, my home. My current house is a two-unit mill house with vinyl siding on a dead-end street. A big shady backyard slopes down to the river. My apartment is downstairs and my tenants live upstairs.

My sons were home births. Micah was born in a rented apartment in a barn in Vermont. Seth was born in a mobile home, a cramped two-bedroom trailer in Hollis, Maine. We hired a midwife both times. After what I had seen in the hospital when I was a student nurse in the seventies, I believed I would be safer at home. I marvel at how far the three of us have come since those humble days.

Micah and his family now live in the place where he grew up, my old house in Hollis. I bought that place three times: once with my ex when it was a trailer, once *from* my ex, and once again when I got a building loan to replace the original mobile home with a real house. I designed the house on a piece of graph paper and found a builder who made it a reality.

I waited for both my sons to finish high school. Then I started looking for a house in town where it would be more convenient for me to get to places, like work, shopping, contra dancing, and singing in an a cappella group. It's a half-hour drive in three different directions to get from Hollis to any good-sized town. Hollis is centrally located in the middle of nowhere. In Hollis, I didn't get much company because it was an entire day trip for friends to visit. And the only thing within walking distance was my car. Around that time, Micah was house shopping. I asked him what he was looking for, and the characteristics he listed described my house. So I sold it to him. I was overjoyed that it would stay in the family. It's not the same place now after he has made so many improvements.

Now, approaching Rockaway, New Jersey, I'm getting tired and distracted. On the highway, I survive a blinding rainstorm. Then comes a rainbow.

June 19: Women Never Did Anything

Danbury, Connecticut, is where I went to college the first time. I majored in music education, and bassoon was my instrument. I lived here for four years. The first year, I was in the dorm, and the rest of the time I shared apartments with other students. I haven't been to Danbury in a long time because it's not on my way to anywhere. Western Connecticut State University is still in the same location, but with changes: new buildings, new parking lots, newly designated one-way streets. A house where I lived on Moss Avenue is not here. Gone. Just a vacant lot with a chain-link fence around it.

I call my mom and say, "I'll be at your place late this afternoon, so Dad can go ahead and have his after-lunch nap."

Southington, Connecticut, is where I lived in a neighborhood of Cape houses from the time I was in kindergarten until I was in the sixth grade. The house is still here, with yellow siding and an enclosed side porch now, but missing the spruce tree that was on the front lawn. Some new houses have sprung up on that street. The corner market, Top's Market, is still here.

Recreation Park, which we always called "The Rec," is close by. We used to walk here to swim in the pond, and now the pond is muddy and weedy and covered with green junk. A new swimming pool is up the street.

Across the road is South End School, where I went through the sixth grade. I loved my fifth-grade teacher, Mr. Lorenzo, because he used to read books to us and he was fun and kind. I remember my mean sixth-grade teacher. I once asked him, "How come there are no women in the history book?"

He said, "Because women never did anything."

I drive by the Little League field. The trees I had climbed are here, but now they're much taller, with no lower branches for climbing. I used to sit in these trees and watch the boys in my class play ball. Girls were not allowed to be in Little League. At the time, I asked why. The adult said, "Girls would hurt themselves." This made no sense to me. I thought, *Boys are more likely to hurt themselves than girls are, because they have fragile stuff on the outside that girls don't have to worry about.* The adult also said, "Girls don't like sports." That also made no sense to me, either, because

I thought, *I love sports, and I'm always one of the very first to be chosen for teams in the neighborhood, when it's just the kids doing the choosing. And aren't I a girl?* As I see these trees and this ball field, I'm flooded with memories of wanting to play Little League, of being left out, and again feel the shame and sadness I felt then.

In downtown Southington, I look for the Bradley Memorial Library and find that the building is a historical society now. How I loved that place as a kid. You could take four books out for four weeks. Every four weeks, my father would take us to get new books. I had always finished my books and was impatiently waiting for the four weeks to be up.

In Newington, where I lived during my junior high and high school years, I spend some time at Mill Pond Park. It's windy and warm. I wander around the pond and across a little footbridge over a waterfall. Back when I was a kid, that spot was overrun with weeds, and I used to go under the bridge by the waterfall to hide behind the weeds and mope. Now the weeds are all cleaned up and there's a sitting area below, with benches that have a view of the waterfall. Back in high school, the marching band members walked over this bridge carrying our instruments from the school to the football field for practice. I didn't march with a bassoon, my usual instrument, so I would be hauling a bass drum, or a tenor drum, or sometimes cymbals. Happy memories and sad memories of this place.

I check out the house where we lived in Newington. A New Englander with barn-red siding and a glassed-in front porch. It seems to be empty. Such nostalgia. In sixth grade, I was happy when we moved to this house because I could walk to the library. At the time, I thought, *I'm in heaven.*

Later, I realized that the move was difficult for me because I was shy and had trouble making friends. That's why I was moping at the waterfall.

Only half a mile from here is the senior living place where my parents live now. As usual, my parents are good sports. Mom climbs up into the front seat and Dad settles himself onto the cot in back. We take the van to Ming Moon, a local Chinese restaurant, where I treat them to supper as part of their last year's Christmas gift.

June 20: Hummingbirds

This morning, I'm on my way to visit my friend Terry. I've known her since we worked together as nurses' aides in the seventies, when we both had waist-long hair. We partied and bar-hopped together on many occasions then. Now we're both alcohol-free.

At Terry's house, I wait in the cool shade, enjoying the breeze in the trees. On her own back in the day, she hired builders to make this white Cape-style house, on a large lawn surrounded by woods. She bounces up the driveway in her white Honda SUV with a kayak on top. She greets me with a hug and says, "You're here already!"

"Yeah, I allowed extra time in case I found something interesting to do along the way, but I didn't. It's so great to see you!"

"Well, come in! Let's see what we can find for lunch. It's great to see you, too!"

She makes veggie burgers and salad and we sit on the deck. She is one of those friends who, even if you don't see her for years, you can talk with as if you saw her just yesterday.

Hummingbirds buzz around her bird feeders. I always feel lucky and blessed to see hummingbirds. Just like I'm lucky and blessed to have a friend like Terry.

Terry is an inspiration to me about what a person can do in retirement. She is a selectman for her little town. "I don't mind being called a selectman," she says. "It's just what people say." All the locals know her.

I never thought she was interested in music beyond dancing with me in disco bars in the seventies. But in retirement, she decided she wanted to learn to play drums. She got a drum set and took lessons. She says, "I'm a percussionist in three community bands."

"Let me know your schedule. I'd love to hear one of your concerts."

We say our goodbyes later in the driveway. "Where are you headed today?"

"I've hunted down a meeting in Rhode Island so I can check it off my list of AA meetings in the Lower Forty-Eight states."

I go to the Meadow's Edge Recovery Center in North Kingstown, Rhode Island, looking for the AA meeting. As

I wait for the meeting to start, a couple of women come by and invite me into a Women for Sobriety meeting that's happening at the same time in a different room. I think, *Why not?* I go in to check it out. Only three of us attend the meeting, Donna, Donna, and me. Donna says, "This program was founded by Jean Kirkpatrick. She's a sociologist who has done a lot of writing on the subject. It's based on thirteen Acceptance Statements. Unlike AA, this program doesn't require women to believe in God. They don't have to say they are powerless, like in the AA Step 1." I judge the meeting to be OK, but not profound or spirited. Of course, one can't evaluate a program by going to just one meeting.

AA's Step 1 says, "We admitted we were powerless over alcohol—that our lives had become unmanageable." Some people think that a woman should not have to say she is powerless because it's too much like saying she is a victim. They want women to see themselves as empowered instead. Me? I don't mind admitting I am powerless, because the empowerment comes from Steps 2 through 12.

June 21: I'm Tempted to Sleep in the Driveway

After a Planet Fitness shower, I come out to find a glorious double rainbow above my van. Maybe I've found the pot of gold.

I think of the time when I was in Hawaii for the NA—Narcotics Anonymous—World Convention with my friend

Jeremy. I was on a city bus in Honolulu, and there was a rainbow visible off in the distance, over the mountains. I was pointing that out to people on the bus, saying, "Look! There's a rainbow!" They were doing their best to ignore me, like I was some kind of crazy bag lady. Later, I discovered that there were multiple rainbows daily in their neighborhood. That would be like a visitor to Maine crying, "Look! There's a pine tree!"

The meeting is scheduled on Narragansett Beach in Rhode Island, by lifeguard chair number one. It's been raining and the sand is wet, so it's decided that we will meet in the nearby pavilion. Some people are standing and some are sitting on the concrete floor of the covered porch of the pavilion. I sit on my raincoat. The meeting starts with a couple of readings about spirituality, then a two-minute silent meditation. They go around the circle so each person can have their turn to share. I hear:

"My ship came in and it went out, and it came in again and went out again, and I was at the bar."

"AA is like Vegas. What happens here stays here."

"I feel the united consciousness in the room."

"I had a very thin owner's manual on life. It had only one page. And that page was blank."

"I was so lonely, I felt like I had a big hole in me. I could feel the wind blowing through."

Loneliness is my perennial problem. I'm reminded of a meeting I went to on a day when I was marinating in excruciating loneliness. It was Valentine's Day, a holiday that should be abolished, because it's a rare person who is not somehow disappointed at the end of that day, maybe because they have no sweetheart, or they didn't get that ring they were hoping for.

The chairperson who spoke said, "I was always an outsider. I never fit in anywhere." Every single person who spoke after her said that they had always felt lonely, left out, a misfit. That was when I came to my conclusion that loneliness is a symptom of alcoholism. But that means it can be treated by using the tools of recovery. Some tools of recovery I have learned are, as I often hear in AA, "Don't drink. Go to meetings. Ask for help." Asking for help can take many forms: reading self-help literature, talking with Faith, calling a friend, therapy. I am not alone with my loneliness.

Beach meetings are sweet. I'm glad, though, that this one is in the pavilion. My problem with beach meetings is that, with my hearing loss, the sound of the waves, and the wind in my ears, I have trouble hearing what is being said.

I take back roads straight north through Rhode Island into Massachusetts. The back roads are hard to follow because they're not always marked. Sometimes they take a turn and I'm not sure if I'm still on the route. Pleasant, though, green, shady woods. How I appreciate the cooler green of New England.

Nothing to do now but head for home. I'm restless and unsettled, and I keep changing the radio station. I'm thinking,

Radio is a bad influence because it's all about the hot mess of politics, or songs about romance, which, in my life, is also a mess. When I get home, no one will be there.

In my town, before going home, I stop for groceries at my local Hannaford market. By habit, I look for the best place in the parking lot to camp for the night. When I get to my house, I'm tempted to sleep in the driveway.

Intermission

Home for the Wedding

Home in Maine, I wake up early. *Oh shit, I'm alone.* It's remarkable how I didn't get socked with that while I was traveling. But times when it does happen, it always passes, and I feel better once I get going. Lots to do in the days that I'm home for the wedding. Mail to be sorted, bills to be paid, checkbook to be managed, laundry to be done. Yard work to be put off till later.

I'm sitting out on the deck overlooking the river in my backyard, and my neighbor, Tyler, calls over to me, "I mowed your lawn. Would you like me to do it again?"

"Yes, I'll pay you."

"No, we're neighbors...but...maybe you'd let me use your canoe?"

"Yes! Good deal. Thank you so much. The paddles are in the shed." One burden lifts. And the mysterious lawn mower has revealed himself.

Out driving now, I see the pink Cadillac up in the air and turn into the parking lot at Micah and Melissa's ice cream shop. The petting zoo here has an alpaca, a rabbit, and two lambs, Hailey's 4-H projects. I find fourteen-year-old Hailey walking her alpaca on a leash. Melissa is waiting on customers. Almost-five-year-old Kennedy runs to hug me. "Grammy!"

Micah hugs me, too. "Welcome home."

"Thanks. It's good to be home, and great to see you! This looks lively." Customers are sitting at picnic tables eating ice cream. Kids are on the playground or harassing the lambs.

"It's a lot of work, though. I was just working on the soft-serve machine. When I get it fixed, I'll show you the house we're working on, if you want."

"Let-me-think-yes."

Minutes later, Kennedy and Micah and I are in his old Subaru wagon, all of us wanting to speak at once. We all have so much to tell. My heart increases in size to take it all in.

I love looking at Micah and Melissa's flip houses, works of art in progress. I get to hear Micah tell all the details, what work they have done, and what still needs to be done. Over the years, as a homeowner and a landlady, I have learned about houses. I am fascinated with everything about houses.

When I meet up with Seth for lunch, my spirits lift even more. Seth is a busy guy. He has his own credit card processing business and it's online, so he can work from anywhere. He has a condo in Puerto Rico and a home in Old Orchard Beach, Maine. He travels all over the country for trade shows.

He has an office in town, in Maine, and routinely leaves the office to walk out to a restaurant and eat lunch. When he is in Maine, that's a good time for me to catch up with him. To stretch out our time together, we stroll around the block after lunch. I say, "Having lunch with you makes my day."

"Is that all it takes?"

"Yes. That is all it takes."

Up at Faith's house later, she lets me talk and talk. And talk. She makes time for me to say more detail about my travels than anyone else has. Her patience with me is remarkable. With other people, I am cautious not to talk too long or complain too much. Or even say the positive things about my life in case they think I am bragging and feel jealous and get irritated with me. I am afraid I will be putting them off. Some people have ways of discouraging me from talking. With Faith, I feel safe to just say it. With her, I feel received.

The wedding is all weekend at a hotel with a large grassy backyard that slopes all the way down to the rocky shoreline of the ocean. I'm staying in what's called the Rose Room, a clean, comfortable, classic room with old-fashioned floral wallpaper and no TV. It has a little deck and a view of the backyard and the ocean beyond.

Seth's boys from high school are here. Seth has long-term friendships. I love seeing these high school footballers as men now, so familiar and yet so different. When I see them standing all together, I think, *Seth's personal Mount Rushmore.*

The evening before the wedding, at a nearby white Congregational church, we practice the pageantry. Nicole's parents, Mike and Leanne, will come in together and be seated. Micah will escort me to my place and then join the groomsmen up front. Joel and Kathryn will follow us in. I'm happy to be escorted in by Micah, my beloved son.

Tonight, there's a rainbow, and a big orange moonrise.

The morning of the wedding, I'm up early. I ramble alone around the grounds, past the shuffleboard and the pool, and down to the dock on the ocean. Lonely, imagining others still asleep with their partners and families, imagining others having someone to talk to.

Breakfast is a buffet in the hotel, and there's a plan for me to meet up with family. People are arriving, and it's so good to see some that I haven't seen in a long while. The energy is cheerful in the dining room, and my loneliness fades.

After he makes his rounds, Seth sits next to me. When he finishes eating, I say, "Let's practice our mother/son dance. We can go to my room." We have all agreed on the song, Paul Simon's "Loves Me Like a Rock." In my room, I play the song on my tinny-sounding little phone, and we bop around a little.

During the ceremony, I wish I could hear more of Seth's vows, but he's facing Nicole, with his back toward me. I hear Nicole, though. Her vows are heartfelt and audible. I hear later that Seth's vows were beautiful.

The groomsmen are all in black tuxes. The bridesmaids are in black gowns. Nicole wears a strapless white gown with a fitted bodice and a full skirt from her slim waist to the floor. A veil flows out in the back from beneath her up-swept hairdo. Nicole's mom, Leanne, and I wear wrist corsages made with white roses.

The after-wedding photo session is heartbreaking for me. The photographer is the boss of the photos and tells everyone who will be included and where they will stand. When it comes to family photos, Joel and Kathryn are in and I am out. Then Joel and Kathryn are out and I am in. I have to ask her, "Could you include me and Joel in the same photo?" And she does, but with obvious reluctance. I just want a photo that includes all of our family. I take a deep breath and keep my head together. At times like this, I hold an imaginary consultation with Faith, and regain my equilibrium.

I have a favorite family portrait. It includes my two handsome sons, and lovely Nicole. It also includes Melissa, Hailey, and Kennedy, all three of them slender and beautiful with their long brown hair. And me in my forty-dollar red formal gown.

Back at the inn, drinks and appetizers are served on the lawn with the ocean view. Everyone is in a party mood. I swing from conversation to conversation and enjoy them all. Plus, I get compliments about how "amazing" I look, which isn't too hard to take.

Inside, the tables look elegant, covered with black tablecloths, with white napkins and white dishes, white chairs, and a generous white flower arrangement on each table.

A seven-piece band with two lead singers plays popular music. Seth and Nicole's dance is intricate, graceful, and well rehearsed. And they're beaming. Their song is "Stand by Me." Nicole dances with her dad to "You Are So Beautiful."

In our dance, Seth and I do a couple of turns, which I lead, and the crowd cheers. And it's OK.

Micah's best man speech is lengthy, funny, sincere. Tales of their childhood. He is Seth's older brother, and he says, "Now it's me looking up to Seth." I am impressed, and my heart balloons with pride for both these guys, my sons.

The band is engaging, and most people dance, including me. People are dancing alone and in groups, too. I'm glad about that because I love to dance, and I get distressed sitting out a dance when people are expected to dance only as couples.

Seth's friend Adam is a hoot, dancing like crazy, and the male lead singer gets out on the floor and dances like crazy, too, which only makes Adam dance more like crazy. They're taking turns, having a dance showdown. Everyone is dancing and smiling like their faces might break. Alcohol helps with that, I believe. Not me, though. I am *au naturel*. I begin to understand how a good band can make a good party.

Both Micah and Seth check in with me a number of times. "How you doing, Mom?"

"I'm doing great. This is an awesome party. I'm so happy you checked in, though. You doing OK?" It sure is comforting to be remembered.

At times I take a break from dancing to visit, and then a break from visiting to dance.

I stay until the band quits at ten. I check out the afterparty in the game room, but I don't stay long. It's a young-people-drinking scene, so I figure it's time for me to head back to the Rose Room. There have been difficult moments for me, yeah, but my head and my heart are full of love, and I am exhilarated. So many people, so many connections, so much love and goodwill. Each person will have a different story to tell. I can only tell my own story.

Now the momentous family event is behind me. My children have their own lives. My grandchildren are well cared for. All bases are covered.

One of my favorite things about traveling is packing. It's enjoyable to imagine all the things I might be doing, and all the things I might need in order to do all the things I might be doing. I am prepared, and the road is calling.

Part Two

July 3: Back in the Saddle

I wake up immersed in self-doubt. I know this will pass. It always does. When people say to me, "This, too, shall pass," I want to say, "Yeah, like a kidney stone." If I wait until a time when I feel good enough to do stuff, there would be too much stuff I'd never do. It's the doing of stuff that makes me feel better.

So I pack up the van and lock the house. At the last minute, I grab my fold-up camp chair from the shed. It's covered with dirt and dead bugs, but I toss it into the van anyway. At times, I would have stayed longer at a place if I'd had somewhere comfortable to sit.

Gradually, I begin to get centered as I drive to my parents' place, talking to Faith in my head. I enjoy driving and singing along with the radio. The motion of the van helps me leave my misery behind.

In my parents' living room, I say, "I have pictures to show you." I pull out the photos I printed for them and tell them tales about the wedding, omitting the loneliness parts. We discuss the wedding, and the participants, in detail.

"I wish we could have gone, but we just weren't feeling up to it," my mom says.

"I didn't want to be the center of attention," my dad says.

"What?" I say.

"I mean, when the ambulance comes. Like that time I had an asthma attack at Andy's."

"Oh. Yeah, well, we all missed you. People were asking about you."

My dad asks, "Will you be seeing Christina in your travels?"

"Eventually I'll meet up with her in Fresno. Her baby will be a year old in a few months." Christina is my foster daughter.

My father says, "You've done so well, and you've done so well by Christina."

"That's good to hear. I'm proud of her. She was yanked out of her home by the state. Her mom was mentally ill. I don't think anyone in her family has ever even graduated from high school. Last time I was in Fresno, I told her, 'You have a job, you're a college student, you have a nice partner, you're a good mother, you have a car and a license. You are a success story.'"

"She might not have been such a success story without you."

"Thanks. We've had a lot of fun together, too. I took her on a tour where we had lunch in all the state capitals of New England. We went to Disney World, and we didn't like it because it was too hot and crowded. We were both more impressed with the glass-bottom boat tour in the Keys. I took her camping. Every child should experience rain on a tent, right? You guys taught me that."

They both laugh. He says, "Right. And you've done so well financially, too, with your savings and your rents to collect."

"Not bad for a part-time nurse, I guess. Sometimes I feel smug."

My dad says, "You should."

It's time for their lunch in the dining room, and time for me to move on.

My mom says, "Thanks for stopping in."

My dad says, "Say hi to Christina. And drive safe."

"I always try." I hug them goodbye and leave to pursue my travel dreams.

Interstate 91 goes straight north into Vermont. On the side of the road, a woman next to a Mustang convertible is waving traffic down. So I pull over. She's fiftyish years old, scantily clad and heavily made up.

When she approaches the van, she says, "It's hot! I think I ran out of gas."

"Do you want to use my phone to call someone?"

"I don't know my boyfriend's number. I lost my phone somewhere. Can you just take me to the next exit? There's a gas station there."

"Sure."

She climbs into the passenger seat. "The world is against me. I even lost my job just because I was defending Trump at work."

I don't engage with her on that subject. She's a nonstop talker, and I just let her spin out.

When I drop her off at the gas station, she says, "Thanks a million."

"You're welcome." Driving off, I breathe a sigh of relief, congratulating myself for being the kind of person who is capable of keeping track of her phone and her gas tank.

In Bennington, I stumble across a twenty-four-hour Price Chopper supermarket and mentally "make a reservation" for stealthy lodging later. *I'm back in the saddle.*

The Wilson House, in Dorset, Vermont, is the house where Bill Wilson, one of the cofounders of AA, grew up. It's a red, three-story house with white shutters and an open porch across the front and around one side. I browse a display of historical photos of the house.

It was a wreck, a total rehab, when two people bought it in 1987 and resuscitated it from its ruined condition. I pore over the photos of all the impressive work they did. It's now being used as a bed-and-breakfast, and it is spotless, run mostly by volunteers.

The barn in the back has been fixed up to be used as an AA meeting room. It's fascinating, with a collection of eclectic furniture and rugs, and various contributions of artwork on the walls. The wooden ceiling beams are covered with license plates from different states. The license plates all feature recovery-related sayings like "WEOWEAA," "ILV-BILLW," "AAMAN."

A women's meeting is starting, and nine of us sit on old couches that have been arranged around a coffee table near the fireplace. I hear things like this:

"I never drank alone, until I did. I never drank before lunch, until I did."

"When a normal person gets a flat tire, she calls AAA. When an alcoholic gets a flat tire, she calls the suicide hotline."

"I'm an alcoholic. My problem is Chris."

It's common in AA meetings for people to introduce themselves by first name. They usually say they are an alcoholic, or something like that. Then everyone greets them by first name. I like this custom because people get to know people, and it is easier to raise your hand to speak once you have heard the sound of your own voice in the room. It's an easy way for this introvert to become known. It was remarkable to me when, in my first AA meeting, I said, "I'm Zinnia, I'm an alcoholic," and people said, "Hi, Zinnia." No judgment, no shock, no disdain. Just greeting and acceptance. Very healing.

I have been to the Wilson House before with Jeremy, who is an ex-sweetheart and now friend, during one of our failed attempts to fix our romance. Since I'm thinking of him, I call him. We have good talks now that we are not attempting to be a couple. He says, "How was the wedding?"

I tell him all the beautiful details about the wedding, just like I wrote for you. Then I say, "Nicole's got a lot of homework to do now."

"What homework?"

"She plans to change her name to Seth's last name. Her name is on all her IDs. It's who she is. It's what she's known by. It's a big commitment to make. It's a big job. She has to change her name on her passport, her driver's license, her professional licenses, her bank account, her credit card, insurance, bills, investments, on Facebook, and whatever other social media she's on. And what about other stuff like her car registration, and business contacts? Her name will be different from what's on her diploma. And what if her long-lost childhood friends want to find her? How could she be found? She's someone else now."

"I never thought about how much there is to it, changing your name."

"Can you imagine a man being willing to go through all that?"

We both laugh. I say, "Seriously. I'll know that women have achieved equality with men when men change their names as often as women do."

"Good point."

Our conversation drifts into recovery topics, as it so often does, since we are both in recovery. "Faith wants me to sponsor people, and I would like to. It would be satisfying and interesting, and I'd be giving back. Or paying it forward, actually. I'm looking for things to do in retirement, too. But I don't know..."

"What's your hesitation?"

"Well, I have been avoiding sponsoring people because when I was working in the hospital, I didn't want one of my sponsees to show up as a patient. Who knows what they might say about me to my coworkers. And also, if I don't even know if God exists, how could I encourage anyone to have faith in God, the way a standard AA sponsor is supposed to do? And plus, I don't read the Big Book because the gender-exclusive language bothers me. How could I ever be a good sponsor?"

Jeremy says, "The right sponsees will come along. Some people would need a sponsor like you. You have a lot to offer."

July 4: There Is Nothing Else in the World I Would Rather Be Doing

This morning, I'm headed to Cobleskill, New York, where my niece and nephew live. I want to bring them something, so I stop off and get a watermelon and a couple of bags of cherries. My niece Crystal is married to Nate, and they have a baby called Spencer. Dave, Crystal's brother, has his own house on an adjacent property.

Dave's house is a log cabin with a long front deck that overlooks the field and has a view of Crystal's place down the hill by State Route 165. He gives me the tour of his place. The cabin needs fixing up, but he has come a long way already, and he's grinning, enthusiastic about continuing. The place is roomy, so I say, "You know, you could make the basement into a separate apartment. Then you'd get the income."

He hesitates. "Yeah...I could...I guess."

I suspect he's skeptical of my brilliant suggestion.

Dave does tech support on computers—don't ask me to explain it—and can do much of his work remotely, from home. He has a workroom where he keeps his computer, as well as a drum set and guitars and a keyboard.

Outside he has four boxes of bees that have recently been wrecked by a bear, and he's pondering how to keep his bees safe.

I borrow Dave's hose to wash the dirt and dead bugs off my fold-up camp chair and leave it outside to dry.

Crystal and Nate have fixed up an apartment in their barn. Nate does construction work professionally. The apartment has three bedrooms downstairs, and a living room and kitchen upstairs with a deck off the living room in the back that overlooks the field and the woods beyond, and has a view of Dave's place up the hill. Baby Spencer is sleeping.

They have a big, mostly mulched vegetable garden, including lots of tomatoes. They make salsa. Originally, they bought the place to raise hops, but they haven't gotten too far with that yet. Crystal will be starting a job in September teaching elementary school health and physical education. She'll be getting health insurance for her family.

Nate gives me a tour of his projects. "We got all these large appliances from a school cafeteria teardown. I don't know exactly what I'm going to do with them yet. But I know they will be put to use." The rambling barn is in need of more repair or remodeling. Nate has ambitious plans. It seems overwhelming to me, but they're all in good spirits and optimistic.

Dave has a jeep and takes me on a tour of the property, up the hill to where the trees are and through the different sections of the field, all with spectacular views of the distant farms and hills. Crystal and Nate own forty-something acres that are mostly hayed by a neighbor. The jeep tour is exhilarating. Sometimes there are moments when I realize that there is nothing else in the world I would rather be doing. This is one of those moments.

Outside at the house, Spencer is awake now, and playing with water toys in the kiddie pool, splashing, laughing, and chirping, as babies do. Dave joins him. It's ninety-five and humid. Burgers and hot dogs are on the grill for lunch and will be served along with the watermelon and cherries I brought.

We watch the Fourth of July parade in Cobleskill. We get icy lemonade from one of the vendors, made from real lemons and tons of sugar. A delight on this hot day. Now there's some discussion about what to do in the evening. "The fireworks won't be till much later," Crystal says. "What are we going to do in Cobleskill until then?" No one has an answer, so we go home.

In the evening, Dave drives Crystal and me to Glimmerglass State Park, where we watch fireworks. We sit on lawn chairs on the long beach by the lake. There's a large grassy area, plenty of parking, picnic tables. Dave brought cold drinks for us. Once again, there is nothing else in the world I would rather be doing.

July 5: Assume That It Is Hot

It's a dark, quiet night in the van in Dave's driveway. No security lights, no streetlights, no passing trucks, no slamming car doors, no beeping car locks. Dave's plumbing is a work of art in progress, so this morning I get a shower at Crystal's. I'm about ready to leave when Dave sails down the hill in his Jeep with my now washed and dried camp chair. "Hey. You forgot something."

"Duh. Thanks."

Crystal says, "When I take Spence to day care, I'll be going right by Route 88 West. Why don't you just follow me?"

"Great idea. Thank you both so much for everything. I love coming here."

Connecting with people is one of the best feel-good parts of traveling. I'm reluctant to say goodbye.

By the end of the day, I've done a long drive, through New York, through that small part of Pennsylvania, and into Ohio. I'm tired and starting to get annoyed with other drivers. Plus, I'm cranky because it's been hot and humid almost the whole time I've been traveling so far. That kind of weather is so common that I don't even bother telling you about it each day, because it's always the same. Hot. If I don't mention the weather, assume that it is hot.

July 6: Henrietta Seiberling

Rockside Station in Independence, Ohio, is where you can get the Cuyahoga Valley National Park scenic train. I have a seat all to myself going south. A bunch of noisy kids are scampering around.

I downloaded the self-guided tour app, but it isn't working well, and it's draining my phone battery, so I shut it off.

Not much to see from the scenic train. Woods, and the Cuyahoga River, with muddy water the color of my decaf coffee with cream. The train stops for a long time, and I have plenty of opportunity to sit and look out the window at the woods, and question, *Why was this place chosen to be a national park?* If the self-guided tour app would work, I might get my answer. My fellow passengers and I learn that a tree has gone down, and it has taken that long to clear the tracks. Plenty of stops, and the train is excruciatingly slow. It proceeds in a straight line to a station where it reverses to where we started.

The train seats are pairs of bench seats facing each other. On the way back, three large people sit with me. It's an intimate setting for such hefty people. When we get back to Rockside Station, I'm done with it. Time to move on to the next attraction.

Dr. Bob's house at 855 Ardmore Avenue in Akron is a National Historic Landmark now. Dr. Bob Smith was the other cofounder of AA, and this house is where the first meetings were held. Ernie, the volunteer, gives me a long-winded tour of the house. He says, "After Dr. Bob and his family left, the house was used as a frat house and a biker gang house, among other things. The house was bought in 1984 for AA. All the things in here are things that could have been owned by Dr. Bob and his wife, Anne." It's a three-story house on a corner lot in a residential neighborhood, up a bit of a rise with—guess what—twelve steps leading up to the open and welcoming front porch.

Ernie and I have a long conversation. He tells me, "It was Henrietta Seiberling who introduced Bill W and Dr. Bob. Henrietta was a member of the Oxford Group, and was already working to help alcoholics, including Dr. Bob. Bill W was visiting Akron on business and craving a drink. He started calling churches looking for some alcoholic to help, to give himself something to do besides drink. He was referred first to Henrietta. She put him in touch with Dr. Bob. Dr. Bob reluctantly said, 'All right, I'll give him fifteen minutes,' and they talked for hours. Henrietta continued to work with them, developing a program for alcoholics." One wonders, *How did Henrietta's name happen to disappear from the folklore story of the origins of AA?*

Ernie doesn't like the AA custom of closing meetings with the Lord's Prayer. In my experience, this prayer is almost universal in meetings. He says, "I have heard that the Lord's Prayer is used as a nod toward the Oxford Group, a religious group that was the inspiration for AA. I don't like it because I don't want to have to forgive others and take all the blame just because I am an alcoholic."

I say, "I don't like using it because it has religious origins, and AA is supposed to be spiritual, not religious. I think it could be discouraging to newcomers who have issues with religion, or who have other religions. I think we've done enough nodding to the Oxford Group by now, don't you?"

The house next door is used for AA archives. Ernie says, "They have also bought the house behind, and that will be used for archives, too. Listen to this: A woman was looking in a used bookstore and found an AA daily reading book and she bought it for thirty-five cents. There was an inscription in the book: 'Please return to 855 Ardmore Ave. R. Smith.'"

The most annoying part of the day is trying to get to the Planet Fitness. It's supposed to be a ten-minute drive, according to my GPS. There is little traffic, luckily, but plenty of construction and detours. Signs tell me which roads are forbidden, but then I'm given no indication of what other roads to take. Some interstate exits and entrances are blocked, with no alternatives. My GPS doesn't know about all the detours, so it's no help. A half hour later, I find myself at the same intersection that I've explored three times already. So I pull out a couple of feet into the intersection and hesitate, debating which way to try next. My light turns red and I'm a little forward from where I'm supposed to be. A driver approaches me from the right to take a left turn in front of me. He has plenty of room to get by, but he stops his vehicle right in front of me, blocking me, and gives me the Hate Stare. You know the one I mean. My mother would say, "If looks could kill…" He keeps it up until I back up the two feet to let him have his way. He doesn't know, or care, that I'm from out of state, have never driven in Akron, have spent a half hour driving randomly and fruitlessly in the same vicinity, am already stymied and defeated. He has no compassion. Road rage never fails to make me cry.

Finally, I decide to choose a road and keep on driving for a long time, no matter which direction, just so I can get away from the construction. After a few more false starts, I find Planet Fitness and my parking spot.

July 7: Like the Post-Holiday Letdown

At two in the morning, the parking lot is being swept with a leaf blower until the street sweeper takes over. I'm up early. Again, so many detours and roads blocked. So again, I take any random road just to get away from the detours, and eventually I make it onto the highway going west, tearful, feeling unloved, unlovable. Shamed by yesterday's road rage and frustrated by lack of sleep.

I get a decaf coffee and live it up with my daily dose of dark chocolate. While driving, I hear "Uptown Funk" on the radio and can't help but sing along. I am convinced that singing, like laughing, changes my brain chemistry. Now I'm starting to think of future things I can do: home improvements, travel, hang out with friends and family, start a business, take a class, learn a new job skill, volunteer, write a memoir, sing, contra dance, get a cat, plant a garden, play the bassoon in a rock band—I don't know. I'm in better spirits. Is it because of the chocolate, the music, singing, or having plans? Probably all of the above.

In Zanesville, Ohio, I hit the AA meeting guide app and find that a meeting starts in three minutes, a half mile away at the Indiana Street Recovery Center, which is on Moxahala Avenue. They're just saying the opening Serenity Prayer as I slide in and locate a seat in the packed room. Topics are chosen: procrastination, attitude, and Step 1. They go around the whole room giving everyone a chance to share, so the meeting runs overtime. These are some of the things I hear:

"If you believe you can, or if you believe you can't, you're right."

"If you're willing to drink yourself to death, that means your life is unmanageable."

"Recovery is progressive."

Often, I hear that alcoholism, or addiction, is progressive, in that it gets worse and worse if not put into remission. It's hopeful and helpful to know that recovery is also progressive, in that it gets better and better.

Rita, a woman my age with real short hair, invites me out to breakfast with her and two men who were at the meeting. At first, I decline. It's my habit to be shy and keep to myself. But then I agree. We drive, in separate cars, to a nonprofit Mennonite café called The Walk. I order a cup of decaf and an amazing large, sweet, frosted cinnamon roll, something definitely not on my food plan. We have a lively discussion about what it was like before AA and how much better it is now. Rita says, "I'm having some medical problems. Sobriety doesn't guarantee that you'll never have problems. But it's way better if I don't drink over it, and I have you people to support me."

I say, "My first AA sponsor used to say, 'If you have a problem and you drink over it, then you have two problems.'"

I haven't craved a drink in decades, but clearly, after hanging out with people who get me, I feel much better. That's one of the gifts of AA for me. I say to Rita, "I'm so glad you invited me. I feel fortified."

This chunk of the trip is getting off to a little bit of a rocky start. Maybe because the wedding was so exhilarating and I felt so connected, and now, again, I'm alone. Like the post-holiday letdown. And now I don't have the wedding to look forward to.

I used to play bassoon in the ballet orchestra for *The Nutcracker.* It was a busy Christmas season with rehearsals and multiple performances, all the hoopla. Then suddenly, when the last performance was over, it would be like my life fell off a cliff. I would feel the emptiness, like I'm feeling today.

Typically, I feel better after an AA meeting, even if I didn't feel bad to begin with. Talking with people and remembering things Faith has told me helps.

July 8: Perfect Place to Get the Runs

This is a perfect place to get the runs. First thing in the morning, I'm going into Planet Fitness, where they have a bathroom. I wonder, *What caused this problem? Was it the questionable rest-area water I've been drinking? Or the massive amounts of cherries I consumed? Damn, and I love cherries, too. Now cherries will be on my "warning, danger" list.*

Luckily, by the time I leave Planet Fitness, things are under control.

I've heard about the mysterious Courthouse Tree in Greensburg, Indiana, so of course I want to cruise by. The courthouse is a large brick building with a tall clock tower, over a hundred feet tall, Trip Advisor tells me. Since the 1870s, an aspen has been growing out of the very top of the clock tower. No one can explain how it got up there, or how it continues to stay alive. I'm a sucker for peculiar stuff like this.

Driving along, I see an ad for Schooner Valley Stables in Nashville, Indiana. Horse riding for beginners! I'm definitely a beginner. I've been on a horse only twice before, not counting when I was little, sitting on a pony that was being led around on a rope at a fair. I pull over and buy a ticket on my phone right then and there.

When I arrive, I see that about twenty of us will be going on this ride, all "beginners." And all of us want photos of ourselves on horses so we can post them on Facebook for our friends to like. Luke is kind and patient when he helps us all get onto horses and explains how to manage them. It takes about an hour for Luke and his staff to get us all saddled up, and instructed, and photographed on our phones.

For about an hour, we ride the trail through the woods, all of us in a row, with Luke and a few other staff members along. The day is hot and muggy, but luckily, it's not buggy in the woods.

My horse is called Strider. He's brown, with some white on his legs and left side. On the trail, he keeps wanting to go off into the woods, and I have to keep redirecting him. Luke notices the situation. He says, "The horse behind you keeps biting Strider on the butt." He escorts me and Strider up farther in the line, away from that diabolical beast. After that, it's much easier for Strider and for me.

This is one of my favorite experiences so far, because horse riding is rare for me, and exciting. And I get to participate and not just observe. And guess what? I do post the photo on my Facebook group, Wander Woman, for all my friends to like.

I'm already in Nashville, Indiana, so I check out the town. It's crowded with tourists shopping, eating ice cream, sitting in restaurants. The shops are artsy, and touristy, and expensive. I stop for a while to watch a busker, a street musician, who is playing a fiddle with strings attached to a puppet on the sidewalk who, as a result of the strings, plays in unison with the human fiddler. Like Mini Me. Imaginative and fascinating. Of course, I give money to buskers. I carry small bills for that purpose. Support your local musicians.

July 9: Waiting to Be Scolded

Signs on the road direct me to the World's Largest Rocking Chair in Casey, Illinois. The rocking chair is in the center of town. "It's made from recycled materials. It's thirty-two feet high and weighs forty thousand pounds," says a bystander with a guidebook. "It can actually rock."

"Do you want to try it?"

She laughs. "No." We take turns getting photos of each other standing under the rocker. We see other World's Largest things: wind chime, pencil, golf tee, gavel, yardstick, knitting needles. She says, "They had to actually knit on them to have them certified as 'World's Largest Knitting Needles.'" Quirky stuff. My favorite.

The morning meeting is at St. Mary's Hospital in Centralia, Illinois. I ask at the reception desk, and the directions are so complicated that a volunteer offers to escort me to the room. It's in a classroom in the basement. On the wall I see a poster of the Jellinek Curve, a U-shaped graph that shows the progression of the disease on the left, going downward, and the progression of recovery on the right, going upward. Small bowls of candy, including chocolate, are on the table in front of each seat. About ten people sit around tables arranged in a square. The format is to read and discuss a section of the AA Big Book.

When it's my turn to share, among other things, I say, "I have a problem with the male, gender-exclusive language in the Big Book, so I don't read it much. God is always referred to as 'Him,' and AA members are frequently referred to as 'men.' I feel left out, like the literature isn't meant for women, like it doesn't apply to me. So I get my understanding of the Big Book by listening to other people quote it."

I cringe, waiting to be scolded. But the man who speaks next says, "I'm glad you said that. I never thought of it that way."

Another man says, "The good part of that is that it keeps you coming to meetings and listening to other people and learning from them." A couple of other men speak about how important women have been to them in their recovery. I'm surprised and delighted at the response from these men. Even some of my women friends at home roll their eyes and change the subject when I talk about gender inequality. I have to come to Centralia to be heard. And plus, I get to eat chocolate.

Some other things I hear today:

"I study the Big Book as if my life depends on it. Because, well, it does."

"Some people come to AA for the socialization. It's like a sober Elks Club."

"Nothing changes if nothing changes."

I have to ask how to get out of the building, and one man is kind enough to show me a shortcut to the parking lot. I

feel embraced, and walk away with song lyrics in my head...
"Limitless undying love which shines around me like a million suns, it calls me on and on across the universe."

The day is hot, needless to say, so I hunt for a place to swim. I locate Carlyle Lake and spend a couple of hours swimming and then sitting in the fold-up camp chair that Dave reminded me to bring, reading in the shade. Life is rough. I take a photo of the chair by the lake and text it to Dave, saying, "Thanks for reminding me!"

July 10: It's Too Hot to Think

Kefir for breakfast. It's cold, wet, sweet, filling. I am in love with kefir.

The Gateway Arch in St. Louis, Missouri, has recently been made a national park, and I'm on a mission to see national parks.

Onto the highway and into St. Louis. When I talk about stealth camping, people say, "Aren't you brave." Driving into, or through, cities is the scariest thing for me about stealth camping. I try to avoid that. But to get to the Gateway Arch National Park, highway driving has to be done.

I make it here and park in the garage that's suggested in the guidebook. I wander around the grounds in the heat waiting for the place to open.

Inside the museum, which is underground beneath the arch, I watch a documentary film about how the arch was made. It's so cold in here that I wish I'd brought my sweater. The museum features displays of American and local history, including a display about Native Americans. I learn that there were over five hundred treaties between the US government and American Indians, and all of them were broken by the US government. All.

A little tram car goes up inside the arch to the top. I've already gotten my ticket ahead of time on my phone. I'm directed to squeeze into a car with a pleasantly conversational couple and two kids. The woman says, "These are our grandkids. They're on summer vacation. Where are you from?"

"Maine."

"I bet it's cooler there."

"Yes, it is, but it's even colder in this museum."

Up on top of the arch, we climb out of the car. We can see out through small windows overlooking the city on one side and the Mississippi River on the other. We can sense the arch swaying, just moving almost imperceptibly. A little unnerving. After five minutes, Grandma says, "We've seen it and done it, right?"

"Right. I think we've seen it all." The five of us pile back into another car and descend.

It's pleasantly cool in the parking garage, so I do lunch parked in the van while texting with Christina in Fresno. She's looking to move and asks me if I'll give her a reference for an apartment. I have no problem at all with that, bless her clean, quiet, responsible, lovely heart. I'm looking forward to seeing her, with my bundle of laundered Goodwill baby clothes for her daughter, Maia. I want to make sure I have her current address when I arrive at the West Coast.

Surprisingly, when I exit the "$6 For A Whole Day" parking garage, I'm told, "It's fifteen dollars because you haven't stayed the whole day." When I realize she isn't joking, I reluctantly hand over the fifteen dollars.

I GPS my way out of St. Louis, thinking, *What did people do before GPS?* and drive north along the river in Missouri. Suddenly the road just stops. Ends. I have to backtrack and detour, guessing which way to turn at each intersection. GPS is not very useful with detours. It is pretty country, though. Farms, hills, trees.

I reach Hannibal, Missouri, hoping to get into the train museum. The sign says it's closed on Tuesdays, and of course, it's Tuesday. I check in at nearby Karlock's Kars and Pop Culture Museum and ask the man about the riverboat cruise I saw advertised on a billboard. He says, "It's right down there, but they leave at four." I look at the clock. It's 3:56. So I leap into the van, race down the side street, park, and run into the office for a ticket, and they let me on. A triumph.

The Mississippi River tour is narrated, with intermittent recorded banjo music. A long tale is told about Indian lovers who were forbidden to see each other. The girl's father was on the lookout for her boyfriend, to kill him. The boyfriend's name was Falling Rock. That's why along the roads you see signs that say, "Watch for Falling Rock." The name of the boat is *Mark Twain*. I like Hannibal. Lots to do in Hannibal.

In the evening, it's too hot to think. That's when movie theaters come in handy. I see the movie *Tag,* and enjoy the air-conditioning while waiting for the sun to set.

July 11: Every Morning Is Like Christmas

Marion, Iowa, is where Sue and John live, and I have an invitation to visit them at their house for lunch at one thirty. This is the friendly retired couple I met on the boat tour in Jefferson, Texas.

I hit a noon meeting at the Marion Industrial Club. The meeting room is downstairs in an industrial-type building in an industrial-type area. Of the ten people, only two of us are women. Going around the room, everyone gets a chance to share, and the chairperson shares last. They share:

"Kathryn will be celebrating forty-six years of sobriety. That includes holidays and weekends."

"I'm hoping to get through the day with a minimum of amends to make."

"They told me when I was a kid that I wouldn't amount to much. But they were wrong. I became an accomplished alcoholic."

"I'm looking forward to hearing what everyone has to say. There is a smorgasbord of offerings in AA upon which we feast."

"If you're sitting here, you are a miracle."

Here is a story about a miracle. One day I was at a meeting in Maine when I saw a younger man who looked familiar. He came up to me after the meeting and said, "I remember you. You were the substance abuse counselor of a group I was in back in the nineties. I was homeless and living in a tent in the woods. I had one of your group handouts in one hand and a gun in the other hand. And here I am."

"I am so glad to see you! That makes my day. Keep up the good work."

I often think of that man. When we don't see our clients or patients again, we don't know whether it's because they are dead or because they are doing well and don't need us.

I pull in at Sue and John's house. They live in a neighborhood of similar houses, new-looking gray-sided houses with two-car garages and wide driveways. The difference is Sue's collection of large rocks along the edge of their driveway. She's interested in geology.

It's spotless and classy inside. They both hug me. I brought them a little flowering African violet from the supermarket, and John smiles and says, "We'll take good care of this."

Sue makes BLT sandwiches, corn on the cob, and fruit salad. She says, "Iowa is corn."

I stay for two hours, immersed in conversation, responding to John's questions about my travels. Sue says, "I'm getting ready to go to a sixty-year-old friend's birthday party."

This is my cue to leave. I say, "We should be Facebook friends."

Sue says, "John doesn't have Facebook, so let's you and I do it." And so we do. They hug me goodbye, and I'm on the road again.

In Wisconsin, I stop at the Dodgeville Serenity Club. It's a white vinyl-sided building with a big parking lot in the back, where the entrance is. The sign on the door shows that AA, OA, Al-Anon, and NA meetings are held here. Inside, a vintage mint-green toilet sits in the corner of the meeting room, without plumbing, of course. Someone has labeled it "Pity Pot" with black marker on the tank. And underneath that, someone has attached a bumper sticker that says "This Too Shall Pass."

Only three of us sit at the big table. This is a women's meeting. One woman says, "I ended a relationship, moved to Wisconsin, and bought a cabin by the lake. It's my dream come true, but it's lonely." Boy, can I relate to that. My house by the river is beautiful, and I love it, but no one is there except me. And my tenants, whom I rarely see.

What this meeting lacks in quantity, it makes up for in quality:

"I always just wanted to remodel the past."

"The things our disease tells us. We're bad. We're worthless. It's like a domestic abuser. We have our own internal domestic abuser."

"You talk about being shy. I had to drink before I could go out drinking."

"Every morning is like Christmas because I've been given a gift of a sober day. Every night is Thanksgiving. I'm always in holiday mode."

One of the first meetings I went to when I got out of rehab was at the Chit Chat Club. And it was also a women's meeting. About a dozen women were at that meeting, so I dared to raise my hand. I said, "I'm new and I could use some phone numbers." One woman picked up a paper napkin and passed it around the table and almost everyone wrote their name and phone number on it.

Later, when I would speak at the Chit Chat meeting about the troubles in my life, I could see these women listening and sometimes getting teary. I felt heard, seen. I felt real. Gradually, I matched the names on my napkin with the faces, and began making calls. That napkin was my Higher Power revealed.

July 12: The Largest Carousel in History

I'm trying to find my way to the House on the Rock. I pull off into a bank parking lot and sit in the driver's seat in my van, looking at the map. A nice bank-dressed lady walks by and stops to ask, "Do you need directions?"

"I'm looking for Route 23."

"Oh, are you going to Spring Green?"

"Actually, yes."

"Everyone goes there—to the House on the Rock, right?"

"Actually, yes." She gives me easy directions. I love the Wisconsin accent. So cute.

My nephew Dave recommended the House on the Rock, so I figure it's worth checking out. It's the oddest, most entertaining place. How can I describe to you something that defies description?

The House on the Rock has three locations: the attraction, the inn, and the resort. I'm interested in the attraction.

Outside is a garden with ponds and a waterfall, and a collection of sculptures, and huge urns with plants growing in them. Inside is a room with historical pictures and documents. I learn that in 1945, Alex Jordan started to build a house on a large, high rock. He had to carry all his building materials up a ladder by himself. People started to be interested in his progress, so he started charging admission. He used the admission money to keep building onto the house.

I proceed through the original house. It has thirteen rooms made with dramatic stone walls, all different. Some have fireplaces. Some are open to the air with trees growing in them. Some have streams of water flowing through.

The first thing I see in the museum section is a mechanical orchestra playing Ravel's *Boléro*. These are real instruments played by machine, and they sound perfect, just like a real orchestra, because it actually *is* a real orchestra, but with no human musicians.

I am thunderstruck and stand to listen to *Boléro* twice. I am astounded to see violins playing themselves. And a drum, a harp, a piano, a cello. All being played by machinery.

This is where I ask the attendant, "Where did he get the money for all this?"

"From admission fees." *Hard to believe.*

Display after display of different instrumental ensembles play real music with real instruments that are mechanically operated. Or is this an illusion? You can buy tokens to play some of them, and some don't require a token. You can go around a corner and see a banjo playing itself in a glass case. Or a guitar. One mechanical orchestra includes two bassoons, and I can't wait to see how a machine can play a bassoon. I have so much trouble with my reeds. Much to my dismay, this one is out of order. *Probably reed trouble.*

Room after room after room shows so many collections and displays. A huge room with a life-sized whale head with a life-sized rowboat in its mouth, and a mechanical orchestra playing "Octopus's Garden." Displays of crowns, Santa dolls, nautical memorabilia, butterflies, and more—too many to remember. A mock town with storefronts with a collection in each shop window: tea sets, cash registers, masks, Norman Rockwell plates, and other stuff. Airplanes and hot-air balloons above. A collection of Burma-Shave advertisements. A limousine covered in ceramic tiles.

And the Largest Carousel in History. The sign gives me this information: 20,000 lights, 182 chandeliers, 269 animals on the carousel, 80 feet in diameter, 35 feet high, and premiered Easter 1981. All 20,000 lights are glittering in a huge, dark, windowless room as the carousel turns. Music is provided by real instruments playing themselves. The carousel animals are not just horses, but mermaids, dragons, and other fantastic creatures. A herd of leftover animals is displayed on a nearby wall. I could stay here all day. A gentleman attendant is dozing in a chair. I guess he does stay here all day.

The Infinity Room is over two hundred feet long and skinny, tapering to a point, and made of three thousand pieces of glass. I look down and see treetops through the glass floor.

In the ladies' room, a wall of glass bottles is all lit up and sparkling.

I don't want to leave the House on the Rock. But the road calls me on.

I move ahead northward toward the Upper Peninsula of Michigan, through farmlands, then hilly forests, listening to that really cute accent on the radio. It's rural, and often I get no phone signal. I'm off to Copper Harbor, on a mission to get to Isle Royale National Park.

Isle Royale is accessible only by ferry. I call to make a ferry reservation for two days from now. "Can I give you my credit card number?"

The man on the phone says, "No, no, that's not necessary."

"I want to make sure I can get on the boat. Should I give you my name?"

"No. There'll be a place for you."

"OK, then, if you're sure."

"Sure, I'm sure."

"OK. See you in a couple days, then." But I am not reassured.

Into Michigan, I make a plan to stay at the Houghton Walmart for two nights because it's somewhat accessible to the ferry. The temperature is in the seventies. Such a relief to be able to hang out in the parked van, relax a while, and then sleep comfortably.

July 13: Friday the Thirteenth

This Walmart is a gathering place for teenage boys in trucks at night. But they seem benign, and not too noisy. Maybe they just have no place else to hang out in this semirural neighborhood.

I have a day to spend in Houghton while waiting for the ferry ride tomorrow. It's kind of like being on vacation from vacationing.

I find a 24/7 laundromat. I do a load of laundry. And since no one is here to stop me, I have a "sponge bath," as my mother would call it, and a shampoo at the sink in the laundromat bathroom.

I get a decaf, make my bed up clean, read my book. I watch a beautiful young woman with a long blond braid sweep trash off the parking lot at Dollar Tree.

Micah was born on a Friday the thirteenth, so I call that my lucky day. Our lucky day. I send him a cheerful text to say "Happy Friday the thirteenth!"

I stop in at the visitor center to find something to do on my day off in Houghton. The Quincy Copper Mine tour is something to do.

On the tour, I'm accompanied by a couple of dozen teenagers who are with a church group. They're well behaved. We're given hard hats to wear, and coats are available. There's a museum with artifacts and a tour of the enormous steam-powered hoist engine.

A train chugs down to the entrance of the mine, and a tractor-pulled wagon brings us in. It's cold, damp, and dark in the mine. Our guide says, "On average, two men a year died in here." It must have been hard times to make people think it was a good idea to be a miner for a living. It makes me grateful that I don't have to do that. I think of that whenever I hear a woodpecker, too. *No matter how hard life gets, at least I don't have to smash my face against wood to eat insects for a living.*

The visitor center person also recommends the A. E. Seaman Mineral Museum. Some roads are closed because they're washed out, with deep ruts here and there. But I find the place somehow. The museum features an impressive display of rocks and minerals and an interesting gift shop. I do some shopping for my granddaughters: carved stone animals for Kennedy and "singing magnets" made of hematite for Hailey. The magnets make a clinking chime when they come together, so I guess that's why they're called singing magnets.

The next thing I want to do is find a Michigan meeting so I can check that off my list.

L'Anse is a cool little town with a waterfront park on the shore of Lake Superior. I get to hang out here for a while with my fold-up camp chair. I visit Pat's Foods and buy some cheesy bread for the ferry trip to Isle Royale, and some locally made jam, a gift for my tenants, who are taking care of my mail. This town has a Subway and a Burger King, but most businesses are local and not chains.

It takes a while for me to find the hospital where the L'Anse AA meeting is supposed to be. I think they must have moved the hospital, because when I get to the address, there's no hospital, so I have to actually ask directions. How retro. I find the hospital and wait in the parking lot for the meeting to start. Not one car is in the front parking lot. No car arrives, so I hit the road and drive to Ontonagon, where I know there will be a meeting later.

The Ontonagon meeting is in the Methodist church. Parking is on the grass. There are six men and me, so I get plenty of attention. One man says, "This one guy goes to the L'Anse meeting and he shows up twenty minutes late or not at all, so it was a good call that you came here." In the meeting, other men say:

"I just drank. It's hardwired."

"If you don't know what to do, just do the next right thing."

"I was resentful I had to pay bills. Then I changed my attitude to gratitude, that I could have heat and electricity and be able to pay for it."

Sometimes I hear people refer to AA as "attitude adjustment." I find that sometimes, for me, just looking at things from a different angle can help. I can choose what to focus on. Like with taking photos. I can take a photo of either the flower garden or the trash can right next to it. But sometimes I don't see the other side of things and it's helpful to have others point them out, things that I am not seeing. I think of Faith, especially, in the helpful department.

After the meeting, they're all curious, so I show off my van. I take a liking to a guy who is probably twenty years younger than me who has been stealth camping, too, and who has been to Maine and worked in Portland's Old Port. We're kindred spirits. A lot of letting go on this trip.

July 14: It's 5:12

I'm up early so I can get to Copper Harbor and catch the *Queen IV* ferry to Isle Royale National Park. Driving out of the Walmart parking lot, I see that it's 5:12 a.m., and involuntarily, I give a little growl of bitterness. That was an inside joke between me and That Guy who broke up with me in an e-mail. One morning as I was sleeping soundly, and probably snoring, he leaned over and kissed me on the cheek and said, "I'm gonna get going now."

I looked at the clock and said, "It's five twelve."

"I know. I have things to do."

He was an active guy, not one for breakfast in bed. So some nights, I might say something to him like, "When are you getting up tomorrow? Five twelve?" Now when I see the clock saying 5:12, I think of him with vexation. He can eat his heart out, if he has one. I'm on an adventure. The best revenge is a life well lived.

The most comforting thing anyone said to me about the breakup was what Micah said one morning. I told him what happened, only briefly, because he's not my therapist. He said, "When one door closes, another one opens."

"Yeah, but it's the wait in the hallway that's the bitch."

"Well, Mom, while you're waiting, Seth and I will take care of you. Because Seth has money and I have power tools."

On the day of that conversation, I had been babysitting my granddaughter Kennedy, and Micah made it a point to return from work an hour early. He took me and his whole family, five of us, for a ride up the snowmobile trail in the woods in the side-by-side. A side-by-side is a utility ve-hicle for off-roading. It was a wild but safe ride. Splashing through puddles and bouncing over bumps and swerving around curves. And I was laughing. I saw that I could still laugh, even in my bereft condition. What a gift. Already get-ting my revenge—a life well lived.

Today, when I get to what I think should be Copper Har-bor, I see just some houses and a restaurant. No sign for the ferry, and no sign *of* the ferry. So I take a right and drive along the road and see no clue, and then suddenly the road just ends. Stops. Just woods here. I turn around and drive back to the place where I think the ferry should be and keep going. I still don't see it, and I turn around again. Finally, I spot someone awake, a woman walking along the road. I ask directions. She points and says, "Oh, it's right down here."

I find the ferry down a tiny lane and behind some houses. A man is directing people where to park on a grassy field across the little road from the ferry.

The boat is not very big, maybe about as long as two city buses end to end, and it's behind a general store type of place and has no sign. No wonder I didn't see it. I'm here early, as usual for me, and I have some time to sit at the picnic table and people-watch.

Looks like all the other passengers are in couples and families except me and this one guy. I overhear him saying, "I've been driving since two this morning from the other ferry location at Grand Portage because there won't be any seats on that ferry for days." I want to try to talk with him, but now he has a knit hat pulled down low on his forehead, sunglasses on, earbuds in his ears, and his arms folded across his chest. I interpret that as a clear signal that he doesn't want to talk. *All right, then.*

Isle Royale National Park is an island in Lake Superior. Lodging and camping are available, and there's a little camp store. I take a long hike. The trail is muddy in places and not well marked. At some points, I have to guess which direction to take. I'm walking roughly parallel to the shore, over some hills covered in weed bushes, through piney woods. It's a clear, blue day. I love the beautiful views of the pines, the rocks, the water. Lake Superior. It reminds me of the Maine coast, like in Acadia National Park, except that this is not the ocean.

Back at the boat dock, I'm waiting for the return trip and enjoying my picnic. A small crowd gathers, and a ranger talk begins. She says, "The animals on the island evolved in a different direction than other animals on the mainland because of their isolation on the island. The boreal chorus frog is a species found only on this island. One species of frog has evolved to be huge compared to others of that kind on the mainland."

On the ferry, the bench seats face each other. A friendly, burly, bearded guy comes and sits across from me. He's a vacationing teacher. We have a conversation about books that we've read. As we chat, the boat enters a thick fog. He says, "I wish I'd brought a book for the ferry ride."

In my day pack, I have an ancient paperback copy of *Heart of Darkness*, from Goodwill. I say, "I'm not using this. You can have it." And I hand it to him.

"Thanks."

"You're welcome."

"Not much to see for the next three hours in this fog," he says, and he opens the book.

I open my John Grisham book, but soon I get sleepy and doze for a while. After all, I left "home" early, at 5:12 a.m.

When I return to the van, I see that the temperature is sixty-seven. As I take the scenic route back to Houghton, I watch the temperature climb to eighty-seven. I'm sad and lonely. I think, *I wish I had someone to talk to about being sad and lonely. But if I had someone to talk to about being sad and lonely, I might not be sad and lonely.*

This will be my third night at the same sleep spot. When it gets dark, I cruise around the neighborhood to blow the hot air out of the van and blow some air-conditioned air in. I'm good for the night.

July 15: Ask Mr. McCarthy

I wake up at three, thinking about my goal of getting to a meeting in all forty-eight contiguous states. I figure it will take five or six hours to get to Duluth. If I'm in time for a morning meeting, I can save myself a day of searching for a meeting in North Nowhere, Minnesota. I'm already in the Upper Peninsula of Michigan, heading for Voyageurs National Park on the northern border of Minnesota, way up by Canada.

So I get up and visit the twenty-four-hour laundromat for another sponge bath. Only one other person is in the laundromat at this hour, a man about my age with long white hair and an iPad. His rusty pickup truck is parked outside. Neither of us has any laundry going. He gives me a quizzical look and then returns his attention to his iPad.

The road is long and dark and deserted, with a lengthy detour that goes off in some other direction. I keep hoping, mile after mile, that the road will come out somewhere. By some miracle, I make it to Duluth.

I discover the meeting location, in a hilly neighborhood of the city, and have time to explore. One block is trendy shops, all closed at this hour. Other than that block, it seems to be a neighborhood of services and brick apartment buildings. Up ahead I hear a man and woman yelling and swearing, drawing a crowd, so I walk in a different direction.

The American Indian Center building requires us to put our names on a sign-in sheet before we enter the small meeting room. About fifteen people gather around a large table. Half of them seem to be Native American. Art is on the walls, and curtains are on the many large windows, making the room shady. The Serenity Prayer is the customary opening prayer in meetings that I have been to, but here there's no opening prayer.

One woman is having her sobriety anniversary, so snacks and goodies are on the table. She reads from the Big Book, speaks for a while, then opens the meeting for discussion. Some people say:

"I was a piece of shit that the world revolved around."

"If the moment of silence is the loudest part of the meeting, you're in the right place."

"I tried substituting 'our mother' for 'our father' and it felt more nurturing."

The Lord's Prayer, with customary hand-holding to close the meeting, is not done, either. The meeting closes with a moment of silence.

I have tried everything I can think of over the years in my attempt to find a Higher Power that I can believe in consistently. I have come to the conclusion that I just don't know if there's a God, and I have allowed myself, finally, to let it go at that. One of the things I like about this meeting is that they have a moment of silence instead of a prayer.

I remember when I was a little kid, I was watching my father fix a leaky faucet and said, "I don't think I can ever be a grown-up."

"Why do you say that?"

"What if I don't know how to do things like fix faucets?"

"You could go next door and ask Mr. McCarthy."

"What if he doesn't know, either?"

"Then he'd suggest somebody else you could ask."

That's when it dawned on me that if I keep on asking, eventually I will get what I need. There is a whole world of people available to help me, and it's my job to find them. This was my first glimpse of Higher Power in the form of people.

When I leave Duluth, I'm looking for the Ash River Visitor Center in Voyageurs National Park. Mile after mile, I pass through forest with rarely a sign of human life. I stop at a state forest information center. The nice ranger fishes out a map and gives me directions. She says, "Technically, that's not my job to be involved with the national park." I'm glad she did someone else's job, because otherwise how would I find it?

I'm just in time for the afternoon ranger walk. Chris is our ranger. He and his wife are volunteer rangers at Voyageurs for the summer. Chuck and Priscilla are on the tour with me. They're a retired couple from Denver. The conversation is all "We...we...we." "*We* did this." "*We* went there." But the 1.2-mile walk on the Sullivan Bay Trail hits the spot for me. Just enough pretty nature to take pictures, and just enough time to walk and chat.

Voyageurs is watery, with river places and lake places. Chris says, "Voyageurs is for boats." *That would be nice, a man with a boat to come back here with me. Preferably one who is a good dancer and is willing to do home repairs.*

Leaving Voyageurs, the trip through the state forest is long and tedious. Nothing much but forest in the forest. I worry that I'm going to fall asleep, until I see a Dollar General and stop for a dark chocolate bar to wake me up, and comfort and distract me. Those rectangular yellow Dollar General signs are like a beacon in a stormy (or boring) sea to me.

July 16: Charmed

It's a cool night in Bemidji, Minnesota, so cool that I almost drag out my sleeping bag, but the blanket is just enough. I'm refreshed, and I leave for Fargo, North Dakota, past fields, pines, and lakes.

In Island Park, in Fargo, I pause at the Angel of Hope statue. The statue is of a child angel with arms outspread, offering comfort to people who have lost a child. Engraved bricks pave the ground around the statue to memorialize those children. It brings tears to my eyes. I can't think what would be worse than losing a child.

The Silver Dollar clubhouse is in a pretty residential neighborhood of large, well-kept single-family houses and nice landscaping. It's a brick, three-story house with an open front porch and brick columns. On the grassy front lawn, a bunch of white plastic lawn chairs are off to the left, for smoking, I assume. A gathering of cheesy lawn chairs can be a signal that this is a sober clubhouse.

The clubhouse is called SDSOS because of a past custom of engraving actual silver dollars and giving them to people who were celebrating a year of sobriety. So it became the SDSOS clubhouse: Silver Dollar Symbol of Sobriety. Now they use those specially made plastic poker-sized chips for months and metal medallions for years, with numbers on them for anniversaries, just like I've seen at other meetings.

The meeting is in a large room in the front of the house on the second floor. The room is crowded. In AA meetings, they take up a collection, called the Seventh Tradition, for rent, literature, and coffee. Usually some kind of a basket is used for this. But the SDSOS club passes around a purple Crown Royal bag, saying, "It gave us so much, we need to give back." That makes me laugh.

After readings and announcements, all the people in the group count off by twos and separate into two discussion groups. In my discussion group I hear:

"There are only two basic emotions, love and fear. I spent too much time in fear. Waiting for the shoe to drop, the world to end."

"Humility is not about thinking less of yourself, it's about thinking of yourself less."

"If you're not feeling right, you need a checkup from the neck up."

That's what I get from meetings, and from Faith—a checkup from the neck up. Meetings have a way of helping me get things into perspective, getting them right-sized.

I'm slightly overdue for an oil change and a van checkup, so after the meeting I approach the cheesy lawn chairs and ask those friendly AA people, "I'm looking for a place to take my van to get it serviced. What place would you suggest?"

After some communal head-scratching, one comes up with, "I take mine to Jiffy Lube. They always do a good job. And it's right nearby."

"Thanks, I'll try that. This is a beautiful house, and a great neighborhood. How are the neighbors?"

"Oh, the neighbors just love us. This lady next door? We mow her lawn. And plus, we never have loud, drunken parties."

Off I go to Jiffy Lube, taking care of business, adulting. They take me right in and show my van some love.

This day in Fargo is charmed. I get a workout at Planet Fitness and a big, healthy, tasty late lunch at Chipotle. In a Goodwill store, I happen upon a comfy brown fleece jacket with a front zipper, and in yellow embroidery on the front left is the Fargo Bruins logo. Their high school team. A great souvenir, and a nice replacement for the zip-up sweatshirt that I lost, probably on the door hook of some restroom, somewhere in the southeastern United States. Charmed because my van and I are both happy and well taken care of.

The long ride to Dickinson, North Dakota, is even longer than I expect because of the time change. When I get to the supposedly twenty-four-hour Walmart, though, I see that it will be closing at midnight, so it's not the best place to hide out. I think, *I could try parking near the auto department so people might think that my van is just here waiting to be fixed.*

I've promised myself I won't stay in a place where I'm uneasy. I'm not comfortable at the auto department of Walmart, probably because the place will seem deserted after midnight, when the store closes. So I hit the road.

It's dark when I get to the rest area/visitor center at Painted Canyon in Theodore Roosevelt National Park. It's cool and windy. A few other cars are parked here, too. The visitor center is closed, but the restroom is available. So here I stay.

July 17: Sing Me to Sleep

In the morning, the rising sun exposes an astounding view behind the visitor center. A surprisingly spectacular panorama of badlands-type formations layered with gray, tan, red, and brown, and peppered with shrubs in shades of green. The sun is just coming up, and I watch as the scenery passes out of shadow into light. The sunlight gradually highlights the colors. So unexpected after the flat, drab, dark road I traveled after leaving the Walmart auto department. I stand transfixed. I take photos of all the different colors that brighten as the sun rises.

I continue on to the Medora Visitor Center, which is deserted at this early hour. But the loop road through the park is not closed off, so I boldly go where no one has gone before, at least not today.

It's stunning to see deer, bison, rabbits, horses. Prairie dog villages, where dozens of them are visible at a time. I am both lonely and amazed. The two times I am most lonely are when there's trouble and I want someone to commiserate with, and when there's something amazing and I want to share it. I get a photo of a deer with fuzzy antlers who comes out near the road to greet me. We're both up early. I don't see anyone else on the road—any humans, I mean.

Once when I was walking in the woods in Hollis, Maine, I came upon a group of deer. It was a sacred opportunity, so I kept as quiet as possible so that I could watch them. I loved them. This was my thought at that time: *I am filled with love. The deer don't love me, but still I am flooded with love. It doesn't matter which direction the love flows, to me, or from me. It's still love.* Now I pull over in astonishment as a herd of bison crosses in front of me. Breathtaking. My heart. I take videos on my phone. Even their snorting and thumping sounds get recorded. Babies seek out their mothers. Some roll in the dust. I know enough to stay in the van.

The scenery is dramatic, too, with plains, hills, badlands, cliffs, a river.

By now other humans are on the road. Whenever I see vehicles stopped, I pause to see what they're looking at. Wild horses are silhouetted on the crest of the hill off in the distance. I step out of the van to take a photo. One person says, "They are shy. They won't come any closer." I didn't know that Theodore Roosevelt National Park would be so wondrous. I'm glad I got here early, when there were far more animals than people to be seen.

After the loop road, I'm back at the Medora Visitor Center, then into the tiny town of Medora, North Dakota. This is a touristy town with a cowboy motif. Admission to the Cowboy Hall of Fame is seven dollars for seniors. I ask the woman at the ticket counter, "So, is it worth the seven dollars?"

She says, "Yeah, I guess." So I go in. I browse displays of guns, saddles, belt buckles. Exhibits of Native American culture, cowboys, rodeos, ranching. A video of western life. Yeah, I guess it's worth it.

Route 85 South is a long road with nothing much but grass and hay bales to see. I stop in at Belle Fourche, South Dakota, to see the geographical center of the country, the country including Alaska and Hawaii. State flags stand waving all around a compass-shaped granite monument, flat on the ground, with an outlined map of the United States and a thing sticking up from where Belle Fourche is on the map. Naturally they have a gift shop.

I'm bound for Rapid City on Route 90, looking to check off my South Dakota meeting. Micah and Kennedy call, so I pull over to chat, grinning. How it cheers me to get a call and have a warm conversation. I haven't told you about each of the calls I've gotten and enjoyed. But they are an important part of my travel. It's so grounding to be able to stay connected.

In Rapid City, during rush hour, I can't find the meeting. For some reason, my phone won't go online, so I can't check the address. Finally, I use my old cigarette-lighter GPS to locate the public library so I can use their computer to look up the meeting. I park outside the library and dash in. Mission accomplished. But when I return to the van, a parking ticket is on my windshield. In my haste, I forgot to feed the meter.

A notice on the ticket tells me that I can drop off the money at a "convenient drop box." A large young man with a bald head and a beard passes by, so I ask him, "How do I find the 'convenient drop box'?"

"I think there's a brown box around the corner."

I drive around the corner and double-park, but I don't know what a "convenient drop box" looks like, besides brown.

I duck into a little sandwich shop, buy a can of diet soda, and ask the young woman at the counter. She says, "There's a green box just a half block away." I thank her and track down the green "convenient drop box," which happens to be black, and put the envelope with the ten-dollar fine money into it.

And by some miracle, I make it to the meeting on time.

My phone starts working perfectly after I turn it off for a while, then back on. Note to self: Keep calm and reboot your phone.

The meeting is at the Alano Club, way down a long driveway and hidden behind some industrial-type buildings. So that's why I had trouble finding it. In the meeting room, long tables are placed end to end. About forty people are seated in two circles of folding chairs, one circle around the tables, and another circle behind them. Someone is chairing the meeting, but I can't tell who for a while because I'm sitting in the back row, behind him. He reads a section of the Big Book, and discussion follows. I hear:

"Fear should be illegal. It causes more trouble. I review all the facts I have collected to support my fear, and pretty soon I believe it."

"I hate when I share at meetings. Some honesty always comes out."

"I am familiar with calamity. I used to live there."

"My life used to have as many ups and downs as a roller coaster. Now it's more like lasagna noodles."

My recovery has made me much more emotionally stable for sure. During the meeting I'm thinking about all the things I have let go of: job, partner, youth. I have some glimpses of thoughts that I could let go of more things:

home, family, and friends, too. I've thought of these as re-quirements for my life. But are they really requirements? Could I move? Could I find new friends? A new home? A new career?

All afternoon the sky has been cloudy, ominous, with random thunder rumblings. In the evening, a serious thunderstorm to sing me to sleep.

July 18: These Lands Are Bad

At Wind Cave National Park, I stand in line for a ticket to the ranger-led cave tour. A man with a toddler-aged son stands in front of me in line. He says, "We got here yesterday and weren't allowed into the cave because the tickets were sold out. It's first come, first served. My wife and daughter are sleeping in at the hotel."

I score a ticket for an early morning cave tour. In the cave, the ranger says, "It's called Wind Cave because of the whistling sounds of the air coming out of the cave. These boxwork formations are characteristic of Wind Cave. See the thin blades of calcite coming down from the cave walls and ceilings that intersect to form rectangles that look like boxes?" I haven't seen that kind of formation anywhere else.

The road out of Wind Cave National Park is hilly and twisty, with grassy plains, and pine forests, and streams.

Photogenic. It's warm and sunny. A scenic pull-off area on top of a hill with a view of all this is a perfect spot for a cheerful picnic lunch.

As I drive, I watch the landscape get drier, less green, more brown and gray.

Badlands National Park is next on my agenda. At the visitor center, a video shows a Native American elder saying, "My family has lived here for generations, and we love the land." I'm thinking, *How could you love this harsh, godforsaken place? It's a sight to see and it's a nice place to visit, but...*

The Park Loop Road is long and hot. I stop a few times to admire the view and to take pictures of scenery. The sun is merciless. So bright, I can't even possibly see on my phone what it is that I just took a picture of.

The Badlands are heavily eroded formations of land, layered with color: purple, yellow, tan, gray, red, orange, white. There is nothing visible growing on them. My sister Sue says she thinks of the Badlands as a spiritual place. *Spiritual maybe because nothing in the physical realm could conceivably live here. These lands are bad.*

The road turns to corrugated dirt coming out of the park, and the land levels out. Dark clouds are visible across the brown, dry field on my right, in the north. I think, *Good. Rain is coming.*

On the radio, I hear, "Thunderstorm warning for southwestern South Dakota."

That's where I am.

"Heavy rain, seventy-mile-per-hour winds, quarter-sized hail, tornadoes. The storm system is moving east at thirty-five miles per hour. Get inside a strong building."

OK, maybe not so good. Quarter-sized hail could wreck my van, and I don't really want to sail off on a tornado to Oz.

I look for a strong building to get inside of. Nothing but fields and an occasional farmhouse.

I pull over and look on the map, and program my old GPS for a town south of where I am. I will be going perpendicular to the storm's direction. And I drive as fast as I safely can on those washboard dirt roads. I don't want to damage my van going over bumps, either.

I'm racing carefully down back roads that change directions at times. The road veers to the right and I am traveling straight into the storm.

Crap. Have faith in your GPS. It's happened before that you've gone north to get south.

At a stop sign, my GPS directs me to take a left. *That's optimistic.*

More bumpy miles to navigate. Another stop sign, and another left. *That's almost reassuring.*

Now I am moving south. More choppy road. What can I do except drive cautiously fast and trust the GPS and hope I can get the storm to stay in my rearview mirror. Finally, I reach a major straight paved road that is heading directly south. And now I know I will be OK.

Somehow, when I cross the state line into Nebraska, I feel safer.

July 19: All the Coffee You Could Drink

The morning meeting is at the New Hope Club, in an industrial neighborhood next to a storage place in Scottsbluff, Nebraska. One woman keeps going around with a coffeepot, refreshing people's coffee. But I have my kefir with me, and besides, I'm decaffeinated. I hear:

"My sobriety comes first. I can't share what I haven't got."

"Hey, I woke up and I am vertical and sucking air."

"I'm going to have to be a man and ask for help."

It is common to hear people say they are reluctant to ask for help. They think they are revealing their weakness, or inconveniencing people. I've had to learn to ask for help. Now I can tell people, "The ability to ask for help is a skill, so when you are asking for help, you are showing your strength. People feel good when they're able to help someone, so asking for help gives them a chance to feel good." Help is what AA is for. But you have to ask, somehow.

I use the bathroom after the meeting, and when I get out, all the lights are off and I'm locked in. I hear people's voices outside, so I pound on the door and call out to them, "Hey! Let me out!" *So embarrassing. Oh well, I'm getting an opportunity to practice asking for help.*

"Hold on." Eventually, one comes up with a key and manages to open the door.

I say, "Good thing you're all still hanging out. Otherwise I might have been locked in here until the next meeting."

"That would have been inconvenient," says one.

"You'd have to pass the time by reading the Big Book," says another.

"You'd get your entire Step 4 inventory written."

"But at least you'd have a bathroom."

"And all the coffee you could drink." They all laugh.

"Then she'd really need the bathroom." More laughter.

After they get done making fun of me, in a good-natured way, I ask, "What's there to do in Scottsbluff?"

"Go to Scott's Bluff."

"Awesome suggestion. Have a great day, everyone. Thanks for rescuing me."

Near a model of a covered wagon, a woman in pioneer costume lectures about the covered-wagon times on the Oregon Trail. A tour group of senior citizens is gathered, so even though I don't have a name tag, I fit right in. "Scott's Bluff over here"— she gestures—"is a national monument, eight hundred feet high, above the North Platte River. Mitchell Pass is a break in the badlands-type geography where the Oregon Trail passed through beside the bluff. The Oregon Trail was disruptive for the migrating wildlife and for the Lakota Indians."

I drive up the road to the summit of the bluff for some scenic photos. I can see the plains, the town in the distance, the hiking trail that goes up the side of the bluff. On the way down, I think, *My bluff-hiking days are behind me.*

I take a photo of my van with the exotic-looking badlands geography in the background and text it to Tommie, the van salesman who'd had that fantasy of me sipping wine in Utah. I tell him, "Thanks for helping me make my dream come true."

He texts back, saying, "That's exciting!"

Then I text him a picture of the inside of my van with the cot and the blue India-print bedspread, my furniture. He says, "Thanks! That made my day! I'm showing this to everyone here!"

"You're welcome."

I drift off into Wyoming. I stop at Subway for a big sandwich that will be my lunch and supper.

It's been forty years since I last saw my high school friend Jayne, who lives in Missoula, Montana. I Google her phone number and call her. Her husband, Tim, answers and says, "Yeah, we got your message on Facebook, and we were waiting for you to call."

Then I talk to Jayne, and she says, "Come stay with us."

"I'll be going to Yellowstone next, and I can come to your house after that. Would that work for you?"

"Yes. We're really looking forward to seeing you again."

I have warm, welcoming friends and a big sandwich. What could be more perfect?

Forty years ago, when I was twenty-six years old, I had a thirty-day Greyhound bus pass and toured the country. That was the last time I saw Jayne. It was the summer between my two years of college when I was working on my associate's degree in nursing.

Most nights I slept on the bus, woke up in a different city, put my backpack in a locker at the bus station, explored the city, then was back on the bus to sleep at night and wake up somewhere else. Those were the days.

Today it's a long slog across Wyoming. Grass, sky, road, grass, sky, road, grass, sky, road, yawn. Billboards show juicy steaks or dripping burgers with the words "EAT BEEF." So I get a craving. After a while, the land begins to get hilly and badland-y.

I arrive at Grand Teton National Park. As I cruise south into Jackson, Wyoming, the sun is setting over the Teton Mountains on my right, and on my left is a herd of bison. I pull over and take that in. I call my parents from here and say, "You won't believe this." I describe the scene. We visited the Tetons in 1966.

Jackson is a touristy little town with a few smallish hotels and lots of restaurants and shops. I make it to a meeting in a dedicated room in the basement of St. John's Episcopal Church. Most of the ten people here are visitors, too. They give me a visitor chip. And they end the meeting with the Serenity Prayer. I like that. During the meeting, I hear people say:

"I come to AA because I never want to drink with me again."

"Sobriety and AA were never on my bucket list."

"When you're in the process of recovery, it's a good idea not to drink."

After the meeting, I ask people for suggestions about where I can park for the night. The Jackson hotels are small enough that it might be noticed that I don't belong. Only one suggestion is made: "Maybe the hospital?"

I check it out and see few cars in the hospital parking lot, so my Maine plate might be noticeable. But I see cars parked on the road that leads up to the hospital. Those cars look like they're not going anywhere. Some are old beater-type cars, some have out-of-state plates. Some look like they haven't been moved in weeks—you know how they get that look. And two trailers are not even attached to any vehicle. So I decide to park on the road.

July 20: Compensation for My Pain and Suffering

I wake up with not even a parking ticket. With no street-lights, it was a dark night, except when cars went by and interrupted the darkness with their headlights. Especially around time for change of shift at the hospital. It was blanket chilly, so I slept well once the traffic died down.

On the way back through Jackson, I spot a house under construction with—oh joy!—a port-a-potty.

The Grand Tetons are stunning in a different way in full daylight. I see a grassy plain for quite a distance and the snowcapped mountains beyond. A shallow, rocky river, with occasional trees sprinkled around. Everywhere I look is another calendar picture.

The drive toward Yellowstone shows me more spectacular scenery. I park to take a photo of mountains reflected in a lake. When I try to return to the van, the scene calls me back to take one more, long look. And then another.

In Yellowstone National Park, it's hot driving, and I begin to smell something burning. I pull over to see if I can tell where the smell is coming from, and now I don't smell it at all. As I drive into the massive parking lot at Old Faithful, I smell it again. One of those what-should-I-do moments, those moments when I wish I had a companion so I could say, "What should I do?" I take a picture of where my van is parked so I'll have landmarks to help me find it later. The parking lot is seriously massive.

Old Faithful is due to erupt, so I walk in that direction first. Me and hordes of other tourists. It's like being at Disney during Christmas vacation, or maybe worse. They claim that Old Faithful will erupt anywhere between every forty-five minutes to every two hours, more or less, and that it's less faithful than it used to be in the past, less predictable. I claim a space on the boardwalk in the hot sun, and I don't have long to wait. I estimate the steam and water shoots up about 150 feet—that's three times the length of the mobile home I used to live in.

As the vast crowds slowly cruise back toward the massive parking lot, I make my way to the service station that I saw near the gift shop. I describe the burning smell situation to a friendly young mechanic. He says, "It's not the brakes, because if it was, you'd notice a difference when you step on the brakes. Your foot would go to the floor. If the oil's OK, then everything's OK. Do you want me to check your oil?"

"Thanks, but I can do that myself. You've been very helpful. Thank you."

I track down the van in the massive parking lot, check the oil, and it's OK. I'm relieved, and treat myself to an ice cream sandwich in the shade as compensation for my pain and suffering.

On to Mammoth Hot Springs, where I climb the stairs and a hilly boardwalk going up. I have to sit down a few times on the way. It's hot, and I'm dizzy and my heart is thudding. I'm glad to see occasional benches. I am strong and healthy, and on level ground I can walk until the cows come home. But I am vexed and embarrassed to say that I am somehow not good on hills. I get winded.

Mammoth Hot Springs is a steaming river that flows slowly over terraces of rock called travertine, all in shades of brown, red, green, and orange. Beautiful. I do get a chance to see all that, and I do not pass out.

Yellowstone is a busy place, crowded with traffic, and many of the pull-off places have not one parking spot available. I can't get a radio signal, so I reach blindly into the box of CDs on the passenger floor and come up with *Tchaikovksy's Greatest Hits*.

I'm enjoying the music as I pass glorious scenery, with no place to pull off. Mountains, rivers, pines. And construction. At one point, traffic is stopped. I turn off the motor and with the windows open, I spoon up my chocolate bar, listening to Tchaikovsky, perfectly content for the half-hour wait.

In 1966, when I was here with my family, Yellowstone was not so clogged with crowds. We had a place to camp right in the park, and our campground neighbor was Harry Tomaras. He had written a book of poetry about Yellowstone and had published it with what my father called the Vanity Press.

At night we stashed our food in the car so the bears wouldn't get it. Harry Tomaras didn't have a car, so he kept his food in our car. One morning, Harry told us, "I heard bears sniffing around your pup tent last night." I didn't mention that to my brother Mike and my sister Martha, who had been sleeping in that tent at the time. Too scary for little kids.

My father took four of us kids hiking up Mount Washburn, and my mom and Andy, the youngest, took the bus up and joined us on top. I remember being impressed with all the wildflowers on the mountainside.

Now, having finished my chocolate, I poke along through to the end of all the Yellowstone construction. I'm driving toward a meeting in Bozeman, Montana, celebrating because I haven't smelled that burning scent again.

The meeting is late, at nine o'clock, and the group is called the Itching Hour. In the fellowship hall of a church, a room is dedicated for various meetings. It's a small meeting with only one other woman. She says to me, "I like your turtle pendant. I love turtles."

I'm asked to read out loud a section of the Big Book known as "How It Works." It's a couple of pages long and contains the twelve steps. This reading uses *His* or *Him* to refer to God, and instead of saying the male pronouns, I just substitute the word *God*, which, to me, can be gender-neutral. Some quotes from the meeting:

"I didn't drink and drive. I couldn't even drink and walk."

"I found out that if you do good stuff, good stuff happens."

"I get bored with a video game once my character has reached the top level. But in AA, there's always another level to aspire to. It's exciting."

People often say that recovery is like peeling the layers of an onion. Another layer of healing will happen next. Sometimes I am impressed with how content and grounded I can consistently be, and still be learning. If you are human, you can always improve, and that's what recovery is.

After the meeting, a young man with long dark hair speaks to me in the parking lot. "I like the way you read 'How It Works.'"

"Thanks. I'm glad you said that. And I appreciate that you ended the meeting with the Serenity Prayer instead of the Lord's Prayer."

"Most meetings do that now."

I leave feeling hopeful.

July 21: Older

First stop of the day, the laundromat. It's Saturday morning and a good time to sit in the van and chat with some folks back home while the washer sloshes. As I transfer my wash into the dryer, a gray-haired man strikes up a conversation with me. He says, "It's so wonderful to be retired and to be able to do anything I want to do."

"Like laundry."

As he folds his clothes, he rhapsodizes about his magnificent escapades traveling on his motorcycle. His laundry is all folded, and he says, "Well, goodbye now," and leaves without inviting me to join him on his glorious adventures. That's OK. I have glorious adventures of my own.

Gates of the Mountains, north of Helena, is a place that was recommended to me by Kris, a nurse I used to work with. She grew up in Montana. But first a stop to feed my van and to eat half of a hefty Subway sandwich.

I come skidding into the parking lot at Gates of the Mountains just in time to get a ticket for the boat tour. The boat floats down the Missouri River heading north—yes, you read it correctly. The tour lasts two hours and is narrated by a vacationing middle-school science teacher, on an open-air boat with a tarp covering it in case of rain.

On both sides of the river are tall, steep, rocky, piney mountains, and cliffs. The science teacher says, "When Lewis and Clark were exploring this area, they kept thinking that the mountains would block them, but the mountains kept opening up to reveal more river. That's how the place got to be called Gates of the Mountains. These cliffs are up to twelve hundred feet high."

He tells us a tale of a group of firefighters who got trapped in one of those valleys and were killed by wildfire. Being a science teacher, he also has loads of information about the local flora and fauna.

Back at the parking lot I finish the second half of my now warm and soggy Subway sandwich. And I set my GPS for Missoula.

It's a two-and-a-half-hour ride through mountains, grassy, with random pines, or rocky—all kinds of mountains. Maybe that's why they call it Montana.

Jayne and Tim live in a single-family house with trees and greenery around it. Their garage is off the back alley, and the house has a front door that faces the street. I pass through the side gate, and Tim is in the backyard smoking a cigarette. He hugs me and says, "You look the same as we do. Older." His hair is now in a ponytail, with streaks of gray.

Jayne is inside with her daughter, Erin, and Erin's friend. Jayne hugs me, too. She also has a graying ponytail. She says, "They're having macaroni and cheese for supper. Would you like some?"

"No thanks. I've already eaten." It wouldn't have been considered polite to show up just in time for supper when I haven't seen them in forty years.

"I'm gluten-free, so I'm not eating that, either," Jayne says. "Let me give you a tour of the house." She describes all the improvements they've made. In one bathroom, they have an enviable refinished clawfoot bathtub. They're remodeling their other bathroom so that it will be handicap-friendly for when they're older.

"Let's go outside. I want to show you my vegetable garden." It's a large, robust garden, and various pots of plants and seedlings are here and there. I'm suitably impressed. We sit in the shade.

Jayne says, "I've been working as a legal secretary and receptionist. I finally finished my degree in elementary education, but I never was able to get hired as an elementary teacher. I worked as a substitute teacher in the music department. I wanted to be a substitute elementary teacher, but they only offered me substitute music."

Jayne and I were in band together in high school in Connecticut, way back in the day. She played French horn and I played bassoon, except when the band marched, and then she played glockenspiel and I played percussion. After school, we used to go to my house and eat toast with cinnamon sugar, or go to her house and listen to The Beatles.

In 1973, I graduated with a bachelor's degree in music education in Connecticut. At that time, Connecticut school systems were flooded with applications for every music teaching position, and I had no desire to move away. Tim had just gotten a music education degree, too, and he and Jayne left Connecticut because Tim found a job teaching music on a reservation in Montana. They've been living in Montana happily ever after.

I worked as a nurse's aide for a while, then went back to school for an associate's degree in nursing. So I had a career as an RN. It was a good career—no complaints about that. I say to Jayne, "Sometimes I am envious of people who have been music teachers, because I missed that boat." Tim and I are now both retired, so the point is "mute," as some Mainers say.

Tonight, sleeping in the van in their back alley is the easiest thing to do.

July 22: Introvert Time

It's Sunday, and Jayne says, "Tim and I are going to our church this morning, the Covenant Reformed Church. Would you like to come along with us?"

"Sure. I think that would be interesting."

"Visitors are asked not to take Communion unless they're church members of a similar denomination."

"OK, understood." I'm relieved.

I have often wished that I could be a part of a congregation, just to belong somewhere. Years ago I was church shopping and spoke with a Congregational minister. I asked him two questions. "How could Jesus have died for my sins when I wasn't even born yet?" and "If Jesus's dying in the past washes away my sins today, what's to prevent me from going ahead and sinning today, knowing that I am already forgiven?"

He had no answer. Next time I saw him, he said, "You know I brought your questions to my minister support group. There was a lot of discussion and finally they agreed, 'Tell her just not to worry about it.'"

In my church shopping days, I learned more about the Bible. I know that there is good wisdom in the Bible. The Bible also says women must not speak in public, and if they have questions, they should ask their husbands, who, by the way, they must submit to. It also gives instructions about how to sell your daughter into slavery. This is part of why I've always had trouble fitting in at church.

I *am* interested in how people worship, though, and I look for ideas that might ring true for me. And I like to sing. I can read music, and I usually sing the alto part on hymns. So I go along with them to church.

Jayne was raised Catholic, and I remember her being religious when we were in school. Back then, we had gone to the theater to see the movie *Jesus Christ Superstar*, and she cried. I didn't think much about that at the time, but now I realize how important her religion is to her.

After the service, lunch is in the fellowship hall. Tim made a pot of baked beans that are delicious because of all the sugar he used. Jayne doesn't eat them, but I do. People are friendly, and there's punch. At one in the afternoon, the "evening service" is held for people who want an evening service, too, but live too far away to be willing to make the trip twice in one day.

Back at their house, our conversation continues. Tim says, "Would you want to go rafting on the river tomorrow?"

"Let-me-think-yes!"

"Great. And also, we're going to a family gathering tonight. A picnic at some in-laws of our son. Do you want to join us?"

"Thanks for the invitation, but I think I could use some introvert time." *They might need a break from me.* "Introvert time can be rejuvenating for me."

July 23: Losing at a Game of Chance

"I fell off a picnic table bench when the fat guy on the other end got up," Jayne says. "That's why I'm going to the chiropractor this morning." So, we don't leave to go rafting until late morning.

It's a big blue inflatable raft, so big it has to be transported on a trailer. It's work for Tim, setting it up. Jane says, "We have to take two cars, one car to carry the raft upstream, and one car parked downstream to bring the people back up to get the car with the trailer to come downstream and get the raft."

"I see how it goes," I say. It seems like there's more preparation time than time on the river.

This is a section of the river with no white water. Jayne says, "I want to avoid white water, at least temporarily, because we had a bad experience. The raft flipped in a whirlpool, and we clung to it for a mile and a quarter in forty-six-degree water. When we finally could get out of the water, the paramedics came and we both went to the hospital."

"I don't blame you," I say.

"I'm OK with white water," Tim says, "but Jayne isn't ready yet."

Where we're putting in, four other rafts with a bunch of teenagers and their adult chaperones are just getting into the river. The kids call out, "There's Mr. A! Hi, Mr. A!" Tim is a bit of a local celebrity as a recently retired itinerant music teacher.

Tim sits in the high seat in the back and steers, while Jayne and I sit up front. The river is slow, with piney mountains on both sides. We see four eagles, a blue heron, a hawk.

We catch up to the four rafts of kids and attack them with water cannons that Tim brought. Because I'm a nurse, the water cannons remind me of huge syringes. They suck up river water, then shoot it out with a plunger. It's fun. For us. I hope it's fun for them, too. They're laughing, and they were already wet before we attacked them.

While Jayne and I are driving the car shuffle, I say, "You are lucky. You have a good marriage."

"Tim and I belong to a religion that doesn't believe in divorce, so if we have a hard time, we get plenty of support."

"The marriage thing is baffling to me. The problems were different each time. People say it's not a failure, but it still seems like it's my failure. Like I've failed at something I can't control."

"Like losing at a game of chance."

"Right. I've done well in other aspects of my life, though. And for that I am grateful."

Her kids have their various problems, and I am truly grateful that I, and my kids, don't have such problems.

After the car-shuffle raft pickup, we go home to drop off the raft and get reorganized. I put my river-dampened trail mix into a strainer in their kitchen sink to dry a bit. Then I treat them to a late lunch at an upscale pizza place that Tim suggests.

Back home, I retrieve my partially dried trail mix, deposit it back into its wrinkly plastic bread bag, and say, "Well, I guess it's time to say goodbye. Thanks so much for welcoming me. I'm glad I got to hang out with you two again." Hugs all around. I feel sad. *When will I ever see them again?*

The ride from Missoula to Kalispell, Montana, is just beautiful. Lakes, mountains, photogenic overlooks. I take some scenic photos, but they do not capture the expansiveness of the real panorama. The Walmart in Kalispell is already popular with visitors—a dozen or so big RVs and a young, long-haired hippie man with a dog, in an old car with New York plates, blasting rock music. I'm home.

July 24: The Brook, the Birds, and the Breeze

I park at the Glacier National Park Visitor Center, where the tour bus will meet us later. I spread my dampened trail mix out to dry on a towel on my cot. My sneakers are still damp, too, from rafting, so I leave them in the hot car and wear my alternate sneakers. I explore a pathway through the woods to a campground, and back. Buy some postcards, read my Alice Walker novel.

The red tour buses are called Jammers. They're like big, long station wagon/limos that seat seventeen passengers. Four bench seats have room for four passengers each—that's sixteen people. And one single passenger seat is in the front near the driver. My fervent hope is that I get that front seat so I can get the best view and not be squeezed between two big sweaty strangers for the whole tour.

The passengers are two families of four, one family of six, and an older couple. And me. Our tour guide decides where people will sit. And guess what? I get my seat. I, being the only one alone, get to be copilot. See, there are some advantages.

Our tour guide/driver is Doug, a middle-aged guy with a cool khaki hat. He has a headset with a microphone, and he speaks into that while he drives, giving us information about the park and making jokes. He has given the kids booklets with games and questions and coloring to work on. He asks them questions and gives them the answers so they can fill in the blanks in their booklets. The kids ask him questions, too.

"Why are they called Jammers?" Kids are good at asking why.

"They're refurbished vehicles from the 1930s," Doug says. "They're called Jammers because they originally had manual shifts, and the gears made a jamming sound as they drove up and down the steep parts of the roads. Now they're all automatic shifts, but they're still called Jammers."

"How many glaciers are in Glacier National Park?"

"There were a hundred and fifty glaciers in the park in 1850, and now there are twenty-five."

"Wow. What's the difference between a glacier and just snow?"

"A glacier forms when the snow lasts a long time and gets packed down and changes into ice. Glaciers can flow, like a very, very slow-moving river."

"Are there any bears here? What are you supposed to do if you see one?"

"Yes, there are grizzly bears. You should make noise when you're walking, because the bears will know you are there and stay away. And don't hang around near a dead animal, because grizzlies feed on them."

The scenery in Glacier National Park, on Going-to-the-Sun Road, is spectacular. Steep, white-capped mountains, a lake, steep drop-offs on one side of the road and sheer cliffs going up on the other side, tunnels through mountains. The Jammer has a sunroof, so we can even see what's above us, looking up at a waterfall. It's a bright, warm day. So glad I'm not driving.

Doug treats me kindly, checking in with me, conversing with me, offering to take photos of me with scenic backgrounds. I crave kindness, then I'm reluctant to receive it, like I'm being too needy or something. Or I'm a burden. Or I'm ashamed because I'm alone. Or all of the above. One of those things I don't understand about myself.

At lunch break, the others go into a restaurant. I wander off and hear the sound of a brook. Through the woods, I see a clear, rocky stream with a path alongside. I find a comfortable, sun-warmed rock to sit on, and eat my picnic lunch. The sounds of the brook, the birds, and the breeze are music to my heart.

When the tour ends back at the visitor center, Doug hosts a ceremony where the kids receive a certificate and a commemorative pin, and pledge to be environmentally conscious Junior Jammers.

After a day in Glacier National Park, I'm returning to my home at the Walmart in Kalispell. Huckleberries are in season, and they're being sold at various places along the road. I've never had the huckleberry experience, so I stop to get some at a farm stand. The old guy says, "They come in two sizes: the twenty-dollar size"—and he shows me a Ziplock bag of about two cupfuls—"or the ten-dollar size," about one cup.

"Can I have half of a ten-dollar size?"

He pours about a half cup into a bag for five dollars. *Like the prices of popcorn in movie theaters.* They taste like sour, tart blueberries. Not very pleasant. But now I've had the huckleberry experience. *I'll put that on my bucket list so I can cross it off.*

July 25: Awkward

Rough night at the Kalispell Walmart. A guy is pacing around near my van yelling into his cell phone for the longest time. Of course, because of the tinted windows, he doesn't know that I'm in here, lying on my cot, with the doors locked. Lying low, literally. Not an unsafe situation, but still distracting. Soon as I doze off, here comes the noisy street sweeper, cleaning up the parking lot.

Libby, Montana, is probably the Vehicles Up in the Air capital of the United States. I notice this kind of thing because of Micah's pink Cadillac in the air at their ice cream shop. So I stop to take photos to text to him. A large Airstream trailer up in the air to advertise an RV park. A red 1940s pickup truck with "Ace" painted large on the door, up in front of a hardware store. What looks to me like a Studebaker, up at a rakish angle, looking like it's about to crash to the ground in front of a restaurant.

The road to Sandpoint, Idaho, is scenic and sunny, with lakes and mountains. The Sandpoint City Beach is a large grassy area on a peninsula with sandy beaches on the lake. And a large free parking lot.

A boat cruise on Lake Pend Oreille is scheduled, and I hop onto that. The boat is about forty feet long, with indoor and outdoor seating. The tour is narrated at times with local history, but mostly, it consists of just cruising around the lake, with the mountain views. They serve drinks and food. I order a root beer float—not on my food plan, but it is exquisite. The captain invites the kids to come up and steer the boat for a while.

A young man is with two older women on the cruise. They're taking pictures, so I offer to take a photo of the three of them. "Are you all related?" I ask.

He says, "This is my mom and this is my grandmother."

"Nice to see families out together," I say. *I love it when I see men out with their mothers, so all the boys can see that it is OK for grown men to spend time with their mothers.*

Grandmother says to me, "Where are you from?"

"I'm from Maine. Just traveling around the country in my van."

"You're traveling alone? I'm so proud of you."

After the boat tour, I go swimming. Then I sit in my camp chair and write out postcards, and read my novel for a while in the shade.

I wait at the Lutheran church for the evening meeting, and only one person shows up. But he's here to practice on the piano. He lets me into the church, but no one is here for the meeting. I call the AA number again, and learn that there's also a meeting at the Gardenia Center. So, I race over and arrive a few minutes late.

The Gardenia Center is a smallish white building that may have been a church in the past. This is a women's meeting. A dozen or so sit in the circle. I sit in the vacant seat, next to a woman who is sharing. She's crying about how miserable she is, and how close to a relapse, sobbing into a soggy tissue.

When she gets done, I realize that they're going around the circle, giving each person in turn a chance to share. And that I'm next in line to speak. Awkward. Wow. But they're all expecting me to share. So I touch this woman on the shoulder for a moment. I say, "I'm Zinnia, recovering alcoholic. I'm visiting from Maine. I'm sorry to be late. I have had a lot of problems and difficulties in my recovery, too. I am so grateful that the AA program and my AA friends have helped me through. There is no problem that I've had that couldn't be made worse by drinking over it." I also speak about how reassuring meetings have been for me as I travel. I hear other women say:

"A problem shared is half a problem."

"Stick with the winners."

"First it was two guys, then a hundred, then a thousand. Now AA is one of the great wonders of the world."

And I agree. Imagine trying to create a worldwide network of assistance available 24/7 free of charge. But we don't have to invent that. It is already there for us. The meeting ends with the Serenity Prayer. Several women are tending to the woman who was crying. I feel compassion for her because that was me at times in the past. I'm relieved that she is being cared for. I see her getting hugs and even see her smile.

July 26: Pretty as a Postcard

I stop at a Subway in Davenport, Washington, to get the $4.99 special big sandwich that will be both lunch and supper. About a dozen old men, even older than me, are planted in their seats, yukking it up with their coffees. I say to the young man who makes my sandwich, "They seem like they're having fun."

He frowns. "There are four groups of them, and they come in every single day. And buy nothing but coffee."

It's a long, boring drive through a vacant, hot, dry, sandy, sunny area called the Desert of Washington—at least that's what the man at the rest stop calls it. He says, "They plant wheat only every other year because there's not enough moisture to plant it every year."

Sometimes I get sleepy driving. The best thing to do is pull over and walk around. But many, if not most, roads don't have a place to pull over. Often there is a scary drop-off on the edge of the road, or railings, ditches, or Jersey barriers. All manner of obstacles on the side continuing for miles and miles. Chewing gum wakes me up a little. And singing along with the radio, or my disco CD. "I will survive! Hey, hey!" Today the driving is very rural, usually with no phone signal, through "desert" and then mountains.

North Cascades National Park is pretty as a postcard. Tall mountains, rocky and steep on top, piney below. Some with white caps. Diablo Lake is a surprising bright jade green. The view looking down on the lake and over to the steep mountains beyond is stunning. At the visitor center, I ask, "How does the lake get its green?"

The ranger says, "The glaciers scrape off bits of rock to form a powder called glacial flour. That gets caught in the runoff and carried down to the lake, where it stays in the water and reflects the color."

The map shows hiking trails at North Cascades National Park, but it looks to me like the terrain is all vertical. As you know, I am not good with elevation gain, so my experience of this park is mostly driving and scenic pull-offs, which I thoroughly enjoy. A ton of photo ops.

At a Goodwill store, I buy a couple of novels and a big brick-red fluffy towel to cover the driver's seat in my van. Even with the air-conditioning on, I'm sweating all the time as the sun slams in through the windshield. But at least the hot dashboard is good for warming my can of chili.

July 27: The Liquor Store and the Cannabis Store

The women's room in the Planet Fitness in Puyallup, Washington, is the nicest one I've seen. Who designed the locker rooms in all those other Planet Fitnesses? Most of them have the showers separate from the dressing rooms, so you have to wrap up in your soggy towel and sneak across to the dressing room, where you have left your clothes unattended while you were showering. Some have no dressing rooms at all, just a shower. In Puyallup, the shower and dressing rooms are right together, so sneaking around in soggy towels is not required.

I'm glad I brought my old-fashioned cigarette-lighter GPS, because I'm without a phone signal most of the day while I'm driving to the south entrance of Mount Rainier National Park. I stop to take a picture of the Hobo Inn in Elbe, Washington. A line of railroad cars and cabooses, all painted different bright colors, are the rooms of the inn. Extreme cool factor.

The park is crowded, but I'm early, so I'm one of the lucky ones who scores a parking spot at the visitor center. All the campgrounds are full, just like in the other national parks. I watch the informational video, another of my favorite things to do. I like the information and the air-conditioning.

I drive around the park. Mount Rainier shows up in the most unexpected places. Around a curve and here's Mount Rainier dead ahead. Another curve and I lose sight of it. Another curve and here it is again.

I make stops where I discover high-mountain scenes, a waterfall, a walk in the woods. And I take time to breathe in the beautiful nature. It's a bright blue day. Mount Rainier rises up through the pines, above the lake, just like a calendar picture.

I'm trying to figure out how to get the best view of Mount Saint Helens. It looks on the map like the road will just dead-end in the middle of nowhere. I spot a ranger station and stop to ask their opinion. They suggest driving around to the west side. A long, twisty road, deserted. No phone signal. No houses. Few cars. The road leads up to a high, spectacular view of Mount Saint Helens, the gray mountain, with grasses and wildflowers below.

After some backtracking and driving through the mountains and the pines, I find the town of Rainier, Oregon, and search out the evening meeting.

A huge traffic jam is clogging up the Lewis and Clark Bridge between Washington and Oregon, but luckily, it's on the other side of the road from where I'm driving. The meeting is at the Rainier Assembly of God. No one here. I check the back parking lot. And here is the meeting. Right near the liquor store and the cannabis store.

The eight people in the meeting are celebrating a member's ninety days of sobriety, and they have a coffee cake, and ice cream melting on the counter. The celebrant chairs the meeting. On a sign-in sheet, you can list your name and sobriety date. After the chairperson qualifies, they go around the room so everyone can share. I hear:

"I needed a meeting. Everything was irritating me. I was upset because the straw fell out of my cup and onto the ground."

"I'm going to have to pick up a coffee cake white chip."

"I was a controlled drinker. I could have just one and walk away from the beer. But my mind was still with the beer. Everything else just pissed me off."

That is one way that I know I am an alcoholic. Whenever I had one drink, I wanted another. If I couldn't get another, I would be irritable and craving for the rest of the day. So I waited till evening for my first drink. I've never been able to understand people who can have just one and be perfectly content.

Ahead to Astoria, Oregon. I notice a large parking lot between the Safeway and a gas station, with couple of RVs already parked here. I think, *Let's give this spot a try. I can't think of any other option.*

July 28: I Am Immersed in Beauty

I sleep soundly until five, when my friend Lydia calls. I forgot to turn off the ringer on my phone, like I usually do at night. It's probably eight where she is, in Maine. I haven't had a serious talk with anyone in a while, and Lydia is someone who encourages me, so I go ahead and dive into the depths of my vulnerabilities. My failed relationship. (What could I have possibly done that was so wrong?) My self-questioning about how I run my AA program. (Why can't I have a faith in God like a normal recovering alcoholic?) My need to "get a life" when I get home. (How will I fill the emptiness with no job and no partner and no family at home?) All questions. No answers. Still, it's great to be heard, and understood. Even at five in the morning.

I miss my regularly scheduled breakfasts with Faith.

Driving through Astoria, one hill in town is so steep that my wheels are spinning on the mist-moistened road.

At the Columbia River Maritime Museum, I see all kinds of displays about the treacherous Columbia River and the Pacific Ocean.

Out in back of the museum, I step on board for a tour of the retired Lightship *Columbia*. The man on the ship tells me, "The land in this area is so flat that this floating lighthouse came in useful."

Remember That Guy, the one who broke up with me in an e-mail with no discussion? (I remember him.) Well, he was a sailor and a lobsterman. So all this maritime stuff is reminding me of him and making me sad. I don't enjoy the museum as much as I want to.

Then south along the coast on scenic Route 101. So many stops for so many photos. I text a picture of this wonderful scenery to my friend Niki, who grew up in Oregon, saying, "Look at this view from Route 101 in Oregon!"

She replies, "I recognize the spot. It's so beautiful. You're lucky. Have fun and be safe!"

There's a traffic jam in Garibaldi for a farmers' market. I stop for some unimpressive Chinese food in Tillamook. I see an old car with the back part transformed into a camper, raised up in the air advertising the Tillamook RV Park. I text a photo of that to Micah.

I cut in toward Salem and down toward Eugene on Route 5. I call the folks back home. "Hi. Just calling to say hi because I had no cell signal yesterday and probably won't have a signal tomorrow, either. I'll be on my way to Crater Lake National Park. I don't want you to worry about me if you can't get in touch with me."

Driving south on Route 5, I reach down into the box on the floor for a random CD, blindly chosen, and slide it in. As I drive over the top of a rise, I see a panorama of piney, rolling hills and hear the opening string chorale of the *1812 Overture*, and I am immersed in beauty.

July 29: All the Other Kids Are Allowed to Do It

At the Walmart in Roseburg, Oregon, I'm dreaming of Indian drums at a powwow. When I wake up, I realize it's the sound of teenagers listening to loud music, with a lot of bass. They're vaping. One circles my van on a skateboard. I want to tell them to quiet down, but I'm the one who is trespassing. So I put in my earplugs and drift back to sleep. Stealth camping is satisfying to me because I always feel like I'm getting away with something.

On the way to Crater Lake National Park, I smell smoke. Signs posted along the road say, "Fire Activity." There's no one to ask. Nothing but trees on either side of the road, mile after mile. I clutch the steering wheel and keep my eyes wide open. When I get to the national park entrance sign, I see two young guys taking selfies. This is a common sight at national park signs. This photo will prove that they've actually been here in person. I stop to ask their opinion. "Is it safe around here? I can smell smoke. But I can't tell where the fire is."

One says, "It's only smoke. The rangers would tell us if it was dangerous." They're headed out of the park as I'm headed in. And they didn't see any fire in the park, so I continue.

In Crater Lake National Park, the air is smoky. The visibility is limited, like a heavy fog made of smoke. I've booked a trolley tour so I won't have to drive on those scary roads and will get to hear an entertaining, informational talk as well. I've heard people rhapsodizing about the blue color of the lake. I can see enough to tell that the view would be spectacular, but with all the smoke, what I see is a grayish, smoky, indistinct scene. The trolley is on a road at a high elevation, looking down steep rocky and piney mountains to the lake below.

Our driver/tour guide tells us, "Crater Lake is 1,943 feet deep, the deepest lake in the United States and the ninth-deepest lake in the world. It is not a crater, but a caldera, caused by the collapse of a volcano. Don't you think the park should be called Caldera Lake National Park instead? The lake is so blue because there is nothing much except water in it. The lake was stocked for a while with six types of fish starting in 1888, and now there are only two types of fish left: trout and salmon. Fishing is encouraged because fish are not native to the lake. See that island sticking up in the lake? It's called Wizard Island because it's cone-shaped like a wizard's hat."

The tour is two hours around the thirty-three-mile rim. I'm glad I'm not driving. I'm starting to dread all those precarious mountain roads. We make stops along the way for viewing and selfies. I take pictures and try to breathe in the expansiveness, but the smoky air makes me cough.

I get a text from Christina, my foster daughter, saying that her days off from work will be Tuesday and Wednesday. So now I'm on a mission to get to Fresno. I'm bound for California.

Several major fires are going on in California. One of the side roads is closed off because of fire, but the other cars keep going on the main road, so I keep going, following the crowd. I'm reminded of times when I was a kid complaining to my mother and saying, "All the other kids are allowed to do it!"

I can hear her say, "If they were allowed to jump off a cliff, would you want to do that, too?"

I slip into the Redwood National Park information center just before they close at five. I pick up a map for my collection. Redwood National Park is here and there. Park areas and areas of towns and private property all mixed in. I choose the Newton B. Drury Scenic Parkway.

On a walking trail, I'm in the forest with the massive, silent redwoods. It makes me want to pray. With all that massive silence, maybe I can be heard. This is one of the times I say to God, "OK, if you're here, now would be a good time for you to introduce yourself." And I wait. And wait.

Back on the road, I see two elk munching on greenery at the side of the road. I stop to watch, and then so do people in several other vehicles.

The ranger station is closed, but a whiteboard gives information about weather and wildfires. Weather: smoky, 99°. A website is listed where you can see maps of the wildfire locations: fire.ca.gov. I look on this website and learn that there are seventeen fires in California. So good to have this information. Better than relying on guessing, following the crowd, or asking random bystanders taking selfies.

I'm having trouble finding a sleep spot. I get no phone signal. The area is rural without Planet Fitnesses or Walmarts.

I stop at a rest area on Route 101. There's no drinking water. A van is in the parking lot with a big sign on it that says, "Praying for food and gas." Two other vehicles have people in them and are packed to the gills with belongings. Homeless? The parking lot is tiny. Just a little too sketchy for me, so I hit the road again.

At a town called Arcata, I get a burger for supper at Carl's Jr. I'm practicing for when I go to visit Christina at the Carl's Jr. in Fresno where she works. I have to get a token to use the bathroom. But after I do that, I'm all set for the night. Across the street is a Red Roof Inn. Hotels are not my favorite places to stay, mostly because I don't feel entitled to use their restroom, but that's where I park. Hiding in plain sight again.

July 30: I Shudder

It works out just fine at the hotel. I wake up once when laughing people slam a car door, and then I sleep again.

Lassen Volcanic National Park is on my agenda. I consult the fire website and see that a fire called the Carr Fire is northwest of Redding. I also find that Route 299, the principal road, is closed near Redding. Looking at the map, I choose a detour that I think will be safe: Route 36 East.

That is an unexpectedly hair-raising ride. Steep, twisty, narrow, and long. It's smoky, and there's construction, sometimes only one skinny, messy, bumpy lane with no flagger to direct traffic. It seems like the workers are trying to move mountains. At times cliffs go straight up on one side and straight down on the other. Just after I pass the mountain-moving construction, eighteen-wheelers come barreling toward me. I have no idea how they will get through all that messy, one-lane construction. Luckily, at the place where they pass me, the road is two-lane. I think, *I bet they detest this detour, too. What would I have done if I had encountered one of these big rigs in the midst of all that mess?* I shudder.

No tours are offered at Lassen Volcanic National Park. I watch the informational video at the Kohm Yah-mah-nee Visitor Center and then eat my sandwich on the patio with a smoky view of the pines and the mountains.

According to the park map, I can take the scenic drive. My first stop is the Sulphur Works. I get close-up views of boiling mud pools and savor the smell of sulphur bubbling in the heat.

I start off to enjoy the rest of the scenic drive, but soon realize *I just don't want to do this.* I'm worn out from steep, treacherous driving. I'm getting treacherous-driving PTSD. *It's not going to be fun for me driving in all these mountains.* I pull into a scenic overlook, overlook the scenery, try to breathe in the expansiveness without coughing, say goodbye, and turn around. I don't get to see much of this park. Too bad. I'm done.

I'm off to Fresno. When I get a phone signal, I make sure to call my parents. "I wanted to let you know that I found out about a fire information website. I can use my phone to see where the wildfires are, so I can avoid them."

My dad says, "Yes, we've been thinking about that. Good to know."

"I'm so glad I have my cell phone. I don't know how you guys managed without one in 1966 when we were out west."

"Well, for one thing, in 1966, the west was not all on fire."

California seems inhospitable. Hot and dry and smoky. Fast-food places lock their restrooms, and the rest areas don't have potable water. I make it to the Planet Fitness in Fresno after dark, and I will see Christina in the morning.

July 31: Babies

I'm waiting for Christina to text me, which she said she will do this morning. I get my breakfast kefir and go to Jiffy Lube.

I had a good experience with Jiffy Lube in Fargo, North Dakota, so I figure that might be a reliable place to get my van serviced so I can be a responsible adult van owner. For some reason, it takes an hour and a half. Three employees are trying to get their air compressor to work, and finally they succeed. Now they can fix my tire pressure. Note to self: 36 psi.

Christina and her husband, Romero, and baby Maia live in a two-bedroom apartment in a housing complex, between an area of single-family houses and a strip mall. I feel awkward at first because it's been a long time since I saw them in November last year when Maia was born. My problem is that, in some situations, I am not sure whether I am welcome, so I look for evidence of it. That's just how I am.

Maia doesn't know me, so I hold back from her, even though I wish I could grab her and hug her. Babies.

Maia goes into the high chair and busies herself with some Cheerios. I stretch out my finger tentatively toward her, but when I touch her hand, she cries for mama, so I back away again. Pretty soon, though, she begins to reach out to touch my finger, too, and we are "shaking hands."

I brought Maia a huge bag of laundered baby clothes from Goodwill. Some clothes she can grow into, and some I hope she can use right away. They were a dollar per item, so I got loads of them. And messy babies need multiple costume changes, so the extravagance is justified. Christina says she doesn't mind clothes from Goodwill. I hope that's true. When she was staying with me, we used to go Goodwill shopping. Most of my own wardrobe is from Goodwill, or yard sales. I miss having Christina around.

She was sixteen years old when she came to me, a junior in high school. I remember when I first met her at the Department of Human Services in Maine. She looked beautiful, with long, brown braids and eye makeup, and she was wearing a pink-and-yellow fairy skirt over jeans.

The social worker asked us each to say something about ourselves. I told Christina, "My kids are grown up and have homes of their own, and I miss having the energy of a teen-ager in the house. That's why I want to be a foster mom. I live within walking distance of the high school and the beach." I saw her smile.

When it was Christina's turn, she said, simply, "I get good grades. I don't do drugs. I don't do bad things." She saw me smile. Turned out those were accurate statements.

In those days, Christina would sometimes come out of her room, open the refrigerator door, and say, "I'm bored."

I would say, "Why don't you go online and see if there's a movie playing that we could tolerate." And we would go to a movie with snacks and cans of soda in her big purse. It seemed so normal and companionable.

Whenever something went wrong with my computer at home, I would say, "Christina, why is my computer doing this funny thing?" She would immediately come out of her room and fix my computer. What's not to love about that? I learned so much from her. Want in-house tech support? Get a teenage foster kid.

Today is Romero's day off, too. He talks about some stuff at work that he's miffed about. "There is an advantage to hiring a bilingual person. I should be paid extra for that." He's the evening manager at an auto parts store. He's from Mexicali, in Mexico, and has a green card that has to be renewed every ten years. He says, "It costs a thousand dollars to become a citizen, but I don't want to anyway. Let him build a wall. It's his country, not mine."

I ask, "Are you planning to speak Spanish with Maia?"

"Yes. And I am getting books so I can teach her to *read* Spanish, too."

"Lucky Maia."

Some dithering and waffling is going on about lunch. They have meatballs in the freezer, so I volunteer, "I'll walk down to the grocery store to get rolls and tomato sauce so we can have meatball subs."

After lunch, I think this would be a good time for me to excuse myself and go do a load of laundry. I don't want to wear out my welcome. Christina and Romero don't see much of each other because they work opposite shifts: she during the day at Carl's Jr., and he evenings at the auto parts place, so that Maia won't have to have a babysitter. I'm off to the laundromat.

In my van, I see that the temperature on the dashboard is 109 degrees. I take a picture of that and post it on my Facebook group page. That's the hottest temperature I have ever experienced. And it's humid, too. Christina hates it.

They're planning to move to Yakima, Washington, soon. He has family there—his mother and a brother. I certainly do not blame them for wanting to move. Like I said before, California is inhospitable—and add to that the crime in Fresno.

While my laundry sloshes around, I am struck with a brilliant idea. I text Christina and offer to babysit Maia while she and Romero take an evening out to themselves. After all, Maia and I have shaken hands and we are friends now. Christina agrees to that.

I'm glad to have a way to be useful and not awkward. My evening with Maia is lovely. Babies.

I stay at Planet Fitness because there's no place for me in Christina's small apartment. Besides, sometimes less is more when it comes to company. You know the saying about guests and fish: After three days, they both smell bad.

August 1: I Wished There Was Some Way I Could Un-Applaud

This time, I'm not planning to go to any meetings in Fresno because I went to a bunch of them last year when I came to visit newborn Maia. California meetings are already checked off my list. One interesting thing about all the meetings at the Fresno sober club I went to is that people were invited to sign a paper before the meeting indicating that they wanted to speak. The chairperson would then call on people from that list, or call on people not on that list. Raising of hands to speak in the meeting was not allowed in any of the meetings at that club. That was the rule decided upon by their group conscience. If I was a club member, I would lobby against this rule. Sometimes people need to talk.

At one meeting there, a woman spoke up and said, "I quit smoking for three days!" She got a rousing round of applause from the group. Then she held up her vaping device and said, "And I couldn't have done it without this."

Silence in the room. I wished there was some way I could un-applaud.

Today, when I get to Christina's as planned, she says, "We were waiting for you. We have to have new tires put on the car. It's probably going to take a couple hours. Do you want to come with us?"

"Go ahead. I'll stay here with Maia if you want." So they do. More time for me with baby. More time for them without baby.

When they get back, Christina and I take Maia to visit the Forestiere Underground Gardens. Last year, we wanted to visit there on my last day in Fresno, but it was closed on Wednesdays, so we were disappointed to miss it. Now is our chance. Especially in this heat, being underground sounds appealing.

We load the stroller into the trunk and buckle Maia into the car seat in Christina's car. Christina and I aren't the type to sit and chat for hours. That's why I like to *do* things with her.

A guided walking tour takes us through underground bedrooms, dining room, kitchen, bathroom, a living room with a fireplace. Hallways with stone archways between rooms. Courtyards where plants and trees grow up through sunlit holes in the "ceiling," which is at ground level. The tour guide says, "Baldassare Forestiere came from Sicily and had experience working on building the subway system in New York City. In 1906, he started building underground in Fresno. His idea was to escape the heat."

And yes, it's cooler than outside. It must be only maybe ninety-five under the ground. But it's still a relief.

Back at home, Romero is playing a video game and exclaiming in Spanish. He had threatened to make BLTs when we returned, and he does.

Being useful, boat tours, and nature walks—these are a few of my favorite things. I suggest, "It's the last day of your 'weekend.' Why don't I babysit Maia for another evening?"

"Yes, thank you."

"You're welcome." I am touched that Christina trusts me with her baby. More time for me to be useful, and to bond with Maia.

August 2: Godforsaken Hellhole

Before leaving Fresno in the morning, I stop in at Carl's Jr. to say goodbye to Christina. That's a mistake. She's busy. I order a cup of decaf, and only hot water comes out of the coffee tank. I go back to inform Christina, and that's how she learns that they're using instant decaf now. We're both uneasy because she's at work. I had a big plan to give her a check to help with their move to Yakima. But the situation feels too awkward, so we just say our awkward goodbyes.

You know all those photos I take? I have a hobby of printing them and making them into old-fashioned note cards. I've brought a bunch of those with me to send to people for their birthdays and whatnot. I choose one and address it to

Christina, and include the check. The message says, "Great seeing you. You have a busy life and a beautiful family. I am glad you are doing so well. This gift is to help with the move." I draw a heart and write my name. I seal it, hold it to my heart, and drop it into the mailbox.

A stop at Walmart to get a battery for my watch. Yeah, I know I can see the time on my phone, but a watch is easier sometimes, and then there's less wear and tear on the phone. I find a tiny white stretchable watch for three dollars, and buy that because it's cheaper and easier than getting a battery. Our throwaway society. But I don't throw the other watch away, just save it to replace the battery later.

Some kids are selling chocolate bars for a dollar at the Walmart entrance for some kind of fundraiser. I ask them, "Are they melted?"

"Not yet. That's why we're leaving here soon."

"Do you have dark chocolate?"

"Yes."

I buy two, knowing full well that they will have to be eaten with a spoon.

Onward to Pinnacles National Park. It doesn't seem like much to me. I search out a spot in the tiny crowded parking lot near the trail entrance. I want to take a hike to see if I can find out why this place has been declared a national park.

The path winds through dry land with weed bushes and scruffy trees. Some rocks have fallen, making a cave-like trail with stairs and tight squeezes. I'm dizzy and shaky and faint. I'm afraid my heart will explode. I'm OK if I slow down and rest often. I don't do well with uphills. *You* know that. It's time for me to admit it to myself. I see few people in this godforsaken hellhole. I trudge all the way up to a small brown pond surrounded by tall, dry, hot rocks. That's where I turn back. I spent fifty minutes slogging uphill going out and it takes only thirty-five minutes plodding back, according to my new watch. The ranger I meet along the way says it's 110 degrees.

The last time I talked with my beloved son Seth, he asked me to tell him when I know where I'll be for the night so that he can arrange a hotel room for me. A generous and welcome offer. After Pinnacles, a hotel sounds inviting, but all afternoon I get no phone signal.

In King City, the temperature is only eighty-five and it's breezy. What a difference an hour's drive can make. There are hotels in King City. I text Seth and leave a phone message, too. It's evening in Puerto Rico, where he is.

I enjoy an early supper at KFC while waiting for him to call back. The KFC Famous Bowl is a satisfying comfort-food treat involving mashed potatoes, popcorn chicken, corn, cheese, gravy. What's not to like? Not for every day, though, certainly. After a while, I come to the conclusion that this is one of those times when Seth will be getting back to me tomorrow.

Time for Plan B, moving on to Paso Robles. It's 101 degrees when I arrive here, too hot and too early to park, so I look up the movie theater and locate it in the center of town.

This is a hopping town center, not one of those ghost town historic districts that I've seen so many of. A large green in the center has businesses and foo-foo shops arranged in a rectangle around it. A band is setting up, and throngs of people are on the green in lawn chairs, with folding tables and wine in stem glasses. *Why do our concerts in the park at home get only maybe a couple dozen people in the audience? Do we not have enough wine there?*

Only four other people, besides me, are in the movie theater. Two couples. The AC is cool and the movie is *Mamma Mia! Here We Go Again*. I am entertained because I appreciate musicals. Near the end, there's a love song between mother and daughter, "My Love, My Life," that makes me cry. Then every character in the movie gets all paired up, the rest of the audience leaves in pairs, and I go off alone to sleep at Planet Fitness.

August 3: A Kick in the Ass Is a Push Forward

A tree is between my van and the security streetlight, and every time the wind blows, the branches shift and the light flashes on me in the dark, so I sleep lightly. But I'm too lazy to get up and move the van. Note to self.

Route 101 and Route 1 take me south past rolling dry hills with dead grass, random scraggly trees, and large farm fields. In the town of Guadalupe, I stop for gas and a grapefruit and a peach. At a rest area, I have to stride around fast while I eat the grapefruit, because it has attracted a flock of bees.

When I try to get to the Channel Islands National Park Visitor Center in Santa Barbara, I'm thwarted at every turn by detours, blocked roads, and blocked exits. It's the Old Spanish Days-Fiesta. While I'm parked in traffic, I watch a long parade with men in Mexican hats on horses, women dressed in traditional Spanish costumes with colorful, full skirts, and horse-drawn carts decorated with flowers.

I figure out how to get onto 101 North to get to 101 South so I can get out of Santa Barbara and go to the other Channel Islands Visitor Center in Ventura. I check out the film here, and gain another map for my collection.

The beach is just across the road, so I slosh along, cooling my feet in the ocean.

I locate the marina and the boat to Anacapa Island. I'll be back tomorrow morning. A couple of dozen shiftless seals are lounging on the dock.

The meeting is at the Alano Social Club in Oxnard. This is a storefront in a shopping center with Hispanic shops. The walls display artwork on wall tiles. For a ten-dollar donation, anyone can decorate a wall tile and have it mounted on the wall. The speaker is a visitor from Hawaii. This is some of what I hear him say:

"Anger blows out the light of reason."

"I drank for thirty-two years. For thirty-two years, I was stuck on stupid."

"My sponsor said, 'Bring the body. The mind will follow.'"

"I had a God-shaped hole."

"My sponsor told me I needed to do more than quit drinking. I needed to learn how to live. Thanks to a kick from that big size twelve."

That reminds me of something a wise man once said: "A kick in the ass is a push forward." That wise man was my ex-husband Bruce.

I met Bruce when I was a senior in college in 1973, about to graduate and terrified of being an adult on my own. I was just beginning to experience the joys of the early stages of my drinking. We had fun, partying and hanging out with his friends. And I was shy as a doe. Naturally I believed that life with him was preferable to life alone. He was a joker, always available, a walking party. Later, I saw the other side of that coin: He was a chronically unemployed late-stage alcoholic. I got tired of paying all our bills, and I left him.

Another typical Bruce quote was, "What happens if I quit drinking and I'm still an asshole?" Sometimes I wish I had known then what I know now about recovery. But I couldn't have known. I was so young, an unenlightened amateur drinker. Bruce died from alcohol.

I have a ticket for the early boat to Channel Islands National Park. I set the alarm on my phone so I won't have to keep checking the time, but I know I'll be awake before it sounds.

August 4: Horizon-in-Sight Insight

In the morning in a grocery store called Smart and Final, I pick up a kefir. The song "Love Machine" by the Miracles is playing loud on the PA system. It's one of my favorites from back in the disco days. I dance up to the cashier. The dark-haired woman at the cash register says, "Didn't you just love the seventies?"

"Oh, yeah."

And now we are singing along. "Ah, ah, I'm just a love machine. And I won't work for nobody but you." I used to embarrass my children when I started bopping around to the music in grocery stores.

Before the boat leaves, I stroll around the marina taking interesting photos of sailboats with their masts reflected in the water, palm trees, flowering plants, and the seals goofing off on the dock.

The Island Packers boat, called *Vanguard*, is maybe sixty feet long with an upper and a lower deck. Kayaks and other equipment, and then passengers, are loaded on. It's pretty full. A woman my age is a crew member. I say, "You must love your job."

"I certainly do," she says. I'm envious.

Anacapa's East Island is only one of the islands in Channel Islands National Park. It's a trip of about one hour. I start to get a little seasick. I remember someone once told me that focusing on the horizon would keep me oriented and help me maintain my equilibrium. I try this, and it works. It occurs to me that this might be a good way to handle emo-tional waves, too. I tell myself, *Don't worry about whether you're happy or unhappy. Just keep the horizon in sight so you can ride the waves instead of letting them bash you around and make you sick. Hey, this is my horizon-in-sight insight.* What is my emotional horizon? My recovery, my gratitude list, my people, my values, my goals.

Back in my bicycle days, I used to ride on a dirt road shortcut going home from work. It was bumpy, so I would lift up from the bike seat and let my knees take all the shocks, and I could keep a level head. *I bet I could be like that emotionally, too.*

Approaching the island, we see interesting rock forma-tions, a natural stone bridge. The boat backs up to a dock, and the *Vanguard* staff helps us step off. A crew member tells us, "There's a volunteer ranger on the island, but we haven't been able to contact him." We climb the stairs up the cliffside.

The ranger is idling around at the visitor center dressed in his pajamas with messy hair, pillow wrinkles on his face, and a coffee cup in his hand. He says, "Yeah, the radio was turned off while I was sleeping. I'll give you all a tour of the island in a half hour or so, when I get dressed." I linger for a long moment, but he's not making any moves in that direc-tion, so I take off on my own.

This rocky island is covered with gulls, bird poo, feath-ers, bird carcasses, and bones. The small, rustic visitor cen-ter has solar panels that are decorated with bird droppings.

The views are impressive, cliffs going down to the sea. Very little vegetation, and no trees or bushes. I knew there would be no shade, so I'm wearing my wide-brimmed straw hat. It's overcast, which makes it less miserable.

In an hour and a half, I've explored the whole island, including photo ops, eating my sandwich, and breathing in the expansiveness. I have a choice of taking the noon or the five o'clock boat back. I can't imagine what I might do out here for another five hours, so I choose noon.

Back at the dock, while awaiting the noon boat, I watch people having fun snorkeling, scuba diving, and playing in their kayaks. On the ride back, we see dolphins.

It takes ages to get to San Bernardino, California. The highway has five or six lanes going in each direction, packed with cars, slowing down and sometimes just parked, waiting. Some motorcyclists invent their own fast lanes here and there, randomly cutting in and scaring the bejesus out of me.

In San Bernardino, I get supper at a Chipotle with a pleasant tree-shaded courtyard, where I stay until it gets too dark to read my Alexander McCall Smith book. I'm again appreciating the fact that I am the kind of person who can linger in a Chipotle courtyard. No one notices me. It's my superpower, being invisible.

August 5: My Angel

On the way to Joshua Tree National Park, I stop to take a picture of a smoky field of wind turbines. The wind is roaring by nonstop, like to blow me over, so I can see why they chose this place to generate wind power. I love it when I see windmills and solar panels.

I arrive at the Joshua Tree Visitor Center just as it opens. The map shows me how to drive along the Park Boulevard loop road. It's hot and harsh, needless to say. The Joshua trees are short, gnarly, spiky-leafed yuccas. I get photos of them and the interesting rock formations behind them, including a rock formation shaped like a skull. I know that you can camp and hike here, but I don't think I can stand to do anything like that. I'm not a desert person, I guess. After the loop road, I've had enough.

I'm apprehensive about going to Death Valley National Park. I figure they call it *Death* Valley for a reason. I have my milk crate with four gallons of water, and I'm on a mission to visit national parks, so I press on.

In Death Valley, I can tell there are mountains off in the distance, but they are shrouded in smoke. The land is parched and cracked. The outdoor temperature is 110 on my dashboard. A sign tells me to turn off my air-conditioning so my car won't overheat. *For real? But I sure do not want car trouble.*

I turn off the AC and roll the windows down. I watch the temperature on the dashboard: 112, 113, 114. I come to a place where the road climbs a steep hill. The heat indicator shows the engine is heating up, too. The dashboard temperature rises: 115, 116, 117. Now the engine heat indicator is in the red zone.

At the Furnace Creek Visitor Center, I stop to let the van rest. A sign announces the current temperature: 121°. That is truly the hottest temperature I have ever experienced.

Yes, it is hot. Signs shaped like red stop signs read:

STOP
Extreme Heat Danger
Walking after 10 a.m. not recommended

I linger to experience the feeling of that heat. You know what it's like when you're baking and you open the oven door to take the cake out and you get pounded with a blast of heat? Like that. I wonder, *How could, and why would, anything live in 121 degree heat? Get me out of here.*

So glad to leave California. Hot, dry, smoking, burning, expensive, crime-ridden. Water is restricted or unavailable. Places are either rural with no phone signal or crowded with traffic jams. No personal need to go back to California, especially now that Christina will be moving to Washington.

I didn't plan to go to Las Vegas. I'm trying to avoid having to drive in cities. This area of California and Nevada is so rural that I can think of no other place to hide out for the night.

The Triangle Club is in Las Vegas, Nevada. I park in the big parking lot in the back. A dozen or so people are spread out around the large echoing room. The chairperson reads something out of the AA Big Book, speaks for a minute, and then starts calling on people. Some decline to talk by saying, "Pass." When I'm called upon, I give my standard spiel about how I'm traveling, and meetings are my home away from home.

One young man raises his voice, saying, "In the old days, people helped other people. When they were homeless, people took them in. No one is going to do that anymore, right? I'm homeless, and none of you self-involved people are going to help me, are you?" He bellows on like this for a while and then stomps out and slams the door. Another man follows him out. The meeting continues. After a while, they both come back in and that young man says, "I'm sorry for talking that way. I do need a place to stay, but it's wrong of me to blame all you people." I think, *Sponsorship at work here.*

Some other people say:

"I haven't found it necessary to pick up a drink. I haven't found it necessary to destroy my life."

"My sponsor said, 'Yes, you have to go to meetings until you want to go to meetings. Then you won't have to anymore.'"

"There's always some way to make yourself feel lonely."

After the meeting, I linger with that knot of people who are smoking or vaping out back. I want to go to Fremont Street because when I was in Vegas with That Guy (you know the one), we missed going there. I ask them, "How do I find Fremont Street?"

"Just put the Golden Nugget in your GPS."

"Where would I park?"

"A parking garage is right nearby."

And I'm on my way. Sometimes I think I should take up smoking so this introvert would have a pretext to hang out with people, to improve my conscious contact with my Higher Power. GOD. Group Of Drunks.

I'm remembering a time a few years earlier when I was in Vegas with That Guy. I was horrified and shamed by the way women were objectified in that city. Men chased tourists down the street, pushing flyers with suggestive photos and a headline that screamed, "WOMEN WANT TO MEET YOU!" The flyers included phone numbers that you could call to buy a woman. Similar posters were all over phone poles. Billboards showed heavily made-up, scantily clad women in sexual poses, advertising shows, bars, restaurants, casinos. There was no escape from the sexualization and selling of women.

I started to talk to That Guy about my feelings. He didn't exactly disagree, but he politely declined to engage in that conversation. I started to feel more alone and more crazy because there was no reality check for me. He was not with me. Back at our room, I found that an AA meeting would be starting soon at a nearby hotel. So I went, and left him watching TV.

A half dozen men were in the meeting, but they assured me it was not just a men's meeting, so I stayed. I was happy to see another woman show up at the last minute. When it was time to share, I spoke about feeling ashamed and horrified, and told the same story that I just told you.

These men became angry. One said, "Oh, don't worry about that. All they will do is dance for you."

Another said, "You have to pay eight hundred bucks for them to actually have sex with you."

"It's just a rip-off."

They were angry *at* the women who were being sold. I started to crumble inside. But I stayed.

After the meeting, that late-arriving woman came to me and hugged me long and hard. She said, "It's not your shame. You have nothing to be ashamed of."

I said, "How do you deal with it?"

"I am a former sex worker. I sponsor sex workers in recovery."

At that moment, I felt blessings wash over me. I had hope for the world. I was heard and held. We are still Facebook friends. Angela. My angel.

But today, I locate the Golden Nugget easily and have to pay only two dollars to park in a nearby garage. Love it. Fremont Street is a pedestrian mall and has a ceiling with images flashing on it. It's noisy, bright, crowded. Everything is open: foo-foo shops, cheesy souvenir shops, restaurants, bars. Music, lights, varieties of buskers. Joyful screaming from the zip line running along over the pedestrians. It's a happening scene. I scarf down a big Chinese supper. And I'm happy.

August 6: Invisible Scenic Vistas Obscured by Thick Smoke

This morning I have to deal with a credit card issue. My credit card company texts me to ask if I recognize a one-dollar charge from the Circle K convenience store. The text says that if I don't recognize the charge, they will cancel my card. I don't recognize the charge, but I hesitate to text them back. I return to Circle K, where I pumped gas last night, and ask why they charged me a dollar. The manager says, "We don't do that."

When I call my credit card company, he says, "The merchant will sometimes charge a dollar to see if the card works, then drop the charge when the purchase goes through. If you know the merchant, you can ignore the one-dollar charge." I almost lost my credit card over this because I didn't recognize the one-dollar charge. That would be inconvenient because I don't have an address where they can send me a new credit card. I would have to use my debit card instead. This is an example of what Faith would call a luxury problem.

My sons recommended using a credit card because it's more secure and gives me points. Seth said, "You can get the whole amount paid directly out of your account each month so you never have to pay interest." I follow their advice.

It's a long drive to Great Basin National Park on a narrow two-way road with nothing on either side for miles and miles. Not even a bush to pee behind. Rarely do I even see another vehicle. At long last, I spot a pull-off with a port-a-potty. It's locked with a padlock. *Who would put a port-a-potty in the middle of this vast, deserted wilderness? And then lock it?* So I pee behind the van. I showed them.

I have plenty of time to think. *Why didn't I do the zip line at Fremont Street in Vegas?* I knew it was there. I knew it would be fun. But actually doing it never crosses my mind until I'm on this long drive. I just didn't think it applied to me. Why? I regret missing out on this. I remember the woman at the meeting in West Chester, Pennsylvania, who had seen the sign for the trapeze school and longed to do it but thought it didn't apply to her. She spoke about her self-limiting beliefs. I wonder, *How much of life do I automatically and uncon- sciously rule out without even thinking?*

At the Great Basin National Park Visitor Center, I speak with the ranger at her desk. "It's really smoky around here."

She says, "I can show you where the fires are," and she turns her laptop toward me. A map shows fires all over the western United States. "Ninety-eight wildfires are going on right now."

"Wow. I'm glad I have the web address so I can see where the fires are and avoid them. Where do I get tickets for the cave tour? Maybe it won't be smoky down there."

She gestures. "That's where you can get tickets."

"Why is this place called Great Basin?"

"It's called Great Basin because most of the rivers don't run out to the sea. Instead they collect in marshes and salt lakes and just evaporate in the desert air. Enjoy the cave tour."

"Thanks."

I'm nervous about going down on the Lehman Caves tour because I've been headachy and I suspect I might get sick. I guess it's probably because of all the smoke. I bring a plastic bag down with me, just in case. In caves, they always tell you not to even touch anything because the oils from your hand would affect the evolving formations forever. No one would want that sheltered, pristine cave environment to be sullied by me puking on it. The formations in the cave are beautiful, and I'm OK.

The weather board at the visitor center reads "Smoke, sunny, 104°." I start out on the Wheeler Peak Scenic Drive. I could drive through perilous mountains in the harsh, dry desert for twelve miles, with invisible scenic vistas obscured by thick smoke, and then drive the same twelve miles back to return. I decide against it, and give up on that idea, and leave.

In Cedar City, Utah, I find the Misfits Group AA meeting. The building is up a hill from a service station, just off the highway, with apartment buildings beyond. The meeting is upstairs above offices that offer services to people with various types of challenges. Other kinds of meetings are held here, too. The meeting room is large and sunny. When the chips are given out for time in sobriety, the group, all in unison, asks the recipient of the chip, "How'd you do it?" And the person makes a brief statement about what keeps him or her sober.

Here's some of what I hear:

"Drugs and alcohol brought out the worst in me. AA brings out the best in me."

"I thought violence was strength, sex was love, and walls were boundaries."

"I thought I was having a breakdown, but I was having a breakthrough."

A man all dressed up in a three-piece suit gestures toward me and says, "Welcome to our visitor. It's nice to see beautiful faces, not just these guys." And with that he nods toward his grinning buddies. *Why would a guy wear a three-piece suit to an AA meeting? Is he a lawyer, or is it a sign of mental illness?* I take his comment as a compliment.

The rest area on Route 70 in Crescent Junction, Utah, is my home for the night. I'm happy because Seth and Nicole booked me a room for tomorrow night.

August 7: Who Is *Thou?*

I take 15 South to Zion National Park and the entrance to the Kolob Canyons Road. The road is blocked off, and a woman stands here with her pickup truck parked nearby. She tells me, "This section of the park is closed because they're replacing the road. I can only allow workers in."

I keep on driving to get to the other entrance and the Zion Canyon Visitor Center. It's congested with people. Taking the free shuttle is required because privately owned vehicles are not allowed. I wait about forty-five minutes with the throng to get the shuttle.

The buses have open sunroofs so I can even see the tops of the huge vertical mountains that we pass. Impressive in person, but less so in photos.

The shuttle makes various stops. The Emerald Pools Trail has views of those mountains layered with color— warm shades of tan, brown, brownish red, reddish brown. A brook, a waterfall, people. Parents pushing strollers. Children scampering under the waterfall shower.

The Weeping Rock Trail rises uphill toward an overhanging cliff that has water streaming down the face of the rock—not a waterfall, just weeping. And more beautiful mountain views from here. On the way back down, I pass an older couple who are laboring up the trail, and the woman says to me, "How much farther is it?"

"You can make it if you go slow. I had to stop to rest a bunch of times, so I pretended I was taking pictures." They both laugh.

The Riverside Walk Trail is an easy stroll along the river, just as the name suggests. A group of people pause to watch a deer taking her lunch in the woods. I've heard that the river sometimes becomes a rushing and treacherous flood, but not today. It's shallow, clear, and lazy.

At the Zion Human History Museum, an air-conditioned theater shows a park overview orientation film. The museum has displays of Native American and pioneer history, and displays about water, and how water changes, and how it changes other things. It's very fluid.

It's easy and quick to get off and on the shuttle, with not much wait time, so I explore plenty of places.

The word *zion* means "sanctuary." In one particularly scenic and expansive place, once again, I speak to God. "If you're here, can you say hello?"

The words of my aunt Gerry's favorite hymn come to me. "When through the woods and forest glades I wander, and hear the birds sing sweetly in the trees. When I look down from lofty mountain grandeur, and hear the brook and feel the gentle breeze." Though I feel that awe, I still don't make the leap from here to the next lyric, "How great Thou art." *Who is* Thou?

Back at the van, I set my GPS for the Best Western where Seth and Nicole have reserved a room for me. Bless them. The GPS usually takes me on something like a main road. But with the help of the GPS and the map, too, the main-est road I can find is the Zion–Mount Carmel Highway, aka Route 9. It's one of those mountain roads with scary switchbacks that by now I am trying to avoid. I don't want to do it.

But I just have to, because the only other option would be to go in a completely opposite direction. So I grit my teeth, grasp the steering wheel, and go for it.

In Mount Carmel, Utah, the Best Western is on a corner in the middle of nowhere across from a Subway, with a convenience store and gas station next door. It has a rustic western motif with columns made from real tree trunks. And yet it's luxurious. My room has two big TVs, a living room/kitchen, a bathroom with a tub, and a bedroom. The first thing I do is hit the swimming pool. Woo-hoo!

At Subway, a busload of Asian tourists has just been served, so I don't have to wait long for my sandwich. Good timing.

I toss in a load of wash at the hotel laundromat. In my room, I do some chores. Write postcards. Make out a check for my property taxes that are about to come due. Fold laundry. Savor the comfort and the air-conditioning.

August 8: Hoodoos

Damn. Another luxury problem. The convenience store doesn't have decaf coffee, or anything to eat except sugary junk. I got myself decaffeinated a few years ago and discovered that all the problems I thought were from aging were actually because of caffeine. Without caffeine, I can sleep better, so I can think better, pay attention better, remember things better. I'm more even-tempered and have less stress and anxiety. I decided to stay quit of caffeine.

I get to Bryce Canyon National Park around noon and take the shuttle around the park. The shuttle isn't required, but I enjoy getting out of the van, and I like being relieved of the responsibility of driving, especially in these scenic locations. I get off to walk at three different shuttle stops: Bryce Point, Inspiration Point, and Sunset Point.

The views are stunning. I'm reminded of the Grand Canyon with the open spaces and the layered rocks in shades of red, pink, and tan, except that the shapes of the rock formations are different at Bryce. At the visitor center, I learn that *hoodoos* are rock shapes formed by hard rock on top with soft layers underneath, so that they erode to leave formations that stand like statues. Hoodoos are found in other places, but Bryce has the largest collection of them on earth.

The sky is hazy with smoke. The only shade is an occasional random scruffy tree, usually with people already under it. The campgrounds are full, as I've seen at the other national parks so far. The walking trails have discouraging elevation gains. And it's hot, as usual. It's time for me to move on.

I know I won't make it to Capitol Reef National Park before the visitor center closes, but I go for it anyway. I don't know what I'll find or where I might stay. I drive mile after mile, seeing no recognizable sign of human life. What a harsh place. Getting close to Capitol Reef, I scope out possible places to park for later. A pull-off? Hotel parking lots?

At the closed visitor center at Capitol Reef, I pick up a map of the park. It's still daylight, so I tour the eight-mile length of the Scenic Drive, stopping often to take photos and breathe in the expansiveness and call out to invite God.

This place is called Capitol Reef because, as the literature says, "The domes of the rock formations resemble the domes of capitols, and the cliffs form an insurmountable obstacle, like a barrier reef."

Though I've seen possible sleep spots before I got to Capitol Reef, I just can't make myself go backward to get to them, so I continue. The view from Route 24 is gray sand and rock, with nothing green. I'm getting thoroughly sick of heat and sun. I'm craving greenery and a cool, cloudy, drizzly day, the kind New Englanders dislike.

At a rest area on Route 70 in Crescent Junction, Utah, the air still smells smoky, and I am wondering, *What could be burning? There are no trees or shrubs or even grass to burn.* This rest area is close to the two national parks I plan to visit tomorrow, so here I stay.

August 9: A Shrub!

At Arches National Park, I drive first to the far end of the park road and work my way back, in hopes of avoiding some of the crowd.

Along the paths, I take pictures of Landscape Arch, Turret Arch, and other beautiful gold-colored formations and arches. The path to Landscape Arch is 0.8 miles and hilly. I can take only about a dozen steps on the uphills before my heart begins to pound. I pace myself. I'm OK when I take my time.

Between Arches and Canyonlands National Park, I pull over into a big parking lot by a restaurant, looking for lunch. I decide not to stay here, and as I'm leaving, I run over a curb with a big thump. I didn't see it because the curb, the parking lot, and the road are all the same color. I'm worried that my tire might go flat, so I check, and it's OK. I keep checking it for a while to make sure it's not losing air, and it's OK. A flat tire would be the worst thing that's happened so far. And it didn't even happen. *How am I so lucky?* Though I haven't needed AAA even once yet on this tour, being a member gives me confidence.

Canyonlands National Park is not far from Arches. Utah has five national parks. OK, by now I think I'm getting a little jaded. Here are more vast, smoky views of dramatic rock formations.

At the different pull-off spots, I keep seeing the same grizzled dude on a motorcycle laden with camping equipment. I notice his Vermont plates because I lived in Vermont for a while, and that's where my son Micah was born.

I dare to speak to him. "You're from Vermont?"

In a German accent, he says, "No, the motorcycle is from Vermont. I borrowed it from a friend. I live in Germany."

"Where have you visited so far?"

"I've been all over. I've been on the road for seven months now. Seeing the country."

"Where have you been staying?"

"I've been putting up a tent in campgrounds."

I gesture toward my vehicle. "That's my van. That's where I've been staying."

"I'm getting worried about fires, though," he says.

"I found a website where you can see where all the wildfires are. Do you have a pencil?"

I give him the information for the wildfire locating website, and he writes it down.

"Well, thanks," he says.

"You're welcome. And safe travels." I confess to you that he is the most interesting thing at Canyonlands. I think I need a change of scenery.

I head back, passing Arches again, up to Route 70 going east into Colorado. As I drive along in Colorado, I spot a green shrub. Involuntarily I shout, "A shrub!" Now I see multiple shrubs. I see a tree and I yell, "A tree!" Now I see multiple trees, red mountains with green pine trees. I breathe sighs of relief to be amidst greenery. I can feel my mood lighten, and my muscles relax.

Seth calls and says, "Do you want to come for Thanksgiving in Puerto Rico?"

"Let-me-think-yes." And my heart smiles.

I've been feeling generally a little lightheaded, dizzy, anxious, short of breath for a while now. I'm sleeping OK, and I wonder if it might be because I'm not eating as much as I do when I'm at home with my refrigerator. I go grocery shopping and buy more big food than usual, muffins, bread, cheese, peanut butter. *Let's see if this helps.*

I've been listening to a murder-mystery book on CD, the only one I could find at Goodwill at the time. But it's distasteful and gruesome, not very uplifting. I've long since given up on the Spanish language-learning CDs because they're too distracting, and I don't want to miss any part of my travels. Often, I get no phone signal and no radio.

Here's a Goodwill, and I stop to see if I can get a less disgusting audio CD, but no luck. Outside the store, on a bench in the shade, I succeed at getting online. I discover a way to download free public domain audiobooks that I can listen to even at times when I have no signal. A triumph.

But I haven't located a place to stay, so I drive on in the dark. My eyes are starting to cross from fatigue when I come to a town called Silverthorne, Colorado. The small-scale Super 8 hotel seems dark and generic enough, so I park here for the night. I'm a little hesitant because so few cars are in the parking lot, but there's nowhere else to go except to keep driving, so I stay.

August 10: Altitude

I wake up and it's still dark and I'm worried. When Seth called yesterday, he told me who would be at his place for Thanksgiving: Nicole and him, Joel and Kathryn, Mike and Leanne, and three other couples who are friends of his. Again, all couples. And me. Sigh. Cringe. We live in a couples culture. I hope Micah and his family will go, too, because then at least there will be children who will not be married, and I won't be the only one single. I'm having a shame and grief attack. Some people I know would use the word *triggered.*

Off to McDonald's for the bathroom and a big cup of decaf. I eat two of the muffins that I got on my last shopping trip. I'm eating more food now in hopes of feeling better physically. Plus, this is comfort food.

I drive about three hours to get to Rocky Mountain National Park, crying off and on. I blow right past the first visitor center, distracted, but keep on going. Such beauty, and here I am crying. I reprimand myself for crying, and that makes me feel even worse. I'm ashamed of feeling ashamed.

The Lake Irene trail is short and not too hilly. And I do love walking in nature. Watching the lake reflect the tall pines, I start to relax and calm down. On the way back up from the lake, I pause to pant for a while. A friendly middle-aged man approaches me and we greet each other, and he says, "What a day."

"It's so beautiful here."

"Nothing like this in Maryland, where I'm from."

"What goes on in Maryland?"

"Well, I'm a veterinarian. I love to come here on vacation. I've been here quite a few times."

"Where have you been staying?"

"Estes Park. It's a small town not too far from here. It's really nice. I recommend it."

I take a deep breath and say, "I can't do hills like I used to."

"Where are you from?"

"Maine."

"Well, you know, we're over ten thousand feet of altitude here."

My jaw drops and the fog clears from my brain. I'm enlightened. It's the altitude that's been bothering me all along.

"What a relief! I'm so glad you said that. I thought maybe I wasn't eating enough calories or red meat or something. Or I might be having heart problems. I've been thinking I might have to take myself to the emergency room."

"No, probably not," he says, laughing.

"Thank you."

"You're welcome," he says.

Because this man claims to be a veterinarian, I consider him a medical expert who has given me an accurate diagnosis. It just makes sense.

Immensely relieved and cheered, I proceed along the scary scenic road through the mountains of the park, pausing for short walks and photos. The sign at the Alpine Visitor Center says "Elevation: 11,796 ft." The wind is howling. In my selfie, what you see is hair blowing across my face and mountains in the background, piney at the lower elevations, then rocky with white patches higher up.

I visit Estes Park, the recommendation from that helpful veterinarian. The town has trendy shops and restaurants, and the river walk is shady and pleasant. I find places to sit and enjoy the sight, the sound, and the smell of the river, more like a brook, really. I poke around in some shops looking at things I won't buy.

Dairy Queen is running $4.99 lunch specials, so how can I resist. My choice consists of chicken pieces on a salad, soda, and a sundae. I ask if I can substitute milk for soda. She says, "Sure," and drags a gallon of whole milk out of the fridge and pours it into a large soda-sized cup. Bonus. Enough milk to last all day. The sundae is a cheat on my food plan, I know. Don't judge me.

It's crowded and I sit next to a couple of senior citizens at the counter. The woman starts a conversation with me. I say, "I've been wondering what to do while I'm waiting to visit my nephew in Denver. What would you suggest?"

She and her husband look at each other and say in unison, "Celestial Seasonings."

She says, "They're in Boulder and they have a tea tour."

"Great idea." Thank goodness for chatty people.

Onward to Longmont, Colorado, where I take time to smell the roses in Roosevelt Park and sit in the shade and write this for you.

The public domain books I downloaded are difficult to hear on my phone with my earbuds, so I buy an auxiliary cable, and now I can listen to them through the radio in my van. I'm so wicked smaht.

The Longmont meeting is at the Triangle Club, a place that's set back behind a parking lot in an industrial area. It costs fifteen dollars a month to become a member of the club, but as always, the AA meetings are free. A sign on the wall reads, "Hang on, but let go." And another sign says, "You only need to go to meetings on days that end in *Y*." A suspended ceiling has artwork on the ceiling squares. For a donation, you can put your artwork up. That reminds me of the art on the wall tiles in the Oxnard, California, club.

The energy is high. People greet each other enthusiastically, hugging, joking, laughing. Their greetings to me are warm and good-humored, too. I say to the guy next to me, "This is the funnest meeting I have ever been to."

"You should come tomorrow morning. It's even funner."

"What a coincidence. I was just going to ask you for suggestions of things to do in Longmont."

Here is some of what I hear these delightful people say:

"Just like I had a high tolerance for alcohol, I had a high tolerance for misery."

"I have to take care of my resentments before they catch on fire."

"The ego says when things fall into place, I'll be OK. The spirit says when I'm OK, things will fall into place."

"Don't be grandiose about your worthlessness."

Just because people are laughing and joking doesn't mean that they are not deep, too. That's something I love about AA. What a great meeting. I think, *I should move here. Umm. Naah.*

August 11: The Funnest Meeting

Back to the Triangle Club for the morning meeting that was recommended to me last night. I notice that on every seat there's a noisemaker, the kind you can get at the Dollar Store that's shaped like two plastic hands on a stick, and they make a loud clacking sound when you rattle them. The energy is high, like at the meeting last night.

The chairperson introduces himself and the room goes noisy with "Yay!" *Clack! Clack! Clack!* Just like midnight on New Year's Eve. Then someone does a short reading, and the room goes "Yay!" *Clack! Clack! Clack!* Every little thing is given a loud rock-and-roll New Year's Eve ovation. And each time that happens, everyone laughs, because it is so ridiculous. What a hoot. This is the funnest meeting I have ever been to.

It's an anniversary meeting, which means that people who are celebrating their sobriety anniversary have a chance to get up and speak to the group. As soon as each speaker begins, the room gets silent, serious, and attentive. And when that person finishes speaking, there's another rock-and-roll New Year's Eve ovation. I hear words of wisdom:

"My son said, 'Why can't you just stop?' I said, 'You know how you're addicted to Xbox? How do you stop?' He said, 'Hit the Pause button.' I said, 'I have no Pause button.'"

"Once I stoop to a low endeavor, it's really easy to do it again."

"I was getting PMS: Poor Me Syndrome."

"I plan to stay in the middle of the herd."

"If you're right, it's hard to change your mind. It's like giving your kid away. But if you just have opinions, you can change them. Then it's only like giving your neighbor's kid away."

"I feel sorry for my sister. She doesn't have this problem, so she doesn't have this solution."

"If you didn't drink or drug today, you are a success."

The contrast between the fun and the serious nature of recovery is stunning. Energized by the meeting, I boogie out to the van and I am on my way.

At Celestial Seasonings in Boulder, tea samples are available in the lobby. I taste a few. I like the Bengal Spice. The best thing about Celestial Seasonings is the artwork on the packaging.

We're all given hairnets, and the men with beards are given beard nets, too, and we're shown into a small theater for a video about the history and doings of Celestial Seasonings. A young woman tour guide takes us through the place where they store and process the tea. Maps on the wall show where in the world different teas come from.

"Different types of tea are kept in different rooms," she says. "The rooms are sealed to keep the aromas and flavors pure."

It's quiet in the room where tea is packaged. "The machinery is all turned off today because it's the weekend. Just a few staff are around, maintaining the machines. What do you think are the Celestial Seasonings top sellers?" she asks the group.

"Sleepytime?" someone says. Others nod.

"Yes, Sleepytime, Chamomile, and Spearmint. The only teas that are real tea are green tea, white tea, and black tea. All the rest are herbal infusions, just to be perfectly correct. Well, thank you all for coming, and make sure to check out our gift shop before you leave."

I take some time to admire all the artwork on the packaging in the gift shop.

Before leaving Boulder, I look for Chautauqua Park because of good reviews on Trip Advisor. When I get near, I see that it's jammed. Traffic stuck on the road, cars parked everywhere possible. I drive around for a while, not finding a place to park. I can't even see where the park is, just streets clogged with traffic. There are supposed to be trails, but the only walking thing I can see is some people trudging up a steep, grassy hill. That would not be for me anyway, because you know how I am about hills. I'm confused. I don't know where to go, or why to go there.

Finally, I ask someone who looks like a park employee, with her reflective vest. She speaks about shuttles and mentions all kinds of streets and directions, and I get even more overwhelmed.

I find a parking lot and ask about a shuttle, but by then, I just want out of the fray. I put my head down on the steering wheel in the hot van, and take a moment to breathe and release some tears of frustration. Soon I have another plan.

People at the Longmont meeting said, "Go to York Street." The York Street Club in Denver is a brick mansion with an open wraparound porch in a shady residential area of big houses and newer apartment buildings. Multiple meetings are scheduled here daily.

There's a smallish parking lot on the side, with an available space. I nose into that spot so that the AA logo sticker on the back of my van is visible. I hope the sticker will show people that I am entitled to park here.

Walking is one of my favorite things. Getting out of the car is good. I'm finally getting to take my walk, though it's not the walk in the park I had been hoping for. The main road is grungy, with traffic, hot sun, noise, businesses. Chipotle for a late lunch.

My stroll continues through a shady residential neighborhood. Green grass, landscaping. In a convenience store, I get my daily dose of dark chocolate and sit on a shady bench in front of a church to enjoy it before it melts.

I hang around the York Street Club sampling different meetings until evening. I leave when it's dark, and cool enough to park for the night.

August 12: Education Is Never Wasted

In Denver, I snag a miraculous parking spot right on my

nephew Thomas's block. It's a quiet neighborhood of older duplexes and triple-deckers.

Mary Kate, Thomas's girlfriend, greets me with a smile at the front door, and says, "Come on up." Thomas is just getting out of the shower. They're both young, slim, and healthy-looking. Mary Kate has long straight hair and Thomas is tall, like his dad, my brother Andy.

The apartment is pleasant with big sunny windows on the second floor of one of those older multiunit houses with character. I see books and bicycles. I ask Thomas, "Where's your piano?"

"No, unfortunately, I haven't been playing..."

"Bummer. Can I treat you both to breakfast?"

Thomas says, "Sure. There's a place we could walk to. Do you feel like walking?"

"Always. Let's go."

The breakfast place has artwork hung all over the walls. Thomas asks, "Which piece of art would you like to take home?"

I glance around and see only abstract art with harsh colors and spiky lines. *They're all bad feng shui.* "Umm. No thanks." We laugh.

We talk about their work. Mary Kate is between jobs, looking for something in a nonprofit agency. Thomas has a degree in art history that he's not currently using for work. I tell him about a conversation I had with my father, his grandfather. "I asked my father if it bothered him that I was working as a nurse and wasting my music education degree, which he had mostly paid for. And he said, 'Oh, no. Education is never wasted.'"

We stroll down to the Capitol. One of the Capitol steps is engraved with the words ONE MILE ABOVE SEA LEVEL. Great time for a photo op. Mary Kate takes a picture of me and Thomas on that step. An innocent bystander takes one of the three of us, smiling, with our arms around one another. I tell Mary Kate my altitude sickness story. She grew up in Colorado, so she's used to the altitude.

Back to their block, I show off the van, my home away from home. They see the simplicity of it, and I can tell they are thinking. *They might be trying on the idea of stealth camping to see if it fits them.* Thomas looks at Mary Kate and says, "What do you think?"

"Hmm," she says.

We hug our goodbyes. Nice neighborhood. Nice life. Nice people. I'm sad to say goodbye, but I feel strengthened by the visit.

Leaving Denver, I hop onto Route 25 South to 160 West to 150, which takes me to the visitor center at Great Sand Dunes National Park. Guess what is here. Sand. I watch the informational movie, of course. People are slogging across the flat area of sand toward the dunes in the distance. I don't want to trudge on sand in the hot sun, and I don't want to labor up dunes. I don't linger here.

Route 17 North goes over flat, dry land to Route 50 heading west, past mountains and lakes, to the town of Gunnison, Colorado. One option is to stay in the parking lot of the

Holiday Inn, then use the bathroom at McDonald's in the morning. Good enough.

August 13: No Pooping

The road to Black Canyon of the Gunnison National Park is mountainous, with scruffy greenery, and scenic. In the park, I drive along the South Rim Road and stop at pull-out places to enjoy the view, and then return to the South Rim Visitor Center. The sun is rising, and the views of the steep black walls of the canyon and the river below are spectacular. While waiting for the ranger tour, I look at the exhibits at the visitor center.

A ranger named Melissa is our guide. We walk along the Rim Rock Nature Trail and pause for scenery and information from Melissa. "The place is called Black Canyon because the canyon is so steep and deep that it's in shadow much of the time, making the dark rock look even darker."

A friend of Melissa's is along on our walking tour. He used to be a ranger, too, and is also a geologist. He says, "The canyons are made of rock called gneiss, pronounced nice, and schist. Be careful how you pronounce that."

During all these western park visits, I've been saving up questions to ask a geologist. Most of the national parks out west are all about rocks, it seems. I ask him, "When you look at a map, why does the east coast of South America seem to fit into the west coast of Africa?"

"Oh, the continental drift. Those two continents were once one continent called Pangea," and he talks about plate tectonics. When I was a kid looking at the globe in my classroom, I imagined continents floating apart on the ocean water. Now I learn that the continents truly are drifting, though I've long since understood that continents do not float on water. He says, "Africa and South America are continuing to drift apart because of a rise in the Atlantic."

Route 50 West is a pretty and easy drive, but Route 550 South is horrifying for several hours. Steep, narrow, curvy. Random huge RVs charging toward me. There's nothing to do but grip the steering wheel, keep on going, and hope for the best. I'm glad I continued my life insurance from my last place of employment.

I arrive at Mesa Verde National Park just in time for the afternoon five-dollar ranger tour. My lucky day. Two ranger tours in one day. I drive the twenty-three miles to where the tour starts at Cliff Palace. The only way you're allowed to go down to the cliff dwelling is with a ranger. There are ladders and steep steps. I'm fine going down.

"These structures are fragile," the ranger says. "Never touch anything with your hands, and never walk on the cliff dwelling." When I was here with my family in 1966, we clambered all over the place all by ourselves. So did all the other visitors. Things have changed in fifty-two years.

"The dwelling was made with sandstone blocks with mortar in between. About a hundred people once lived at

Cliff Palace. Those people were smaller than we are today—we can tell by the size of the doors and the rooms. Their average life-span was about thirty-two years."

I have to rest on the way back up to the parking lot. A number of times. This place is at about seven thousand feet of elevation.

While driving out of the park, I catch a glimpse of a sign that says "Showers." And they're even free. I'm intrigued by signs I see posted in each shower stall. They direct me not to poop in the shower, in various languages, including the international stick-figure sign for no pooping. I get all showered and shampooed, without even being tempted to poop in here.

Route 160 has a lovely rest area with a few short trees and a gravel walking trail. I see two signs. One says "Hiking Trail Entrance." But the one that says "Beware Rattlesnakes!" discourages me from taking a stroll. I would love to stay put here all night, rattlesnakes and all, but then I see another sign that says "No overnight parking." So I move on.

August 14: Petrified

Last night, a bunch of teenagers were going around the Walmart parking lot putting a small chocolate bar and a note on each windshield. The note says "#SpreadSunshine." I waited impatiently until they left, and then took the candy and the note off my windshield. If I left it there, it would give away my secret, that I'm here all night. My cover would be blown.

On the road to Petrified Forest National Park, the Four Corners is only twenty miles out of my way. That's the place where four states come together: Colorado, New Mexico, Utah, and Arizona. Getting closer, I see that they're charging admission, and I start to feel resentful about commercialism. Then I see that the proceeds will go to the Navajo reservation and I think, *Well, that's OK then.*

I park near the outhouse. Concentric benches are set up on a slight incline toward the middle, where the names of the states are written in concrete and also on a big metal medallion in the center of that. Naturally, I stand with my feet in four states. Who wouldn't?

From here, down Route 491 in New Mexico and then Route 40 into Arizona.

Petrified Forest National Park is another hot, dry, harsh location. I'm reminded of the Badlands as I drive past gray-reddish-tan layered, eroded mountains. A rusty ancient car stands by the side of the road with a sign that says that Route 66 used to be right here. Among low-growing shrubs, a line of simple old-fashioned T-shaped wooden telephone poles disappears into the horizon. That's where Route 66 went, back in the day.

I pause to speak with a retired volunteer ranger in the blazing sun, amidst chunks of petrified logs. "I'm fascinated with how wood can get petrified."

"Well, 218 million years ago, the continents were all one. Back then, Arizona was at a similar latitude with where Costa Rica is today, and it was a rain forest. Big logs fell into the river. Volcanic ash settled on them and other sediment seeped in, and the logs turned to quartz. The continents drifted apart."

"What makes the different colors?"

"The color varies with the different types of minerals that created it."

I stop at the gift shop and come across a container of polished petrified wood pieces. I am in love with them. Petrified wood is beautiful, with the wood grain visible. The earth has been through so many changes. It makes climate change seem like a small issue in the big picture. Don't get me wrong. I'm certainly not saying we should be able to be careless with our environment. It's a big deal for humans now. Far from perfect myself, I'm driving an internal-combustion engine.

In the seventies, Jayne and I went to an environmental protest demonstration where a combustion engine was buried. Afterward, people got into their cars and drove away.

I try to take the least "scenic," least terrifying route to Saguaro National Park, Route 77 going south. It's beautiful, and hardly frightening. First, pine trees with grass underneath, then mountains. Then lightning and more mountains. Rain, just enough for interval wipers. A rainbow. A charmed evening, and I'm enchanted.

August 15: A Magical Fairyland

Morning rush-hour traffic is moving slowly on the divided road around the outskirts of Tucson. The directions in my national park guidebook say to take Escalante Road, but I hear on the radio that Escalante Road is flooded. That's worrisome, but my GPS takes me a different way, so nothing bad happens. Just clouds and thunder.

It's raining by the time I reach Saguaro National Park, so I wait it out at the visitor center. The ranger says, "A saguaro cactus is the immense, iconic one you see standing with its arms upraised in western movies." He demonstrates. "They've been monitored since 1942 in an attempt to figure out why so many of them have died."

When the rain eases up, I take my trusty visitor center map and go exploring on the Cactus Forest Scenic Loop Drive. I scout out places to park and walk.

It's a magical fairyland in the mist, clouds, and off-and-on rain. I'm entranced. I can see Mica Mountain in the distance, in the clouds. I'm surprised by the largest rabbit I have ever seen, with the tallest ears. And plenty of types of cacti, in various arrangements and still lifes, to marvel over and photograph. In that comfortable weather, I can linger.

August 16: The Difference Between Meditation and a Manicure

At a rest stop before Las Cruces, New Mexico, I see the Recycled Roadrunner, a big sculpture on a hill overlooking the city, made out of all recycled debris: sneakers, electronics parts, and whatnot. Extreme eccentric factor.

I try to figure out something to do in Las Cruces, or in nearby El Paso, Texas, but I'm overwhelmed by heat and traffic. I set off for Carlsbad, New Mexico.

Going east on Route 62/180, I get stopped at a border patrol checkpoint. The man asks, "Are you an American citizen?"

"Yes."

"I'm going to take a look into your van." He shields his face with his hand and squints into the back. I think, *There's nothing unlawful here, but how can he tell, through those tinted windows?* Somehow satisfied, he waves me on. I drive away breathing a sigh of relief, even though I had no cause to worry in the first place.

Small dust tornadoes are twisting on both sides of the road. Multiple dust storm warning signs say "Zero visibility. Get off road. Turn off car. Foot off brake. Stay buckled." I'm prepared. I will know exactly what to do.

There's rain in the distance, getting closer, with lightning and thunder, and it hits so hard I can barely see. I search out a place to pull over and wait it out. Once I'm safely off the road, I am free to appreciate the excitement of the storm until it passes.

So I can complete my goal of attending AA meetings in all forty-eight contiguous states, I find the Alano Club in Carlsbad, New Mexico. It's a low-budget, dirty building in a neighborhood of one-story houses with rectangular yards. No one else is here until the very last minute, when six other people show up. At this meeting, they do "sticks": Popsicle-type sticks with topics written on them. Each person randomly picks out a stick and then speaks on that topic. I hear:

"They say the only requirement for AA membership is a desire to stop drinking. Well, I didn't have that desire, but my probation officer had that desire for me."

"I didn't put down the drink so I could beat myself up with both hands."

"I got rid of that huge gorilla, but now I have this ugly butterfly on my shoulder telling me to drink. This program teaches me what to put between that thought and that action."

"I learned to practice self-care, not self-indulgence. Like the difference between meditation and a manicure."

At first, in recovery, I had a lot to learn about self-care. I didn't know the difference between selfishness and self-care. When I was in rehab, a guy in my group asked me, "Whose needs come first, yours or your kids'?"

"The kids'."

He said, "What about your need to be a good mother?"

Food for thought for me. Since then, I have seen how people who have their own needs met have so much more to offer others. That's how I want to be.

Later in that rehab group I expressed concern about my ability to maintain sobriety. "What will I do when my son gets married?"

The same guy asked, "How old is your son?"

"Five," I said. They all laughed.

"One day at a time," he said.

After the Carlsbad meeting, I have achieved my goal of getting to at least one AA meeting in all forty-eight contiguous states. I have lived the experience of being held by my Higher Power, the group.

August 17: Unmoving Physically, but Emotionally Very Moved

It's noisy and bright at the Carlsbad Walmart. Someone pulls up right next to me blaring what sounds like bagpipe jazz, and keeps it up for way too long. After I doze off, the street cleaner roars by multiple, loud times. *Maybe I should have stayed at the Marriott parking lot next door instead.* I leave here early.

I arrive at Carlsbad Caverns National Park at seven, thinking it's eight because of my time-zone confusion. I have trouble getting my head around the time-zone situation sometimes. I am way early.

On the road to the visitor center, I see a herd of some kind of curly-horned goats munching on the sparse vegetation by the side of the road.

I stop the van and watch them with the windows rolled down. No other humans are in sight. I stay in the van so I won't scare them off, and I commune with them with my heart open, unmoving physically, but emotionally very moved.

I think back to when I was in Kenya with my friend Sharon. Our friend Sam had been in Kenya when he was in the Peace Corps, and he wanted to bring some of us there to show us around. Sam had a jeep and we went on safari, on dirt roads and sometimes off-road. The luggage was attached to the top of the jeep. Sam's ten-year-old son, Jake, and I often rode on top with the luggage.

Sam said, "Animals have no instinctive fear of motor vehicles. They just see cars as movable boulders or something. It's when the human gets out of the car that the animals get defensive." It was exhilarating on the jeep roof with a view of elephants, giraffes, zebras, ostriches, and lions, who were not afraid to come close as long as we were in or on the car.

When the Carlsbad Caverns National Park Visitor Center opens, I buy postcards in the gift shop, look at the informational displays, and get a ticket for the self-guided Big Room Cave Tour.

I take the elevator down. The cave rooms are huge. The whole section I'm in is the size of six football fields. It's a cool, easy 1.25-mile walk. Railings along the pathways keep me from getting lost, or wrecking any stalagmites. White lights highlight all the beautiful formations, the stalactites and stalagmites. I wear different shoes so I won't spread the white-nose bat fungus from other caves I visited. All the cave places I've been to are concerned with this, and they ask you to disinfect your shoes. I'm always happy to comply for the sake of those poor diseased bats.

After that, Guadalupe Mountains National Park. The two parks are right close together. I watch the film at the Pine Springs Visitor Center.

I pick up a map of the place. It shows that there's not much driving to be done in the park, but there are plenty of hiking trails in the mountains, and places to camp. I wander in the heat along the Pinery Trail behind the visitor center.

The Frijole Ranch History Museum is the ruins of a small ranch. Rustic, stark, Spartan, hot, harsh, remote, lonely. A nice place to visit, but I sure as hell would not want to live here.

Route 54 South brings me to Fort Stockton, Texas, where I plan to spend the night. I have the entire evening to hang out here, so I do laundry at Fabian's Laundromat while reading my novel, and then eat a whopping great Chinese buffet dinner. As the temperature cools, I pace a couple of loops around the perimeter of Rooney Park, then sit at a picnic table to write this for you.

August 18: Packing

I drive down Route 385 all the way to Big Bend National Park. The first visitor center I come to, Persimmon Gap, is closed, but I spot an outhouse, so I stop in. Two guys are hanging out here, one with a motorcycle and a younger one with a customized bicycle packed up with gear. We chat a while and the motorcycle guy says, "Texans are not all as mean as we seem. But we're all packing."

"Packing?" I say, wondering, *Where are they all moving to?*

He says, "Carrying guns. Because the cartels are pushing drugs across the border. A sheriff was decapitated."

This is not how people in Maine are talking.

Big Bend National Park holds another long, hot, scenic drive, with mountain parts and flat parts with scruffy weed bushes. I stop in at the Panther Junction Visitor Center, then head out toward the Santa Elena Canyon Trail. At one point, a deer leaps out in front of me and I have to brake hard. I'm laughing, because I'm glad I missed her. I pull over to rearrange all my furniture in the back of the van, where it fell over or slid forward.

There are historic buildings to visit—the Sam Nail Ranch and the Homer Wilson Ranch. They're ruins of small, rustic stone buildings, reminding me of the Frijole Ranch I saw at Guadalupe. What a harsh life.

The Rio Grande flows through the Santa Elena Canyon. It flows between steep canyon walls and then through flat land with sparse vegetation. The water is the color of my decaf coffee with milk. The river is low, and people are wading in it. I've heard that the river can be dangerous when it floods suddenly because of rain upstream, so I keep my feet out of the muck.

The Rio Grande is the border between the United States and Mexico, so I look around for "bad hombres," as our president called them, who might be illegally invading our country or bringing in drugs, crime, and violence. But the only people I see are some tourists picnicking or wading on the US side.

After my day trip to Big Bend, I've been to all but one national park in the forty-eight contiguous states. The one I am missing is Dry Tortugas, on an island far off from Key West. Faith has been there, and she said it's not much to see. I hadn't planned to go there, it's so out of the way, so my personal national park goal for this trip is achieved. It's always good to have something else to aspire to. Dry Tortugas.

I drive back up to Fort Stockton for supper. I see several thunderstorms far off in the distance along the way, but my road doesn't take me into them. Some rain would sure feel good, though.

Micah calls. I left him in charge of taking care of my tenants. "They're having trouble with their fridge," he says. "But don't worry. It's not an emergency. I'm on it." He and Seth are planning to go out with the boys in Portland's Old Port tonight. Hailey, my granddaughter, brought her two 4-H project market lambs to the fair in Skowhegan. A Sysco truck knocked over the electric pole to their tenant's place. Seth and Micah are going to go into business together, buying houses to rent. Life goes on without me.

August 19: Such Beauty, and Such Heartbreak

It's hot at first in Odessa, but I have a nice cross-breeze from the rear vent windows. I hear it start to rain and think, *Ahh.* It's still raining when I get up. So nice.

In Lubbock, Texas, I stop in at the National Ranching Heritage Center at Texas Tech. In front, by the parking lot, are statues of cattle, and a cowboy on a horse. I get a picture of that for my sister Sue, the horse lover.

Inside the building, I see artwork and a museum of ranch-type gear, including a display of fancy cowboy boots, which I know my friend Lee would love. I pick up a map for the walking tour outside. Period buildings represent the history of ranching, and inside these buildings are displays of tools, furniture, dishes, and things that would have been used in the early days of ranching.

I continue north, past Rita Blanca National Grassland in the Texas panhandle and in Oklahoma. Guess what I see here. Grass. And beautiful clouds and sunset, a vast sky. A huge flock of tiny birds rising up, another small gas station out of business. Such beauty, and such heartbreak.

On my phone, I see that there's supposedly a twenty-four-hour Walmart in Liberal, Kansas. *That must be where all the liberals live.* But I keep on going to a rest area I see on the AAA map, on Route 54 near Kismet, Kansas. I want to get away from all the light pollution in hopes of seeing the stars.

There are lights at the restroom, lights of idling trucks, and lights in the distant town. I'm probably not going to be able to see the kind of stars that people brag about, the big-sky, clear-air western stars. My stealth camping technique has me hiding amongst parked cars at night, and in these places there's too much light pollution. I would have had to plan ahead to get a campsite in the parks I visited, because by the time I get there, they're all booked up. So I guess this kind of stargazing will remain on my bucket list. Superstitiously, I think it's good to have something remaining on my bucket list, because what would happen if I finished the list?

August 20: Something Beautiful Everywhere

Onward through Kansas. On the radio, people are screaming about politics. Someone got killed. Singers brag musically about their wonderful romance. Advertisers seduce us into buying sugar and caffeine. This all makes me teary. I'm feeling lost and uncertain. I can tell that my travels are winding down, and then I'll be home, and then what?

I drive through towns so small that the only way I know I'm here is that the speed limit is down to thirty-five.

Looking for something to do in Wichita, Kansas, I find the Museum of World Treasures. It's surprisingly easy to park in the parking lot. I see dinosaur bones and fossils, memorabilia from wars, rocks and minerals, and statues of the Buddha. I post a photo of one beautiful, intricate, white Buddha on my Facebook group page, and people make comments like, "Who knew there was anything like this in

Wichita, of all places." There is something beautiful every-where, even in Wichita.

Again because of construction, I have trouble getting out of Wichita. I stay on Route 54 through Oklahoma, Kansas, and Missouri. Route 54 must be the new Route 66. It's long and has an assortment of businesses, some of them named after Route 54. This is the type of road I enjoy, because there is so much more human life to see than on the big interstate highways. I'm glad to have maps to use to find these roads, because my GPS would just take me the fastest way, probably highways, and I would miss out.

Still moving east, I'm even more cheered up when I see agriculture, and more green. It's overcast and in the seventies. Nice. Just as I get to Camdenton, Missouri, in the evening, it starts to rain. Rain falls on me like a blessing. I enjoy camping in the van in the rain, feeling snug in the coolness and hearing the sound of rain on the roof. In the past when I was camping out in a tent, I sometimes woke up with my face in a puddle.

August 21: Out of the West

It's still rainy when I leave Camdenton. It's overcast and in the seventies all day. I see green. Soothing green. Corn and other crops, trees. I am relieved to be out of the West.

Seth calls. "Is it OK for me to leave my truck in your driveway for a few weeks while I'm in Puerto Rico?"

"Of course. Too bad I won't be seeing you before you leave, though."

"We'll be in touch. Come see me in Puerto Rico."

I'm sad because the trip is almost over. I'm running out of traveling energy and don't know what to do next. Sad to think about being home alone with too much time on my hands. Sad because politics are a hot mess and people are so hateful, and I feel like dropping out. People are a hot mess, too. The West is on fire, literally.

To pass time in the evening, I see a movie called *Crazy Rich Asians*. In the movie, Rachel's boyfriend's mom says Rachel's not good enough for her son because Rachel has a passion for her career, and family should be more important. The boyfriend has a big family in Singapore and they want him there. Rachel has only her mother in New York City. But of course, he proposes and she is thrilled. Cliché Hollywood. They plan to stay in New York, turning their backs on his family. *How is that going to work out for them?* I wonder.

August 22: We Are in Agreement

On Route 41 in western Indiana, for miles and miles, windmills spin over crops, mostly corn, as far as the eye can see. That seems like the most practical use of land I can imagine. I like the idea of renewable energy and feel a small ray of hope for humanity.

Trip Advisor advises Fernwood Botanical Garden in Niles, Michigan. I look at a model train, a stick sculpture, gardens and flowers with bees and butterflies. And of course, a gift shop. I mosey on down the walking trail to the St. Joseph River and stand to watch the water move, imagining that soon I will be watching the river flow past my backyard. *How will that feel?* Breathe. "Keep it in today," as they would say in AA. "Present moment, wonderful moment," as Thich Nhat Hanh would say.

It's time for another visit to Jiffy Lube. The guy in the South Bend, Indiana, Jiffy Lube has a unique opinion about the kind of oil I should be using and how often I should change it. He says the other guy in the other Jiffy Lube was wrong, which is the same thing that the other guy said about the previous guy. *Won't it be nice to be home where I can deal with the same mechanic every time and I'll have no confusion.*

My nephew Sean is a student at Notre Dame near South Bend. Sean is roughly the age of my sons, and they had some fun and made some mischief when they were little. I locate his building on North Eddy Street. He lives in an upstairs apartment on a block of restaurants and bars, the kind of place where I can imagine Sean feeling right at home. He likes the nightlife and the social life.

I text him, and he comes out and greets me with a hug. Sean is tall and blue-eyed, and has shaved his blond head.

He leads me on a walking tour of the campus. We see the mural of Jesus blessing a big grassy green. People are sitting quietly or kneeling on kneelers at The Grotto, where a cave of candles glows. The marching band is gathering for practice, and a herd of huge brassy sousaphones is shining in the low sun.

While walking, we talk. Even about religion and ethics. Sean says, "I'm not religious, but I'm glad for my religious background. I took a class in ethics because Notre Dame is Catholic, whereas Harvard MBAs don't have to care about such things."

"It's like that in the AA program. Doing the right thing is a requirement for a good quality of sobriety." On this, we are in agreement.

Sean took a college class in Japan earlier this summer. While he was there, his wife, Ming, went to visit her relatives in Taiwan. I ask, "How is Ming doing?"

"She's looking for work in Massachusetts, and I'm planning to go back there when I finish my master's degree. My parents will be glad we're back in the neighborhood."

"That's for sure."

I treat Sean to supper in an on-campus pub-style restaurant called Legends of Notre Dame. It's been an interesting, pleasant evening. He walks me to where my van is parked, and I show it off to him. He's suitably impressed. "Looks like you've got everything you need."

"I'm happy to have had a chance to connect with you, Sean," I say as we hug goodbye.

August 23: The Same Shoes

How frustrating this morning is. Because the roads are so straight in Indiana, I believe Route 20 East will be an easy, straight shot. But here's a detour. I have to go south. I keep looking for another detour sign to tell me where to go next. I expect to take a left, then another left to get back onto Route 20. Mile after mile. Like forever. I've gone twenty minutes due south when I want to go east, and I never see any other sign.

I pull over and set my GPS. She has me going on tiny dirt roads, like someone's driveway. *No.* Eventually, I come to a gas station/convenience store where I ask for directions. If all else fails, ask for directions. I'm directed back to Route 20 at a place that is past the roadblock part. Finally.

During all this wandering, I've been noticing the beauty of the countryside. The low, rising sun makes everything glow. The mist in the hollows, crops, trees, homes. Horses and buggies. Girls in Amish dress on bicycles.

On Route 20 East again, I come to a town with another road closure, this time with no detour signs, no clue as to where to go next. I wander around for a while, looking for a way to get back onto Route 20, and fail. Do they just expect that people will automatically know where else to go? So I give up on my first-choice route and set my GPS for Route 90, the toll road.

Having "wasted" an hour and a half trying to stay on Route 20, I find myself on a road with a million tolls. Tolls at random intervals along the road, and tolls every time I take an exit for gas or whatnot. A heavily traveled divided highway, the kind of road I've been trying to avoid. It's a long slog, but I want to put some miles behind me so I can stop near Seneca Falls for the night. I have a date for a family gathering in New York in two days.

After I cross into New York, I find Route 20 again. I'm grateful for the AAA maps. I hit the AA app and find a meeting in five minutes, two miles ahead, so I go for it.

This is the East Avon Way Out group at the First Presbyterian Church in Avon, New York. It's getting dark, and the lights inside the church welcome me and draw me in. The meeting room is accessible by passing through the kitchen, where I see plates of cookies and smell the coffee. A commonly heard remark when I was in rehab was, "Wake up and smell the coffee." Even though I don't usually eat cookies or drink caffeinated coffee, I can still take comfort from the fact that they are offered.

A gray-haired greeter in a flannel shirt shakes my hand and introduces himself. About forty or so people are here, only about half a dozen women. The young, stylish woman sitting next to me says, "We have the same shoes." And sure enough, she is wearing the same sparkly black flip-flops that I got for five dollars at Walmart. (Don't tell anyone I actually spent money at Walmart.) Suddenly I feel young and stylish. I hear people say:

"At my first AA meeting, I said, 'I'm Karen, I'm an alcoholic.' It was the worst thing I ever said, and the best."

"Being in denial is like being asleep. I don't know I've been there until I wake up."

"AA is the largest fellowship no one ever wanted to join."

I feel blessed, once again, by the fellowship of AA. I have the reassurance that when I am home alone, with no job, no partner, no family living with me, there will be a place I can go where I can be with people who get me. Even, possibly, people who might have the same fashionable footwear. This meeting has been medicinal for me. This is one reason why I still go to meetings, even though I have not craved a drink since 1985.

And thus, with my spirits restored, I drive on through the darkness.

August 24: Would Not Be Allowed to Speak or Vote

I stop for breakfast at Sweet Sue's Diner. Sweet Sue is working all alone, including cooking, waiting, and cleaning tables. She's my age, and has a long red braid hanging down her back. She asks me, "Do you want a whole or half order of home fries with your omelet?"

"Whole, please." When she brings my plate, I'm shocked to see the monumental pile of potatoes on it. No way can I even make a dent in this mountain of taters. The whole breakfast is less than six dollars. I give her a 100 percent tip, handing her the cash as I leave, because she's so busy. And I'm full of food.

I roll into the town of Seneca Falls early. It's easy to park on a side street around the corner from the Women's Rights National Historical Park.

I spent the early years of my life feeling ashamed because I objected to the limitations put on girls, and to the way girls and women were sexualized and trivialized. People would argue with me and I would hear "You're maladjusted," or "You're just looking for trouble," or "Why can't you just be normal?" But gender inequality stood out to me like a stone in my shoe. I didn't have to go looking for it. I was shamed for complaining about it. I thought I was some kind of a freak. But here I am at a national historical park dedicated to the very real problem of gender inequality. I start to cry, and after a while I give up trying to stop crying. I cry from the relief of finally being validated, from the grief for the decades spent in shame.

On the corner is the Wesleyan Chapel, a brick building with a big open room inside. This is the building where the first Women's Rights Convention was held in 1848, and where the Declaration of Sentiments was written and signed.

The visitor center is a brick building with a museum and gift shop inside. Between these two buildings is a green grassy lawn sloping down toward the Waterwall that's on the side of the visitor center. The entire Declaration of Sentiments and the names of all the signers are engraved on a wall of stone that has water running across the face of it.

A young man presents an excellent ranger talk about the history of the Women's Rights Convention. "Lucretia Mott was an elected delegate to the World Anti-Slavery Convention in London in 1840. Elizabeth Cady Stanton went there with her brand-new husband, Henry, who was also an elected delegate. The organizers of the convention refused to seat any women. The first day was largely spent arguing about what to do with the women who were present. Finally, it was decided that all women, including all female elected delegates, would be seated in the gallery, but would not be allowed to speak or vote. Lucretia Mott and Elizabeth Cady Stanton met in that gallery.

"In 1848, Jane Hunt invited some ladies to tea in her home: Lucretia Mott, Elizabeth Cady Stanton, Mary Ann M'Clintock, and Martha Wright. They talked about gender inequality and the need to have a convention to discuss this. They decided to 'Do it now.' And the convention was held ten days later." How I wish I could have been a fly on the wall at that historic tea party.

The ranger continues, "At the convention, the Declaration of Sentiments was presented and signed by about a hundred people, women and men. This declaration asked for things to change, and listed the inequalities. You can read them here, engraved in the Waterwall." He gestures behind him. "At the time, women did not vote, hold office, attend college, or speak in public. A married woman could not disobey her husband, divorce her husband, keep her children, sue in court, make contracts, own property, keep her own earnings. If by some chance a woman earned any money, legally, the money belonged to her husband, or, if she wasn't married, to her father.

They had some discussion at the convention about women's right to vote, and not all present were in favor of it. Frederick Douglass spoke in favor of women's right to vote."

The museum at the visitor center has displays of women's rights memorabilia, and right in the center of it all are life-size bronze statues of a group of some people who were important at the time of the convention, including Elizabeth Cady Stanton, Frederick Douglass, Sojourner Truth. I'm mesmerized by the statue of Sojourner Truth. I get the sense that she's looking right at me.

Meanwhile, back at the Wesleyan Chapel, a naturalization ceremony is in progress. People are becoming US citizens. A barbershop quintet of old White men sing. Everyone is smiling, especially the judge who leads the ceremony. Representatives from the League of Women Voters are here to register people to vote as soon as they are eligible. People are tearful and hugging when the ceremony is done.

I don't want to miss seeing Elizabeth Cady Stanton's house, so I set off walking. It's a white house with black shutters and an open front porch in a neighborhood of similar houses. It's spotlessly clean inside with some period furniture to give you an idea of how it might have been furnished in those days. She was a married woman with seven kids, and she played the piano, too. *Where did she get her energy?*

On the walk back, I pass the statue that shows Amelia Bloomer introducing Elizabeth Cady Stanton to Susan B. Anthony. Elizabeth and Susan became lifelong friends, working together for women's rights. Amelia Bloomer is the woman who decided to shorten her long skirts and wear loose-fitting pants underneath. Amelia is why the pants were called bloomers. It was considered shocking, at a time when all women were expected to wear ankle-length skirts in all situations at all times. Imagine trying to do anything with all that cumbersome fabric tripping you up constantly.

The Women's Hall of Fame is in the town of Seneca Falls, too. I hunt for a picture of my heroine, Frances Old-ham Kelsey. From the caption, I learn more about her. She was Canadian, born in 1914. She applied to the University of Chicago to do graduate work in pharmacology. She was accepted into the program because they thought she was a man named Francis. After graduating, she was working for the FDA at the time when thalidomide was coming up for review.

This drug was used to treat morning sickness for pregnant women. It had been approved by many other countries, but Frances said there wasn't enough research for her to approve it. She said no. Under more pressure, she still said no. Later on, this drug was shown to cause severe birth defects, and thousands of children worldwide were affected. New drug approval regulations were passed in 1962, thanks to Frances, my heroine.

August 25: The Farm

I show up for the family gathering at "the farm" in Cobleskill, New York. This is the place where my nephew Dave and my niece Crystal live.

Nate, Crystal's husband, is making sausage from a pig that his dad raised. "You'll have to stay for supper. We're having a farm supper with smoked pork, ham, purple mashed potatoes, corn, tomatoes—all from the farm."

"Of course. That sounds great."

My parents, and my brother Mike and his wife, Alison, arrive. Dave takes us for a jeep tour up and over the hills of their farm.

"This is beautiful," my mom says.

In the backseat, Mike and I both hoot in falsetto, "Lookit the view! Lookit the view!" like we're little kids, still in 1966.

"I hope you show us what you've done with your house," my dad says.

We stop to take a look inside Dave's log cabin. The upstairs is just about finished now, and nicely, too. The bathroom is a work of art completed. He is rightly proud of his house and says, "I love it here."

I say, "I'm envious of your situation, living in a beautiful place with family around and friends right near."

Supper is on Crystal's back deck overlooking the hills of fields. The menu is just as Nate described. Of course, I stay for supper.

John, their friend and neighbor, helps me figure out on the map the best way to get into New York City tomorrow. He says, "What are you planning to do in the city?"

"I'm visiting one of my other nephews, Richard."

After supper, I leave my people, waving and calling out their goodbyes on the deck. I'm hoping to reach a rest stop on I-84 near East Fishkill, New York. The Taconic Parkway is long, and it's getting darker. By the time I get to the rest stop, it's fully dark and I'm exhausted.

August 26: You Seem Normal to Me

I leave the rest area early. I think, *I'm not nervous. I'm just holding the steering wheel real tight and keeping my eyes wide open.* I'm excited going over the bridge and seeing the Manhattan skyline in the distance. Even though it's early on a Sunday morning, there's fast-moving traffic and multiple lane changes to be maneuvered. *What are all these people doing up so early on a Sunday? And where are they all going in such a hurry?* I thought I would never dare to drive into New York City in this lifetime, but here I am parking on the street right in front of Richard's apartment building in Brooklyn. Bonus: Parking is free on Sundays.

I'm wicked early because I wanted to avoid traffic. I hit the AA app and choose a meeting and start walking. I enjoy being in the city. I notice morning glories on someone's porch, a fire hydrant spouting, interesting graffiti.

People out getting their coffees, walking their dogs. A park where mothers watch their little kids play. Community gardens.

The meeting is the Feelings Group on Quincy Street. I step down stairs into one of those half-submerged Brooklyn-type apartments. It looks like some walls have been removed, because the meeting room is larger than an apartment-sized living room. The floor is old gray and red linoleum tiles. About twenty people, most of them Black, sit in a circle of folding chairs. I've been wondering where the Black AA members hang out, because usually I see few, if any, in meetings. I find them in Brooklyn. And Jackson, Mississippi. I hear people say:

"I thought I probably shouldn't quit drinking. What if I go to New Orleans someday?"

"I knew I was the one person I couldn't listen to."

"There's a lot of bait in the water. Don't bite."

"The best way to quit drinking is to quit drinking."

"I may not be much, but I'm all I think about."

They all stand and hold hands, and the meeting closes with the Serenity Prayer, and after the prayer, they all shout, "Stay!"

Back at Richard's house, I get the tour. He has a two-bedroom apartment he shares with a friend. I take a picture of him on the balcony overlooking the elevated train tracks, the tracks my van is parked beneath. So Brooklyn-ish. Richard is the son of my brother Andy, the cellist in Knoxville, and the brother of Thomas, the one I visited in Denver. Like them, he is tall and slim, but he has his mom's curly hair.

I offer to treat him to brunch, and we do the half-hour walk to a restaurant with tables outside in the shade. He works in Manhattan and doesn't have a car. Why would you, in NYC? We talk about deep things: questioning God, looking for love. He's exploring online dating and says, "You should try that."

We walk back to where my van is parked and I say, "My turn to give you the tour now." I slide the back door open and describe all my preparations while Richard checks it out.

We hug our goodbyes. He says, "Drive safe."

"Thanks, I plan to. So good to see you."

It's hair-raising getting out of the city, but I make it and nothing bad happens, so I call it a success.

I contact Jeremy, my ex-sweetheart and now good friend, thinking I might stop in and see his new house in Massachusetts on the way home. He greets me in the driveway, and we step inside to talk.

After we get caught up a bit, he asks, "How many miles did you put on your van?"

"Just about twenty-five thousand. But I rarely traveled over four hours in any one day."

"How many times did you have to call AAA?"

"Not once, luckily. Having car trouble can be an adventure, but if I have a choice, I'd rather choose a different kind of adventure. It's so reassuring to have AA and AAA on my side. It makes all the difference."

"I'm sure."

He tells me about the work he is doing with Narcotics Anonymous. He manages their website. Instead of calling himself the "webmaster," he calls himself the "webservant." He has lengthy recovery in NA and has done a world of service work. We went to two NA World Conventions together, one in San Diego and the one in Honolulu where I saw rainbows from the city bus.

In San Diego, we hung out with twenty thousand addicts in one room. The organizers had arranged for people around the world to be present through technology. The operator greeted people by phone while giant video screens showed a picture of the world turning and then zoomed in on their locations. Guam, Japan, a jail in Texas, and other places all over the globe.

After all the locations were greeted, and we heard those NA members cheering, we all said the Serenity Prayer together, twenty thousand–plus addicts worldwide at the same moment. It gave me chills.

I tell Jeremy about my memorable AA experience in Cambodia. At the time, he was in the hospital, being kept in a medically induced coma while awaiting a liver transplant. I had made a commitment to do volunteer work at a medical clinic in Cambodia with some other nurses from Maine. I was reluctant to travel, but I could do absolutely nothing for him here but worry.

When I got to Cambodia, I saw that the other thirteen people on the trip were in holiday mode and drinking. Because I was a psych nurse, not a "medical" nurse, I was nervous about the medical clinic. I was also distraught about Jeremy's condition. Though I wasn't craving a drink, I was on another emotional planet from all my partying colleagues. I tried to manage my emotions for a while, thinking, *I have a strong recovery, I should be able to do this.* But I had limited success and decided to reach out for support.

I called the AA number, and a man named Howard hooked me up with a woman named Jeanette, because in AA it's men with men and women with women. I explained my situation to Jeanette on the phone. She said, "What hotel are you in?" I told her, and she said, "I'll be there in fifteen minutes."

Ten minutes later, a six-foot-tall woman came striding into the lobby with her motorcycle helmet under her arm. Jeanette and I took a walk along the river in Phnom Penh. I told her more detail about my situation and why it was so upsetting to me. In her New Zealand accent, she said, "Well, you seem normal to me."

And at that moment, I felt normal again. My feet were on the ground. Halfway across the planet, a phone call and a ten-minute wait was all it took for me to be with my tribe. My Higher Power. Jeanette had six months of sobriety at the time, and I had twenty-five years, and with one sentence, she fixed me right up.

She said, "I'm glad to talk with you as well. Let's make a plan to meet up later in the week and go to a meeting." She is still my Facebook friend.

And Jeremy got his liver transplant. Now he tells me his memorable AA meeting anecdote. "I was newly sober and still raw, and it was Halloween night. At the meeting, some people were wearing costumes. The man chairing the meeting was dressed as a clown, with a big rainbow Afro, a red nose, red cheeks, huge shoes, and a puffy polka-dotted outfit. When he started speaking, he said, 'When I was drinking, I felt like I couldn't be myself.' And the crowd roared with laughter. Then he said, 'People never took me seriously.' More howls of laughter. Everything he said was hilarious, coming from a grown man in a full-on clown suit. Then he said, 'When I was two, my mother left me.' Suddenly the room went quiet and attentive and respectful. He told his story, and was heard. He was being himself, and being taken seriously."

Jeremy says, "I'd be interested to hear about any regional differences you noticed at the AA meetings."

"I can't really say that I saw any differences that were regional. Even in the same town, the meetings can vary, you know, like there are speaker meetings, tag meetings, discussion meetings, all kinds of meetings. I did notice some different accents in different regions, but most people spoke like the accent they hear on the TV news, or on the radio."

"I know what you mean. I think that accent is called General American."

I tell Jeremy about my visit to the Women's Rights National Historical Park, just like what I wrote for you. I'm all choked up and emotional when I describe what I learned and how I felt. I can tell Jeremy is an empathetic audience. Some people just don't want to hear about it—most people, in fact.

It's late, so I say good night and retire to the van in his driveway.

Drifting off to sleep, my mind shows me a montage of images: mountains, a horse, a carousel, a green lake, a deer, stalactites, art, cacti, rainbows. I hear a medley of sounds: birds, an orchestra, snorting bison, thunder, a waterfall, a baby's laugh.

I see visions of faces: family, friends, AA colleagues, a cashier, a mechanic, a ranger, a tour guide, a waitress. The faces of people who care and wish me well. Like the sun, they are always there, even when I can't see them. In this kaleidoscope of faces, I see my Higher Power, and I am embraced.

August 27: Breathe a Sigh

My last day of traveling. Some things haven't changed. I didn't find my true calling. I didn't find my true love.

I congratulate myself on my achievements. I am free to risk adventure because I can trust myself to stay safe, to take care of business like an adult, to manage my emotions.

I know all this because I have practiced using these skills, and I get to keep them. What I have gained is courage, optimism, faith in the Higher Power of my understanding.

Home. I see the waist-high weeds where my last year's vegetable garden was, a box full of mail on the porch, my lawn recently mowed. Inside, everything is just as I left it. I sit on the deck and watch the river roll, and breathe a sigh. This traveling is done. Now the adventure begins.

Appendix A

Serenity Prayer

God, grant me the serenity
To accept the things I cannot change,
The courage to change the things I can,
And the wisdom to know the difference.

The Twelve Steps of Alcoholics Anonymous

1. We admitted we were powerless over alcohol—that our lives had become unmanageable.

2. Came to believe that a Power greater than ourselves could restore us to sanity.

3. Made a decision to turn our will and our lives over to the care of God as we understood Him.

4. Made a searching and fearless moral inventory of ourselves.

5. Admitted to God, to ourselves, and to another human being the exact nature of our wrongs.

6. Were entirely ready to have God remove all these defects of character.

7. Humbly asked Him to remove our shortcomings.

8. Made a list of all persons we had harmed, and became willing to make amends to them all.

9. Made direct amends to such people wherever possible, except when to do so would injure them or others.

10. Continued to take personal inventory and when we were wrong promptly admitted it.

11. Sought through prayer and meditation to improve our conscious contact with God as we understood Him, praying only for knowledge of His will for us and the power to carry that out.

12. Having had a spiritual awakening as the result of these steps, we tried to carry this message to alcoholics, and to practice these principles in all our affairs.

The Twelve Traditions of Alcoholics Anonymous

1. Our common welfare should come first; personal recovery depends upon A.A. unity.

2. For our group purpose there is but one ultimate authority—a loving God as He may express Himself in our group conscience. Our leaders are but trusted servants; they do not govern.

3. The only requirement for A.A. membership is a desire to stop drinking.

4. Each group should be autonomous except in matters affecting other groups or A.A. as a whole.

5. Each group has but one primary purpose—to carry its message to the alcoholic who still suffers.

6. An A.A. group ought never endorse, finance, or lend the A.A. name to any related facility or outside enterprise, lest problems of money, property, and prestige divert us from our primary purpose.

7. Every A.A. group ought to be fully self-supporting, declining outside contributions.

8. Alcoholics Anonymous should remain forever nonprofessional, but our service centers may employ special workers.

9. A.A., as such, ought never be organized; but we may create service boards or committees directly responsible to those they serve.

10. Alcoholics Anonymous has no opinion on outside issues; hence the A.A. name ought never be drawn into public controversy.

11. Our public relations policy is based on attraction rather than promotion; we need always maintain personal anonymity at the level of press, radio, and films.

12. Anonymity is the spiritual foundation of all our Traditions, ever reminding us to place principles before personalities.

Permission

Appendix B

Zinnia's Guidelines for Life on the Road

1. Pay attention when driving. Duh.
2. Drive as slowly as you want. If that bothers anyone, they can call their sponsor or therapist.
3. Keep the van serviced.
4. Lock the van.
5. At night, put your van key and glasses where you can find them quickly.
6. Follow your gut when it comes to safety. No chances.
7. Use sunscreen every day.
8. Wear flip-flops in the shower.
9. Be clean. Wear clean clothes.
10. Get a workout or some kind of exercise every day.
11. Keep the van neat and organized.
12. Drink at least two liters of water every day, early in the day.
13. Avoid caffeine and sweets. Except dark chocolate.
14. Write every day.
15. Say yes.

Where I Spent the Night: Part One

May 13: On the street, Yorktown Heights, NY

May 14: On the street, West Chester, PA

May 15: Dawn's driveway, Fairmont, WV

May 16: Megan's driveway, Bloomfield, KY

May 17: Megan's driveway, Bloomfield, KY

May 18: Andy and Helen's house, Knoxville, TN

May 19: Andy and Helen's house, Knoxville, TN

May 20: Andy and Helen's house, Knoxville, TN

May 21: Walmart, Central City, KY

May 22: Rest stop on Route 40 West near Forrest City, AR

May 23: Embassy Hilton, Hot Springs, AR (gift from Seth and Nicole)

May 24: Rest stop, Ozark, AR

May 25: Duck Creek Casino 24/7, south of Tulsa, OK, then Creek Nation Travel Plaza

May 26: Walmart, Ardmore, OK

May 27: Walmart, Ardmore, OK

May 28: Walmart, Sherman, TX

May 29: Walmart, Atlanta, TX

May 30: Walmart, Carthage, TX

May 31: Walmart, Orange, TX

June 1: Visitor center, Natchez, MS

June 2: Magnolia Grove Meditation Center, Batesville, MS

June 3: Walmart, Tupelo, MS

June 4: Walmart, Demopolis, AL

June 5: Walmart, Foley, AL

June 6: Walmart, Marianna, FL
June 7: Walmart, Valdosta, GA
June 8: Walmart, St. Marys, GA
June 9: Planet Fitness, Savannah, GA
June 10: Planet Fitness, Charleston, SC
June 11: Planet Fitness, Myrtle Beach, SC
June 12: Walmart, New Bern, NC
June 13: Joel and Kathryn's house, Wanchese, NC
June 14: Joel and Kathryn's house, Wanchese, NC
June 15: Planet Fitness, Danville, VA
June 16: Planet Fitness, Centreville, VA
June 17: Walmart, Denton, MD
June 18: Planet Fitness, Rockaway, NJ
June 19: Mike and Alison's driveway, Newington, CT
June 20: Planet Fitness, Kingstown, RI
June 21: Home for the wedding

Where I Spent the Night: Part Two

July 3: Price Chopper, Bennington, VT
July 4: Dave's driveway, Cobleskill, NY
July 5: Planet Fitness, Mentor, OH
July 6: Planet Fitness, Akron, OH
July 7: Planet Fitness, Milford, OH
July 8: Planet Fitness, Terre Haute, IN
July 9: Walmart, O'Fallon, IL
July 10: Walmart, Hannibal, MO

July 11: Walmart, Dodgeville, WI

July 12: Walmart, Houghton, MI

July 13: Walmart, Houghton, MI

July 14: Walmart, Houghton, MI

July 15: Walmart, Bemidji, MN

July 16: Painted Canyon Visitor Center, Theodore Roosevelt
    National Park, ND

July 17: Planet Fitness, Rapid City, SD

July 18: Walmart, Scottsbluff, NE

July 19: On the road to the hospital, Jackson, WY

July 20: Walmart, Bozeman, MT

July 21: Jayne's driveway, Missoula, MT

July 22: Jayne's driveway, Missoula, MT

July 23: Walmart, Kalispell, MT

July 24: Walmart, Kalispell, MT

July 25: Planet Fitness, Spokane, WA

July 26: Planet Fitness, Puyallup, WA

July 27: Safeway, Astoria, OR

July 28: Walmart, Roseburg, OR

July 29: Red Roof Inn parking lot, Arcata, CA

July 30: Planet Fitness, Fresno, CA

July 31: Planet Fitness, Fresno, CA

August 1: Planet Fitness, Fresno, CA

August 2: Planet Fitness, Paso Robles, CA

August 3: Planet Fitness, Oxnard, CA

August 4: Planet Fitness, San Bernardino, CA

August 5: Planet Fitness, Las Vegas, NV

August 6: Rest area on Route 15 south of Cedar City, UT

August 7: Best Western Hotel, Mount Carmel, UT (gift from
    Seth and Nicole)
August 8: Rest area on Route 70, Crescent Junction, UT
August 9: Super 8 Hotel parking lot, Silverthorne, CO
August 10: Walmart, Longmont, CO
August 11: Planet Fitness, Denver, CO
August 12: Holiday Inn parking lot, Gunnison, CO
August 13: Walmart, Cortez, CO
August 14: Walmart, Globe, AZ
August 15: Rest area on Route 10, Dragoon, AZ
August 16: Walmart, Carlsbad, NM
August 17: Walmart, Fort Stockton, TX
August 18: Planet Fitness, Odessa, TX
August 19: Rest area on Route 54 near Kismet, KS
August 20: Walmart, Camdenton, MO
August 21: Walmart, Danville, IL
August 22: Planet Fitness, Big Bend, IN
August 23: Walmart, Canandaigua, NY
August 24: Planet Fitness, East Syracuse, NY
August 25: Rest area on I-84 near East Fishkill, NY
August 26: Jeremy's driveway, Carver, MA
August 27: Home

Attractions I Visited: Part One

May 13: Lunch with family in CT

May 15: Dawn's farm in WV

May 16: Megan's house in KY

May 17: Jazzercise class with Megan in KY

Bernheim Arboretum in KY

May 18: Andy and Helen's house in TN

Not Watson's restaurant in Knoxville, TN

Tennessee Theater, Knoxville Symphony Orchestra concert in Knoxville, TN

May 19: Johnson City Symphony in Johnson City, TN

Sycamore Shoals State Historic Park, TN

May 20: Ijams Nature Center in Knoxville, TN

May 21: Mammoth Cave National Park in KY

Green River ferry in KY

May 22: Cape Girardeau, MO

May 23: Hot Springs Duck Tour and Wax Museum in Hot Springs, AR

Hot Springs National Park in AR

Embassy Hotel in Hot Springs, AR (gift from Seth and Nicole)

May 24: Garvan Gardens in Hot Springs, AR

May 25: Little House on the Prairie Museum in Independence, KS

May 26: Honor Heights Park in Muskogee, OK

Renaissance Faire in Muskogee, OK

Turner Falls in OK

May 27: Methodist Church in Ardmore, OK

Lake Murray State Park, and Tucker Tower, in
Ardmore, OK

Movies in Ardmore, OK

May 28: Eisenhower State Park, TX

May 29: Atlanta State Park, TX

May 30: Walking tour in Jefferson, TX

Riverboat tour in Jefferson, TX

Jefferson Historical Museum in Jefferson, TX

Supper with John and Sue in Marshall, TX

May 31: Rosenberg Library Museum in Galveston, TX

Walking tour of Galveston, TX

Pier 21 Theater in Galveston, TX

Galveston Seawall in Galveston, TX

Ferry to Bolivar Peninsula from Galveston, TX

June 1: Allen Parish Wall of Honor at the visitor center in
Allen Parish, LA

Louisiana History Museum in Alexandria, LA

Hotel Bentley in Alexandria, LA

River Oaks Square Arts Center in Alexandria, LA

Steve's Lube in Alexandria, LA

June 2: Bluff Park in Natchez, MS

Farmers' market in Natchez, MS

Natchez Trace Parkway

Magnolia Grove Meditation Center in Batesville, MS

June 3: Oxford, MS

Elvis's birthplace in Tupelo, MS

June 4: Riverwalk in Tuscaloosa, AL

June 5: Fairhope Municipal Pier and Rose Garden in

Fairhope, AL

June 6: Destin Harbor Walk in Destin, FL

Beach in Port St. Joe's, FL

June 7: Florida Caverns State Park in FL

Jack Hadley Black History Museum in
Thomasville, GA

Rose Garden in Thomasville, GA

June 8: Okefenokee Swamp State Park, boat, train, and
nature tours in GA

St. Marys Museum and Walking Tour in St. Marys,
GA

Movies in St. Marys, GA

June 9: Jekyll Island tour in GA

Georgia Sea Turtle Center on Jekyll Island, GA

Driftwood Beach on Jekyll Island, GA

Faith Chapel on Jekyll Island, GA

June 10: Botanical Gardens in Savannah, GA

Edisto Beach in SC

Carriage tour of Charleston, SC

Charleston City Market in Charleston, SC

Jazz Vespers in Charleston, SC

June 11: Congaree National Park in SC

Myrtle Beach, SC

June 12: Southport–Fort Fisher Ferry in NC

Wilmington boat tour in Wilmington, NC

June 13: Joel and Kathryn's house in NC

Elizabethan Gardens, outdoor play at Roanoke, NC

June 14: Joel's hearing aid doctor in Virginia Beach, VA

Museum of Contemporary Art in Virginia Beach, VA

Sidewalk art show in Virginia Beach, VA
June 15: Edenton, NC
Dismal Swamp State Park in NC
Dan Daniel Park in Danville, VA
June 16: Natural Bridge State Park in VA
Shenandoah Caverns in Quicksburg, VA, includes
Yellow Barn Museum and American
Celebration on Parade
June 17: Washington, DC, Mall:
Vietnam and WWII memorials, Holocaust, Castle
Gardens, Flagler, Freeman, Hirshhorn, Air
and Space with Planetarium, Botanic
Garden, National Gallery of Art, Museum of
the American Indian
June 18: Harriet Tubman Underground Railroad stop in
Denton, MD
Delaware Shore Drive
Lewes Ferry to NJ
June 19: Danbury, CT
Southington, CT
Newington, CT
Mike and Alison's house in CT
Parents' house in CT
June 20: Terry's house in CT
Umbrella factory in Charlestown, RI
June 21: Narragansett Beach in RI

Attractions I Visited: Part Two

July 3: Parents' home in CT

      Wilson House in Dorset, VT

July 4: Dave, Crystal, and Nate's house in NY

      Parade in Cobleskill, NY

      Fireworks at Glimmerglass State Park in NY

July 5: Corning Glass Museum in Corning, NY

July 6: Cuyahoga Valley National Park in OH

      Dr. Bob's house in Akron, OH

      F. A. Seiberling Nature Realm in Akron, OH

July 7: Decorative Arts Center of Ohio in Lancaster, OH

      Hopewell Culture National Historical Park in OH

July 8: Decatur County Courthouse tree in the tower in

           Greensburg, IN

      Schooner Valley Stables in Nashville, IN

      Nashville, IN

July 9: Carlyle Lake in Carlyle, IL

      World's Largest Rocking Chair (also world's largest

           wind chime, pencil, golf tee, gavel,

           yardstick, knitting needles) in Casey, IL

July 10: Gateway Arch National Park in MO

      Riverboat cruise in Hannibal, MO

      Movies in Hannibal, MO

July 11: Sue and John's house in IA

July 12: The House on the Rock in Spring Green, WI

July 13: Quincy Copper Mine tour in Hancock, MI

      A. E. Seaman Mineral Museum in Houghton, MI

L'Anse Waterfront Park in L'Anse, MI

July 14: Isle Royale ferry from Copper Harbor, MI, to Isle Royale National Park

July 15: Voyageurs National Park in MN

July 16: Jiffy Lube in Fargo, ND

July 17: Painted Canyon Visitor Center in Belfield, ND

Theodore Roosevelt National Park in ND

North Dakota Cowboy Hall of Fame in Medora, ND

July 18: Wind Cave National Park in SD

Badlands National Park in SD

Street fair in Alliance, NE

July 19: Scotts Bluff National Monument in Scottsbluff/Gering, NE

Grand Teton National Park in WY

July 20: Yellowstone National Park in WY

July 21: American Computer Museum in Bozeman, MT

Gates of the Mountains boat tour on the Missouri River in Helena, MT

Jayne and Tim's house in MT

July 22: Covenant Reformed Church in Missoula, MT

Rocky Mountain Elk Foundation Museum in Missoula, MT

Carousel for Missoula and Missoula Historic District in Missoula, MT

July 23: Rafting with Jayne and Tim

July 24: Glacier National Park Jammer tour in MT

July 25: Lake Pend Oreille boat cruise in Sandpoint, ID

Sandpoint City Beach in Sandpoint, ID

July 26: "Desert of Washington"

July 27: Mount Rainier National Park in WA

Mount Saint Helens in WA

July 28: Lewis and Clark National Historical Park in OR
Columbia River Maritime Museum in Astoria, OR

July 29: Crater Lake National Park trolley tour in OR
Redwood National Park in CA

July 30: Lassen Volcanic National Park in CA

July 31: Christina and Romero's house in CA
Jiffy Lube in Fresno, CA

August 1: Forestiere Underground Gardens in Fresno, CA

August 2: Pinnacles National Park in CA
Concert in the park in Paso Robles, CA
Movies in Paso Robles, CA

August 3: Old Spanish Days-Fiesta in Santa Barbara, CA
Channel Islands Visitor Center in Ventura, CA
Ventura Beach, CA

August 4: Anacapa Island, Channel Islands National Park, CA

August 5: Joshua Tree National Park in CA
Death Valley National Park in CA
Fremont Street in Las Vegas, NV

August 6: Great Basin National Park in NV

August 7: Zion National Park in UT
Best Western Hotel in Mount Carmel, UT (gift
from Seth and Nicole)

August 8: Bryce Canyon National Park in UT
Capitol Reef National Park in UT

August 9: Arches National Park in UT
Canyonlands National Park in UT

August 10: Rocky Mountain National Park in CO
Estes Park, CO

Roosevelt Park in Longmont, CO

August 11: Celestial Seasonings tea tour in Boulder, CO
Pearl Street Mall in Boulder, CO
Quilt Museum in Golden, CO

August 12: Thomas and Mary Kate's house in CO
Capitol steps in Denver, CO (elevation 5,280 feet)
Great Sand Dunes National Park in CO

August 13: Black Canyon of the Gunnison National Park in CO
Mesa Verde National Park in CO

August 14: Four Corners (UT, CO, AZ, NM)
Petrified Forest National Park in AZ

August 15: Saguaro National Park in AZ
Funny Foot Farm in Tucson, AZ

August 16: The Recycled Roadrunner in Las Cruces, NM

August 17: Carlsbad Caverns National Park in NM
Guadalupe Mountains National Park in TX
Rooney Park in Fort Stockton, TX

August 18: Big Bend National Park in TX

August 19: National Ranching Heritage Center at Texas Tech University in Lubbock, TX
Rita Blanca National Grassland in TX and OK

August 20: Museum of World Treasures in Wichita, KS

August 21: Movies in Danville, IL

August 22: Fernwood Botanical Garden in Niles, MI
Jiffy Lube in South Bend, IN
Notre Dame in South Bend, IN
Sean's house in IN

August 23: Amish country in IN

August 24: Seneca Lake Park in Geneva, NY

> Women's Rights National Historical Park in Seneca Falls, NY
>
> Naturalization ceremony at the Wesleyan Methodist Church in Seneca Falls, NY
>
> Elizabeth Cady Stanton's home in Seneca Falls, NY
>
> Statue of Amelia Bloomer introducing Elizabeth Cady Stanton to Susan B. Anthony in Seneca Falls, NY
>
> National Women's Hall of Fame in Seneca Falls, NY
>
> Jane Hunt's house in Waterloo, NY
>
> Harriet Tubman's house and the nursing home she founded next door in Auburn, NY

August 25: Farmers' market in Cazenovia, NY

> Art Park in Cazenovia, NY
>
> Dave, Crystal, and Nate's house in NY

August 26: Richard's house in NY

> Jeremy's house in MA

August 27: Home

AA Meetings I Attended

Alabama: Jack Warner Parkway, Tuscaloosa, June 4
      Common Ground, Daphne, June 5
Alaska: None yet!
Arizona: Alano Club, Tucson, August 15
Arkansas: Sellers Street, Hot Springs, May 24
California: Fresno Fellowship, Fresno: many times in
      November 2017
      Oxnard Alano Social Club, Oxnard, August 3
Colorado: Triangle Club, Longmont, August 10 and August 11
      York Street, Denver, August 11
Connecticut: Universalist Church, West Hartford, May 13
Delaware: Westminster House, Newark, May 15
Florida: The Camel Club, Santa Rosa Beach, June 6
Georgia: Northside Group, Valdosta, June 7
      24-Hour Club, Savannah, June 9
Hawaii: Not this time!
Idaho: Gardenia Center, Sandpoint, July 25
Illinois: St. Mary's Hospital, Centralia, July 9
      O'Fallon Trailer, O'Fallon, July 9
Indiana: First United Methodist Church, Mooresville, July 8
Iowa: Marion Industrial Club, Marion, July 11
Kansas: Morgan Avenue, Parsons, May 25
      North Hoover, Wichita, August 20
Kentucky: Presbyterian Church Annex, Danville, May 18

Louisiana: Twin City Clubhouse, Alexandria, June 1

Maine: My home group at Seventh-day Adventist offices,
     Westbrook

     And many, many others over the years

Maryland: Mann House, Bel Air, May 15

Massachusetts: Main Street, Southbridge, June 21

Michigan: United Methodist Church, Ontonagon, July 13

Minnesota: American Indian Center, Duluth, July 15

Mississippi: YANA Club (You Are Never Alone), Jackson, June 2

     South Broadway Street, Tupelo, June 3

Missouri: Downtown AA Hall, Cape Girardeau, May 22

Montana: Fellowship Hall, Bozeman, July 20

Nebraska: Laramie Street, Alliance, July 18

     New Hope Club, Scottsbluff, July 19

Nevada: Triangle Club, Las Vegas, August 5

New Hampshire: Derry Friendship Center, Derry, June 21

New Jersey: St. Bartholomew, Ho-ko-kus, May 14

New Mexico: Arid Club, Las Cruces, August 16

     Alano Club, Carlsbad, August 16

New York: St. Patrick's, Yorktown Heights, May 14

     First Presbyterian, Avon, August 23

     Quincy Street, Brooklyn, August 26

North Carolina: New Street, New Bern, June 12

North Dakota: Silver Dollar Symbol of Sobriety, Fargo, July 16

Ohio: Choices Club, Akron, July 6

     Indiana Street Recovery Center, Zanesville, July 7

Oklahoma: Okmulgee Avenue, Muskogee, May 26

     Maxwell Street NW, Ardmore, May 26

Oregon: Rainier Assembly of God, Rainier, July 27

Pennsylvania: West Chester Church of Christ, West Chester,
    May 14

Puerto Rico: Serenity Club, San Juan (on a different trip!)

Rhode Island: First Baptist Church, North Kingstown, June 20
    Narragansett Beach, Narragansett, June 21

South Carolina: Old Central, Charleston, June 10
    Alano Club, Myrtle Beach, June 11

South Dakota: Alano Club, Rapid City, July 17

Tennessee: Greater Warner Tabernacle, Knoxville, May 20

Texas: Anchor Group, Gainesville, May 28
    Serenity Club, Texarkana, May 29

Utah: East Cobblecreek Drive, Cedar City, August 6

Vermont: Wilson House, East Dorset, July 3

Virginia: Trinity United Methodist Church, Danville, June 15
    St. Andrew's Lutheran Church, Centreville, June 16

Washington: Our Club, Spokane, July 26

Washington, DC: Dupont Circle Club, June 17

West Virginia: John Manchin Senior Health Care Center,
    Fairmont, May 15
    Serenity Club, Dunbar, May 16

Wisconsin: Serenity Club, Dodgeville, July 11

Wyoming: St. John's Episcopal Church, Jackson Hole, July 19

CPSIA information can be obtained
at www.ICGtesting.com
Printed in the USA
FSHW010824010321
79031FS